The Business
of Women

The Business of Women

Marriage, Family, and Entrepreneurship in British Columbia, 1901-51

MELANIE BUDDLE

UBC Press • Vancouver • Toronto

20 19 18 17 16 15 14 13 12 11 10   5 4 3 2 1

Printed in Canada on FSC-certified ancient-forest-free paper (100% post-consumer recycled) that is processed chlorine- and acid-free.

Library and Archives Canada Cataloguing in Publication

Buddle, Melanie, 1971-
    The business of women : marriage, family, and entrepreneurship in British Columbia 1901-51 / Melanie Buddle.

Includes bibliographical references and index.
ISBN 978-07748-1813-1

    1. Businesswomen – British Columbia – History – 20th century. 2. Business-women – British Columbia – Social conditions – 20th century. 3. Businesswomen – Family relationships – British Columbia – History – 20th century. 4. Women – Employment – British Columbia – History – 20th century. I. Title.

HD6054.4.C3B83 2010   305.43'3380971109041   C2010-901124-4

Canada

UBC Press gratefully acknowledges the financial support for our publishing program of the Government of Canada (through the Canada Book Fund), the Canada Council for the Arts, and the British Columbia Arts Council.

This book has been published with the help of a grant from the Canadian Federation for the Humanities and Social Sciences, through the Aid to Scholarly Publications Programme, using funds provided by the Social Sciences and Humanities Research Council of Canada.

UBC Press
The University of British Columbia
2029 West Mall
Vancouver, BC V6T 1Z2
www.ubcpress.ca

Contents

Illustrations

FIGURES

Acknowledgments

This project has been with me longer than I ought to admit. It began in the late 1990s at the University of Victoria during my doctoral studies. It has been with me through jobs, the births of my children, and moves across the country. Now, I am happy to set it free.

I am grateful for the support of many fine colleagues who have listened, encouraged, and prodded me toward publication. The parts of this book that are strongest are a reflection of the great advice and support I have received, but of course, any failings are mine alone. Peter Baskerville, my dissertation supervisor, was respectful when the occasion required, and irreverent whenever possible. Over the years, he made many suggestions that improved my scholarship and my trust in my ideas. Other faculty members at the University of Victoria had a hand in shaping this project, serving as committee members and as sounding boards: my thanks to Lynne Marks, Pat Roy, and Annalee Lepp. I am also grateful for the suggestions from Helen Brown of Malaspina University College. I want to thank members of the Canadian Families Project, especially Eric Sager, for including me at CFP meetings and conferences and helping me feel I was part of a community of scholars. My thanks also to Marc Trottier and Donna Mandeville, in "L-Hut" at the University of Victoria, who helped me to navigate the Canadian Families Project database.

Time has passed, and the list of academics to thank has become longer. As a part-time instructor at Trent University, I have experienced collegiality, support, and friendship from the members of the Canadian Studies and History departments. They have willingly shared advice, given me the chance to share my research at departmental colloquiums and events, and asked appropriate questions that led me to consider my work in new ways. Thanks in particular to those who provided grading work when I wanted it, detailed advice, letters of reference, and coffee breaks: Dimitry Anastakis, Sally Chivers, Chris Dummitt, Finis Dunaway, Fiona Harris-Stoertz, Jennine Hurl-Eamon, John Milloy, Janet Miron, Kirk Niergarth, Van Nguyen-Marshall, Bryan Palmer, Joan Sangster, Kevin Siena, Tim Stapleton, Jim Struthers, and John Wadland. Trent University has also provided me with many engaging students to teach: I am grateful to the undergraduate students who have had to endure my lectures on gender and business.

The project finally began to become a book, thanks to UBC Press, particularly to Jean Wilson, Darcy Cullen, and Laraine Coates, who provided much encouragement and prompt feedback. Thank you as well to the anonymous reviewers of the manuscript, who took the time to make meaningful comments that I have tried to incorporate.

I would like to acknowledge the financial support of a Social Sciences and Humanities Research Council of Canada doctoral fellowship, which aided my graduate studies. Thanks also to the Canadian Federation of University Women, the BC Heritage Trust, and the University of Victoria for scholarships that helped me to complete the research. My thanks to the staff of the Vancouver City Archives and the British Columbia Archives, who sometimes watched me fall asleep – pregnant and exhausted! – on top of archival files.

A long list of friends and colleagues provided encouragement, friendship, food and drink, and childcare. Dominique Clément first urged me to take a bigger step toward publication: his advice was timely and eye-opening. I'd like to thank Robin Fisher, who supervised my master's thesis and was the catalyst to my decision to pursue further study, and Alison Prentice, a good friend and a role model, whose work in Canadian women's history has been a huge influence. Others helped in innumerable ways and will recall endless conversations about "my book": David Berger, Dana Capell, Mike Eamon, George Fogarasi, Candace Gritter, Barry Laverick, Erica Martin, Wade Matthews, Jacki Millar, Nick Mitchell, Tanya Mitchell, Sandra Patrick, Maggie Quirt, Kristin Semmens, Kate Siena, and Shona Taner. My parents, Bill and Liz Buddle; brother, Chris Buddle; sister-in-law, Becky Stone; and my in-laws, Bonnie, Ron, Dave, and Winnie, have also had to hear about this project for too long: I gratefully acknowledge their advice, meals, emotional support, and practical daycare assistance.

Lastly, how can we best thank the ones who suffer through the worst parts of these projects and yet continue to love us unfailingly throughout? I owe so much to those who live with me, and thus, with my research: my fabulous husband, Drew Ginter, and my beautiful kids, Taren and Cameron. I adore them, and I would not be able to do anything without their cheers of love and pride.

The Business
of Women

I

Businesswomen in British Columbia

W hen I began to research self-employed women in British Columbia, I supposed that most would be single, just as other working women across Canada often were, particularly in the first half of the twentieth century. Since marriage usually ended gainful employment for women, I hypothesized that some, willingly or unwillingly, remained single and turned to self-employment to support themselves. For much of the century, marriage was an occupation for women. It provided financial security in the form of a wage-earning spouse, but it was also an occupation in terms of the amount of unpaid work that married women did in the home. If marriage was a form of economic security, then self-employment was an alternative form of security and possibly, as historian Joy Parr has said in the context of wage-earning work, a way to "escape" conjugality.[1]

What I discovered about women who worked for themselves contradicted my initial assumptions. Being single (never-married) was not a particularly likely condition for self-employed women, and the latter cannot be understood in the same light as wage-earning single women in British Columbia or in the rest of Canada. Self-employed women were older than wage-earning women and were more likely to be married, widowed, or divorced. My initial position needed to be re-evaluated, and this book is the result of that re-evaluation. My focus is entrepreneurial women in a frontier zone, British Columbia in the first half of the twentieth century. This was a place and a time period in which rates of self-employment were relatively high for women, as were rates of marriage. Businesswomen's identities as mothers, wives, and widows affected their entrepreneurial decisions in meaningful ways.

The term "businesswoman" was increasingly used in the early 1900s to refer to women who worked as wage earners in professional occupations. The word implied a certain kind of working woman: well-dressed, white, middle-class professional working women were called business girls or businesswomen. In the second half of this book, I write about business and professional women's (BPW) clubs, and I interrogate the use of the word "businesswoman" and its numerous meanings. However, in general and unless specifically stated in references to BPW clubwomen, I use the terms "businesswoman," "entrepreneur" and "self-employed" interchange- ably throughout this book to refer to women who worked for themselves rather than working as wage earners for someone else.

This story centres primarily on white women in the province. Indigen- ous women and non-white immigrant women ran businesses, but these women are hard to find in the historical sources I used. I have highlighted non-white businesswomen whenever possible, and it seems that their ages, marital status, and familial demands paralleled those of white entrepre- neurs. However, their businesses were usually even more marginal than those run by white women, and imperfect census taking and differing understandings of whether marginal laundry businesses, farming, hunting, and fishing were entrepreneurial have distorted the ways in which these women's stories were recorded. Investigating their experiences and using a diverse set of qualitative records (including oral history) would be a worthwhile process. In general, there is great potential for other scholars to analyze the individual experiences of non-white female entrepreneurs. I hope such scholars might use my study as a starting point from which to compare the experiences of non-white women to those of the white businesswomen that I analyze in the pages that follow. If my work helps to explain the roles of marriage, family, age, and region for a great many white businesswomen in the province, then further work might explain how these factors also mattered for non-white women. More detailed qualitative examinations might yield interesting portraits that would enrich this story, but it should be assumed that the women I discuss are white unless otherwise noted, in part because of the research methods employed here and my reliance on club records, published sources, and census data.

Simply being in the labour force in the early twentieth century was un- conventional for women, and business ownership was constructed as a masculine endeavour. Businesswomen chose unconventional paths in life, and self-employed women formed a small proportion of all women workers *and* of all business owners in every decade under study. This should not, however, deter us from examining them more closely. That entrepreneurs were a distinct minority of the female labour force does not mean that they did not resemble other women, but women's labour force experiences were and are diverse and deserve to be examined from different perspectives. Businesswomen struggled to survive and often operated small, home-based businesses in occupations that had been sex-typed for centuries as feminine work. They frequently ran businesses because they could not find other avenues of work and needed to support family members, not because they were rebelling against traditional roles as wage earners or as wives and mothers. As I demonstrate in the first half of this book, the need to support family – described in Chapter 2 as the "family claim" – was the primary reason women opened businesses. Self-employed women and contemporary observers invoked the language of family responsibility to justify entrepreneurship, whether it was in particularly feminized industries such as sewing, cooking, or cleaning or in more male-dominated occupations such as farming. The ways in which family – the presence of dependent children and the presence, or sometimes absence, of a spouse – influenced women's business decisions is a theme that threads throughout this study.

Finding indications that marginal businesses – which most women's businesses were – provided something more than basic survival is difficult. Evidence of personal fulfillment is lacking, particularly for lower-class entrepreneurial women. It may not have been an important factor for the owners of small businesses in the province. But even when their operations were marginal, and personal satisfaction may not have been the primary goal, some degree of choice is evident in women's decisions. Businesswomen chose to open their own enterprises in a time period when most women did not, and "however miniscule or ephemeral" their businesses,[2] they gained the advantage of becoming their own (and sometimes someone else's) boss.

My initial research prompted me to ask whether female entrepreneurs went against the grain of what British Columbians felt was appropriate feminine behaviour. How important was gender to women's entry into self-employment? Were self-employed women perceived as less feminine in behaviour or appearance than wage-earning women because they operated in a distinctly masculine sphere? As David Burley has argued, notions of masculinity were closely linked to the idea of the businessman.[3] In some ways, female entrepreneurs in British Columbia resembled male entrepreneurs more than they resembled other women in the labour force.

Some ran businesses in male-dominated arenas, such as shopkeeping or farming. Even women who ran businesses in female-dominated trades, such as sewing or operating boarding houses, were relatively rare in the very fact of their entrepreneurship. They ran businesses in towns that were not exactly teeming with other businesswomen. However, while women in British Columbia were like men in choosing entrepreneurship, they could be feminine and also businesslike. Sara McLagan founded the Vancouver daily *The World* with her husband in 1888 and, as a widow, became sole owner in 1901 and the first woman in Canada to run a daily newspaper.[4] A colleague described her as a "most womanly woman and yet one ... who can talk politics with men."[5] Businesswomen and the commentators who described them reassured the public that even women who worked in male-dominated business worlds could be feminine in action and appearance.

I also considered region. British Columbia provides an interesting window on the actions of female entrepreneurs. There were proportionately more adult married women in the population (and in the gainfully employed population) of British Columbia than in the rest of Canada in the first half of the twentieth century. And women were more likely to be self-employed in the province than in the rest of the country between 1901 and 1951. I propose that the higher incidence of female self-employment in British Columbia was connected to the frontier characteristics of the province. The low numbers of women, the correspondingly high rates of marriage, and the market demand for the types of services women typically provided (such as food preparation and boarding and lodging establishments) led married or once-married women to open their own businesses in relatively high numbers in British Columbia. The effects of these early patterns continued to be felt in the province. Women's prominence in entrepreneurship continued until the mid-twentieth century, long after the gender imbalance had righted itself.

The year 1901, the dawn of a new century, is an apt place to begin this study. The records for the female labour force in pre-1900 British Columbia are scant, and the white female population in the province was particularly small.[6] Moreover, in the pre-1901 period, "white women's experience was defined by limited opportunities for labour and financial dependence."[7] While such limitations still existed after 1901, some women in the province responded to the limited opportunities for waged labour by turning to self-employment. If depending financially on men was untenable, they actively sought out other options for financial survival. The economic and social possibilities available to white women in the province, beyond simply arriving on "bride ships" to be married off to miners, were just beginning to be realized as the new century began.[8] And the 1901 census records, which provide detailed data on occupations, help illuminate women's work options in this important time period.[9]

At the beginning of the twentieth century, it was also a relatively recent phenomenon for married women to be able to legally own businesses and property. As Chris Clarkson has shown, a wave of reforms in British Columbia between the 1860s and the early 1900s extended property ownership and inheritance rights to married women. Clarkson argues that British Columbia's legislators extended property, inheritance, and political rights to white women in the name of capitalism, to "encourage the individualistic pursuit of material gain," thereby boosting the province's economy, supporting family growth, and increasing immigration.[10] He states that legal reforms geared toward the rights of white settlers, including expanding married women's rights to own property, had the effect of reducing Aboriginal power and land ownership.[11] In other words, white women gained some legal headway while indigenous populations lost out as British Columbia developed legally and politically.

In 1873, the Married Women's Property Act was passed in British Columbia. Some of its aims can be interpreted charitably: it gave married women property rights that would help them survive abuse or desertion, legalized their participation in business, and generally seemed emancipatory. But its other important purpose was to allow married men "to protect property from creditors by transferring it to their wives."[12] Thus, while both Clarkson and Peter Baskerville suggest that in cities such as Victoria married women owned property in high numbers in the late 1800s, it seems women's ownership was tied more to the desire of their husbands to protect property from creditors than to their support for women's emancipation.[13] Despite this, my work shows that there was a link between marriage (at least on paper, even if husbands were absent) and entrepreneurship. Married women were finally able to own both property and businesses legally. The wave of acts and amendments that Clarkson highlights led to what he has called "a changing mentality among women. From the 1870s onward, British Columbian women were independently invoking their rights."[14] The beginning of the twentieth century was a good time for married women to own businesses even if, in practice, the property laws were not always applied equitably.

This study ends with the 1951 census. By mid-century, the gender imbalance in the province had virtually disappeared. Although British Columbia still retained frontier characteristics and high rates of female

self-employment, wage-earning opportunities had increased as a result
of the Second World War, and self-employment rates for both women
and men were declining. British Columbia was modernizing, the workforce was changing, and women's work and life options were arguably
much different after the war. A study of the second half of the twentieth
century would reveal equally interesting but different facets of female
self-employment.[15]

The first half of this book gives a sense of the many experiences of self-
employed women in British Columbia during the period 1901 to 1951.
Surveying the options for women, the frontier nature of British Columbia
in the early twentieth century, and the kinds of work that women did in
the province is critical to understanding the context within which women
entered self-employment. Most worked in small-scale, survival-oriented
enterprises in order to support families. They are rarely discussed in business history, and the women's voices are soft and difficult to hear because
they did not join clubs or leave substantial records of their businesses.
They were in many ways members of the working class. Entrepreneurship
may in some cases elevate the status of workers, but by and large these
were working-class women running very small, home-based businesses
that often involved teaching, sewing, cooking, and cleaning.

In British Columbia, frontier conditions opened some doors for female
business ownership. In Chapter 2, I use census data to develop a fuller
picture of these women and to explore the links between marriage, family, and entrepreneurship. The family claim in the context of self-employment is examined. I also explain the lack of women on the frontier
in the first half of the twentieth century and connect demographic information to women's employment options. This is also related to marriage
and family: the comparatively small number of women in the province
meant high rates of marriage, but these marriages did not necessarily
last. Women with children were sometimes left to support their families
alone.

In Chapter 3, I look at the conditions of work for self-employed
women in British Columbia and the types of work open to them. Self-
employed women were, like wage-earning women, clustered into a narrow
range of occupations. However, while businesswomen participated in
womanly trades and frequently capitalized on what were deemed feminine
skills, they worked in a predominantly male work world and were more
likely than wage earners to work in male-dominated occupations. Self-
employment connoted independence and manliness; businesswomen thus
challenged women's place in the working world. In the latter half of the

chapter, I look carefully at entrepreneurial women's options in the province, given the sex segregation of the labour force more generally.

In the second half of the book, I examine the business and professional women's clubs in British Columbia, highlighting a particular group of white, middle-class businesswomen. Certainly, for some entrepreneurs, such clubs would have seemed irrelevant. Working-class women (self-employed or not) and non-white women, even when not specifically banned, were either not welcome or not interested in these groups. Moreover, the women who joined the BPW clubs were not all self-employed, as I discuss in Chapter 4. However, the clubs provide a glimpse into the organizational, work, and family lives of a particular demographic: ambitious but respectably conservative middle-class white women, some of whom were self-employed and some of whom needed to work, just as working-class women did.

Despite their relatively privileged status, not all middle-class white women were married to a breadwinner. While many more of the BPW club members, compared to the workers described in Chapters 2 and 3, chose entrepreneurship for personal reasons that may not have been entirely financial, this was still a hard road to walk, particularly before the Second World War. Were these women radical? Were they working just for fun? Were their businesses important to them because they provided a job? As Chapter 4 indicates, their social lives and organizational lives as club members provide insight into what it meant to be an entrepreneurial woman in the early decades of the twentieth century. While this group was small and did not always represent the larger group of self-employed women discussed in the first half of the book, it is still the case that the actions of the BPW clubwomen tell us something about all women who engaged in entrepreneurial occupations in the province.

Clubwomen's social activities and their efforts in the arena of women's employment conditions suggest how they understood their own roles in the business world. While members maintained a respectable "outside" image, some elements of "inside" club life were devoted to criticizing and overturning the more obvious signs of inequity that they dealt with in their daily lives. Parodies of male-dominated business traditions, described in Chapter 4, illustrate that club members were acutely aware of the gendered world that shaped and limited their working lives. While such actions, if they were noticed at all, may have seemed frivolous to non-members in the rest of the province, club activities provide a deeper and more nuanced response to the questions of gender and business than census data can provide.

Chapter 5 demonstrates that business ownership was perceived as a masculine realm of work; despite this, businesswomen found ways to present themselves as both feminine and businesslike, characteristics that would seem antithetical. The way for women to assert their place in an entrepreneurial context was to stress that they could be businesslike in an appropriately feminine manner. Entrepreneurial BPW clubwomen in British Columbia, as well as outside observers, relied on conventional understandings of appropriate gendered behaviour as a way to legitimize their place in the business world.

I conclude that women's work experiences in the first fifty years of the twentieth century were affected by the frontier characteristics of the province. The regional component to this study is important: businesswomen exercised options in British Columbia that were not exercised in quite the same way in the rest of the country, partly because of the province's demography. Furthermore, recent increases in female self-employment rates, and the increasing media interest in female entrepreneurs and "mompreneurs" in Canada, indicate the relevance and timeliness of this study.

There are undeniable differences between the marginal, frequently home-based penny capitalists documented in the first half of this book and the more privileged female entrepreneurs and BPW club members described in the latter half. However, working-class, survival-based businesses and upscale salons and clothing stores all reflect a set of similar themes in the lives of self-employed women in British Columbia. First, while some women worked primarily to support themselves, most used the income from their businesses to support family members, often children. Second, women who were entrepreneurs, whether they took in boarders, operated private schools, or ran tastefully appointed retail shops, were older and more likely to be married or once-married than were wage-earning women. Third, entrepreneurial women, by running their own businesses, were in a distinct minority not only among all workers but also among all working women, an important and interesting point. Given the marital status and ages of most self-employed women, they would have had fewer options for wage-earning work. And in British Columbia in particular, wage-earning jobs for women were not plentiful in the early half of the twentieth century. This helps to explain the elevated rates of self-employment in the province compared to the rest of the country, regardless of size or status of business. Finally, all self-employed women had to consider operating businesses that fit societal ideas about what women were supposed to do. Whether they ran women's clothing stores or businesses tied to women's supposed domestic strengths, they tended to move into businesses that were appropriately feminine, again regardless of the size of business.

HISTORIOGRAPHY

Canadian researchers have rarely singled out businesswomen as a subject of study, and there are presently no competing works in the fields of business/labour/gender history. This material does not duplicate other works like it because other scholars are not researching the history of self-employed women in British Columbia or even in Canada generally. The history of women and work in British Columbia, especially that which deals with the twentieth century, is also sparse. Two useful collections, *In Her Own Right: Selected Essays on Women's History in BC* and *Not Just Pin Money: Selected Essays on the History of Women's Work in British Columbia*, were published in 1980 and 1984, while Gillian Creese and Veronica Strong-Boag's collection *British Columbia Reconsidered: Essays on Women* was published in 1992.[16] As useful as these collections have remained, their continued prominence indicates that more recent research on women and work in the province is scant. Research on women and self-employment is more so. One recent addition to the field is Lindsey McMaster's *Working Girls in the West: Representations of Wage-Earning Women.*[17] Her work goes beyond earlier studies that primarily documented women's presence in the workforce, but it does not address entrepreneurship.

My study does answer the call of Creese and Strong-Boag to take gender into account in British Columbia.[18] It also builds on more recent important contributions to family and gender history in western Canada. Adele Perry's *On the Edge of Empire: Gender, Race, and the Making of British Columbia, 1849-1871* is invaluable in its examination of colonial gender and race relations, although it does not move into the twentieth century. Chris Clarkson's *Domestic Reforms: Political Visions and Family Regulation in British Columbia, 1862-1940* touches on gender and family in British Columbia. Even so, these more recent contributions rarely separate female entrepreneurs from the female labour force.

While others have researched some aspects of female business ownership in the province, they have focused on nineteenth-century businesswomen and have rarely noted the relatively high rates of female entrepreneurship in British Columbia. Sylvia Van Kirk argues in "A Vital Presence: Women in the Cariboo Gold Rush, 1862-1875" that women had an impact on gold rush society "out of all proportion to their numbers," but she does not directly compare entrepreneurial women in British Columbia to women elsewhere.[19] While useful for understanding women in a particular time and place, Van Kirk's article does not make larger connections to the rest of the province or to the rest of Canada and deals only with the 1860s and early 1870s.

Peter Baskerville has examined mid-nineteenth-century businesswomen in an urban context.[20] His 1993 article on enterprising urban women in British Columbia is an exception to the general paucity of scholarship on entrepreneurial women, and his observation that historians have assumed women did not pursue entrepreneurial activity is still valid.[21] Baskerville also addresses the relationships between self-employment, marriage, and bearing children and suggests that studying self-employed women provides a way of "uncovering, at all class levels, the hopes, fears and aspirations of individuals within families."[22] His recognition of the importance of these variables prompted, in part, my considerations of marital status, age, and family among self-employed women across a broader time period.

Beyond these works, most research on entrepreneurial women in the province has been limited to biographical sketches, celebratory vignettes in local history publications, or short commentaries in studies about work or about women in the province more generally.[23] It has also largely been confined to studies of the nineteenth century. Robin Fisher noted in 1993 that British Columbia's historians should be thinking about getting into the twentieth century; we are now starting to do so, but in the field of gender/business history, the steps have been tentative.[24]

Research into how gender shaped women's entrepreneurial choices is almost non-existent. And despite the value of the works mentioned here, book-length studies that interrogate employment, family, and gender in British Columbia are lacking. The contribution of my research is threefold: it broadens our understanding of gender and work in the province; it broadens our understanding of women's family obligations in twentieth-century British Columbia; and it contributes to a little-known facet of the larger historiography of women in the labour force, female self-employment. There is a need to differentiate between types of women's work. Gender alone cannot unify all working women's experiences, and self-employed women were not the same as their wage-earning counterparts. The "proportionately smaller female population exercised a variety of options in tailoring their British Columbian life-course," and my work demonstrates that businesswomen also exercised these options in multiple ways.[25]

Scholars who are beginning to interrogate the intersection of gender and business history still form a small group. Research published in this area has been almost entirely American, and much of it dates to the late 1990s. The US literature suggests that gender is not widely acknowledged in the field of business history, in which women are largely absent except as helpmeets to men. Mary Yeager states in the introduction to *Women in Business* that there is "no theory of entrepreneurship, no theory of the firm, no theory of contracts or of marriage, no theory of the family, no feminist theory that adequately explains the history of women in business."[26] Similarly, gender and business historian Wendy Gamber suggests that "historians of women in business who venture forth in search of inter- pretative contexts are apt to return empty-handed."[27] Female entrepreneurs "fall between a number of historiographical cracks," which may explain the dearth of scholars willing to combine the fields of gender and business history.[28]

New directions in the field were explored in a special 1998 issue of the *Business History Review* that addressed the cross-disciplinary aspects of studying businesswomen. In this issue, Gamber suggests that three sub- disciplines of historical inquiry – business, labour, and women's history – can provide insights, but that inherent contradictions between subdisci- plines complicate the task of writing about women in business. Interest in the field has also developed hand in hand with the development of gender history. Joan Wallach Scott's seminal 1986 article "Gender: A Use- ful Category of Historical Analysis" first opened the doors for historians to develop "gender as an analytic category."[29] And in her contribution to the *Business History Review*, Scott suggests that gender "is a useful category of analysis in business history, but also that using it is no easy matter."[30] She reminds us that "reconciling questions about women's access, experi- ence, and status with questions about firms, markets, and economies is not an easy task."[31]

Women in Business, a three-volume collection edited by Mary Yeager, brings the themes of gender and business together and draws on the Amer- ican historiography of the mid- to late 1990s. Yeager suggests that with "more women and men in academia alert to issues of gender and culture, the boundaries distinguishing the sub-fields of history blurred."[32] By the 1990s, historians of women had "begun to recover the histories of business buried in the interstices of the economy, in local neighbourhoods, in mo- tels and hotels, in the beauty and funeral parlours, laundries, and boutiques" and, she adds, the "engendering of business history had begun."[33]

There have been other American contributions to the field, dating from the mid- to late 1990s. In addition to articles that may be seen as "thoughts on the history of business and the history of women," as one is subtitled,

Gamber also wrote *The Female Economy: The Millinery and Dressmaking Trades, 1860-1930*.[34] She has specifically examined female entrepreneurs from a gendered perspective. Others in the field include Angel Kwolek-Folland, who has written about the rise of office work and white-collar professional women.[35] She defines business broadly to include wage-earning and self-employed women. In her 1998 book *Incorporating Women*, she includes the business experiences of "entrepreneurs, women as members of family businesses, the business aspects of professionalization and women's roles as slaves, laborers, wage earners and managers."[36]

Gamber maintains that many scholars have been unable "to 'see' women as the proprietors of business concerns, let alone place them in any interpretive context."[37] The resulting problem is that "existing accounts (most of them the work of women's, not business, historians) either mention businesswomen in passing or celebrate the achievements of those who enjoyed unusual visibility or success."[38] I have attempted, as Gamber proposes, to place businesswomen in an interpretative context, examining them in relation to men, in relation to other women, and in relation to their families. This has not been done in histories of Canadian business, in which women are mentioned as exceptional actors either in the arena of business or in the arena of womanhood. Michael Bliss dismisses businesswomen almost completely in *Northern Enterprise: Five Centuries of Canadian Business*. The book jacket proclaims that Bliss surveys "the entire history of business in Canada" and tells the story of "enterprising men and women willing to take incredible risks."[39] This is not the case, for his attention to women is limited. He does not therefore actually survey the "entire" history.

Bliss notes that some wealthy male entrepreneurs who had hoped to pass down the family business "had no children or were dynastically crippled by having given birth to daughters."[40] Bliss, who presumably meant that the wives of these entrepreneurs gave birth, argues that when sons "were not there to ... take the helm it was necessary to go outside the family." Daughters were "not thought to have managerial potential or aspirations. What right-minded woman, almost certainly destined for marriage and motherhood, would think of business as a career, even if she did have a head for it?"[41] Bliss did not allow for the possibility that women could be mothers, wives, *and* businesswomen. In fact, marriage and motherhood did not impede most businesswomen. Sometimes it was the presence of unreliable husbands or dependent children that led women to entrepreneurship.

Other Canadian business histories have also given little space to female entrepreneurship, although they have not dismissed businesswomen as confidently as Bliss. *A Concise History of Business in Canada* by Graham Taylor and Peter Baskerville, published in 1994, is a broad study of the connections between Canadian business development and the evolution of capitalism. Like Bliss, Taylor and Baskerville cover an extensive period, from the 1600s to the 1990s. Their work focuses on larger themes rather than on microstudies of individual businesspeople. The individuals who get attention in the book are "heroic" men of business, those who acquired vast wealth and power; Sir Adam Beck, C.D. Howe, and other elite white men of business are mentioned in passing, as are family dynasties led by men, such as the Crosby or McCain families.[42]

While Taylor and Baskerville stress the growth of big business, they note the continued importance of individual small business owners to Canadian business history. However, it is primarily in the book's epilogue that they address the importance of examining new "challenges" to Canadian business history, such as gender relations and the importance of female-run businesses. In 2008, Baskerville revisited the connections between gender and business in *A Silent Revolution? Gender and Wealth in English Canada, 1860-1930*. The book is not solely about self-employed women, but it is about property and business ownership as it relates to women's acquisition of wealth. Baskerville details the ways in which women controlled wealth and exercised their economic rights with a rather high degree of independence, correcting our sense that Canadian women were not major economic players in the late nineteenth and early twentieth centuries.[43] This is one important part of female entrepreneurship, although the vast majority of female business owners in my study were running small businesses in which survival rated more highly than wealth acquisition. Managing investments was not on their radar.

The size of businesses is important to the field, and some scholars have done important research on small-scale entrepreneurs. John Benson defines the penny capitalist as a "working man or woman who went into business on a small scale in the hope of profit (but with the possibility of loss) and made him (or her) self responsible for every facet of the enterprise."[44] This is a good term for understanding female entrepreneurs, who were often penny capitalists. Benson includes women in this definition, found in his 1983 publication *The Penny Capitalists: A Study of Nineteenth-Century Working-Class Entrepreneurs.* He also specifically discusses Canadian women's experiences in *Entrepreneurism in Canada: A History of "Penny*

Capitalists." Benson suggests that women were pushed into penny capitalism, running "food and accommodations" types of businesses usually because of extreme poverty brought on by the death or disappearance of a spouse. But "nagging poverty" also drove married women to run small businesses, and he argues that many small enterprises are not quantifiable and are missed by census data.[45]

This is corroborated by Bettina Bradbury. In her examination of working-class families in mid-nineteenth-century Montreal, she points out that raising animals, gardening, domestic production, and taking in boarders were all methods of "retaining an element of self-sufficiency" for working-class families.[46] Even though they may not have been recognized as forms of entrepreneurship in the census, Bradbury argues that such strategies were forms of penny capitalism – although she does not refer to them as specifically entrepreneurial.

Labour historians have discussed working-class female penny capitalists in many contexts. While they have researched boarding-house keepers and women who sold butter, milk, and eggs or sewed in their homes, they have rarely identified them as entrepreneurial. When Canadian historians have acknowledged the existence of such entrepreneurial initiatives, they have examined them as non-wage contributions to family survival, as Bradbury has, or as temporary actions on the part of very poor women to cushion the blows of immediate financial crisis or seasonal unemployment, as Benson explains. My work reconceptualizes these interpretations of women's endeavours. Removing them from the history of the family economy and highlighting the ways in which their endeavours were entrepreneurial affords women a legitimate place among the self-employed: they ought to be viewed as in and of the business world, rather than being seen as home workers or secondary earners.

THEORETICAL CONSIDERATIONS

Incorporating the history of women with the history of business, without simply adding in women and celebrating the fact that they were in the field at all, is part of the challenge of a gendered history of female entrepreneurship. Joan Wallach Scott argues that the history of businesswomen cannot rest on the "emancipatory impulses of women's history."[47] Yet she also notes that while the study of separate spheres and the celebration of women-specific experiences of entrepreneurship may not be useful approaches, it is clear that "some kind of segregation did still exist in the world of business ... Specialization rested on sex-segregated markets."[48] Businesswomen were different in some ways from businessmen, and the differences deserve exploration. However, the interaction between men and women and between gender and business must be given consideration. The great benefit to applying an understanding that business is not gender-neutral to the history of business is that it permits the historian to view female entrepreneurs as businesspeople and as women. Making allowances for gender does not necessitate a retelling of the story of men in business; rather, it allows us to bring women into the history of business, focusing on them and accounting for the influence of sex and gender. Acknowledging gender means acknowledging that women's activities as entrepreneurs may or may not differ from men's, but that both men and women are involved. The challenge is to understand the experiences of female business owners in relation to male business owners, dealing with the differences without separating the two groups into entirely separate spheres.

For all these reasons, this study incorporates gender into the history of business. I argue, as have other Canadian gender historians, that women's lives are "no less rich or complex than men's, and that women's lives do not necessarily share the same rhythms."[49] Certainly, the importance of gender history in particular lies in the way in which it can "take us beyond the study of the subject 'woman.'"[50] While I acknowledge the importance of studying both men and women as gendered subjects and accept that they interact in the history of business in all kinds of gendered ways, this study nonetheless privileges the history of women. If the goal of gender history is in part to study relations between the sexes, it is also, as Gisela Bock maintains in her seminal essay on women's history and gender history, to study relations within the sexes. In arguing for a gender-encompassing approach rather than a gender-neutral approach, women's history can be "gender history par excellence."[51] Women's lives are as rich, complicated, and diverse as men's, and yet little has been written about the diverse experiences of businesswomen. It is possible and necessary to insert gender as a category of analysis into the history of businesswomen and to privilege only their stories over the already-established historiography of male businessmen.

Gender has become entwined with two additional analytical categories: class and race or ethnicity. As the authors of the Canadian collection *Gender Conflicts* emphasize, "just as gender is equally, though distinctly, constitutive for men and women, so, too, class and race or ethnicity inform the lives of all women."[52] Although *Gender Conflicts* was published in 1992, these words reflect a trend that has not waned in the intervening years: gender, class, and race have been intertwined in much of the Canadian social history published since the early 1990s.

Class is a difficult analytical category to apply to the history of business-women. Many female entrepreneurs ran very small businesses that lay at what Gamber refers to as the "murky boundaries of public and private, profit-seeking and philanthropic, wage labour and entrepreneurship, legitimate and illegitimate enterprise."[53] As Yeager points out, business-women's lives tell us "more about hopes and expectations than spectacular achievements; more about the property-less than the property-blessed ... more about petty market traders than rich merchants; more about service than manufacturing ... more about family strategies than managerial strategies."[54] Yet the fact that some women pursued "an option [self-employment] that suggested a somewhat individualistic outlook" and "wittingly or unwittingly set themselves 'above' those they served" means that self-employed women are not easily categorized.[55] In a narrow Marx-ist sense, businesswomen own the means of production. Since they are not members of the wage-earning proletariat, self-employed women are capitalists and, by extension, members of the middle or upper classes. The small size of their businesses and the fact that many businesswomen did not have employees suggests that they were members of the petite bour-geoisie (a less privileged group amongst the capitalist class), or as Benson suggests, penny capitalists.

For Marx, the petite bourgeoisie, which included small business owners, worked in order to survive, and members of this group sometimes had divided interests.[56] Thus, the question for our purposes: "At what point does a small businessman [or woman] stop being petty bourgeois" and become either a member of the upper class, Marx's capitalists, or a mem-ber of the working class, Marx's proletariat?[57] Should we, as Joan Scott asks, view businesswomen as workers or capitalists?[58] Clearly, definitions of class are complicated and point to another of the historiographical cracks that hinder the study of businesswomen: labour history has not integrated the histories of working women who happen to be self-employed into histories of working-class, wage-earning women – or, if they appear, their entrepreneurship is minimized. "Despite their proprietary status," female proprietors often remained within the working class.[59] Most female entrepreneurs in British Columbia did not acquire wealth by running small boarding houses, laundries, or hair salons. Most of the women documented in the first half of this study were "petty proprietors."[60] They operated small and financially vulnerable home-based businesses.

It is also the case that a businesswoman's relationship to the means of production and her level of financial success are not the only markers of class status. Social status, not linked directly to income, is part of one's class position. Marriage, family, and community affiliation inform one's class and status, and the types of businesses women owned could also indicate their social status and their degree of class privilege. In general, this study addresses women's social status and the sizes and types of businesses they operated. This does not mean I want to ignore women's class position; instead, my understanding of class is related to the size and type of business and the social position of the business owner more than the profitability of the business. A small hat shop with an elite clientele in an affluent retail area was very different from a small boarding house in a working-class neighbourhood, despite the fact that they might have generated similar levels of income. The women documented in the first half of my study may not have consciously considered their class position, but they did operate small businesses in which it seems that survival and a measure of independence took precedence over achieving great fortunes or increasing social status. They also lived with and worked with what we might call the proletariat. In some senses, these women were the proletariat of female business owners. On the other hand, women who belonged to BPW clubs sometimes ran small businesses with little profitability, yet it appears they considered themselves (by association or community prominence and by a sense of status and privilege) members of the middle class. The members of the BPW clubs discussed in the second half of this book were middle- and upper-class women, a particular group of professional, white, educated women of privilege in British Columbia. They would have felt they had little in common with working-class businesswomen, even though the profits and sizes of their business were similar.

Furthermore, although the ability to legally own property was important and may demonstrate that some women who held real estate had higher levels of status or income, owning property was not a necessary prerequisite of owning a business. I am less concerned here with the legal question of ownership than with women's declarations of their status as entrepreneurs in the census, business directories, and media. If they saw their work as entrepreneurial and if the census recognized them as self-employed, then for all intents and purposes they owned businesses, if not the buildings in which they operated.

That female business owners "defy easy categorization" in all kinds of ways should not lead us to abandon the question of their class status.[61] It is imperative to keep class status in mind, just as it is imperative not to assume that all businesswomen were automatically marginalized or that all businesswomen were automatically removed from the working class by virtue of owning a business. It is the case, however, that we do not have records for many of the most marginalized. Few businesswomen left records of their lives in print, and educated middle- to upper-class women left more written records of their lives than did lower-class women. The less numerous businesswomen who joined the BPW clubs do not represent the majority, but they are the women who left documents that tell us about their lives and aspirations. In this respect, the voices of the self-employed businesswomen heard most in this book are the voices of a relatively privileged group.

Race and ethnicity have also gone hand in hand with gender as categories of historical analysis. This study could be accused of ignoring more nuanced aspects of race and ethnicity in the history of businesswomen. However, just as gender history is not only the study of women, the history of race is not only the study of women of colour. My research focuses on Anglo-Canadian women who occupied "a position of race privilege."[62] That they were white women is not an indication that race was absent or that race cannot be used as an analytical category. The members of the BPW clubs did not interrogate their whiteness or their privilege; rather, they accepted it as fact. But they were privileged, nonetheless, and their race *and* class privilege was entwined with gender. In researching the history of white women, we may be tempted to bemoan their powerlessness as women, but we must also address their power as *white* women.

Of course, non-white, non-Anglo-Canadian women also operated businesses. Their stories do not appear in the records of the BPW clubs. They are among the more numerous, and more marginal, self-employed women documented in the first half of this study. The 1901 census recorded specific examples in British Columbia of First Nations women who were enumerated as hunter/fisher/farmers and who declared their status as self-employed.[63] The 1931 census included, in its data on British Columbia, the number of stores operated by "persons of Chinese and Japanese Origins." These figures show that about 12.9 percent of all Japanese and Chinese storekeepers in the province in 1931 were female. When all storekeepers in British Columbia were considered, a slightly lower percentage (12.3) were female.[64] Non-white women also appear in other sources, such as city directories: in 1918, *Wrigley's British Columbia Directory* listed Mrs. K. Ushijima, who operated a dry goods store and worked as a dressmaker in Vancouver.[65] One Japanese woman's small business is portrayed in

Tomoko Makabe's *Picture Brides*. Hana Murata describes the dressmaking business she opened in the late 1920s in Vancouver. Murata was twice-divorced, an unusual situation for any woman at the time, and she decided she was "going to work no matter what" rather than risking a third unhappy marriage.[66] She expresses pride in her independence: "I'd managed to stand on my own two feet and was confident I could make my way in life."[67] She ran the business for almost twenty years.[68] Murata also explains that in Vancouver "there were a lot of Japanese dressmakers, they say about 40 in those days, but not many like me, a woman working alone."[69]

There are, then, glimpses in the data of the importance of studying race and entrepreneurship in the province.[70] Yet in a larger sense, the data on female entrepreneurs in the province is extremely limited. First, there were relatively few female entrepreneurs in British Columbia, and within this small group, non-white women were an even more distinct minority. In addition, census data does not identify entrepreneurial women according to categories of ethnicity and race, with the exception of scattered information in some places, such as the 1931 census data on Japanese and Chinese storekeepers.[71] Lastly, few archival sources illuminate even the patterns of white middle-class entrepreneurs in the province. This study begins the task of incorporating women into the history of entrepreneurship but stops short of unravelling the many ethnic and racial identities of businesswomen in the province.

My research relies on quantitative sources (the Census of Canada) and qualitative sources, including the BPW club records of Vancouver and Victoria, newspaper articles, and archival collections. I provide a context within which more detailed studies of individual entrepreneurs can be researched; while individual women are discussed here, there was a need for an overview of the patterns of female self-employment in British Columbia and for a basic understanding of what kinds of women ran businesses and why they ran them. In addition to the published census returns from 1901 to 1951, I use the Canadian Families Project database – a 5 percent sample of the 1901 census – which includes far more detail about individual people, dwellings, and families than do any of the published census returns. One problem with using the 5 percent sample is that it does not include *all* self-employed women in the province or in the rest of Canada. By extension, it does not capture all types of female-operated enterprises that existed in 1901. There were relatively few entrepreneurial women in either region in 1901, and therefore the number in a 5 percent sample is also small: the database captures sixty-eight self-employed women living in British Columbia. However, the 1901 published census returns include almost no information on women in the labour force and no information on female self-employment. The Canadian Families Project database is therefore the best available source of census information on female self-employment in 1901. Moreover, it represents occupations that were most central in female self-employment; dressmakers, boarding-house keepers, and farmers are all represented.

While female-run enterprises such as retail clothing stores, private nursing homes, hospitals, and schools do not appear in the database, British Columbia business directories for 1901 demonstrate that they did exist. The Misses Crickmay were listed in the 1900-1 directory as proprietors of the Cottage Hospital in Nelson; widow Jane George ran a fruit and tobacco store in Nanaimo; and Mrs. David Matheson ran a ladies' furnishing business in New Denver. Other enterprises not captured by the database include "Birck & Daniels Ladies Furnishing," run by Alice Daniels and the widowed Anne Jane Birck, and a "select Preparatory School," run by Mrs. Frith in Vancouver. Other women were listed in the directory as grocers, hotel proprietors, restaurant owners, and owner-operators of old-age homes and schools.[72]

Some of these enterprises would shift in importance in later decades, but their relatively small numbers in 1901 explain their absence in the 5 percent sample of the 1901 census. Other occupations that did appear in the database also appeared in the 1900-1 directory and would remain significant for decades: according to both census data and directories, many women were employed (and some were self-employed) as dressmakers, nurses, stenographers, teachers, boarding-house keepers, and farmers in 1901 British Columbia.

The first half of this book should be seen as important contextualization for the lives of businesswomen of all classes in British Columbia. The second half closely examines a group that had more options because of race and class privilege and whose members were therefore slightly different from most female entrepreneurs in the province. It fleshes out BPW clubwomen's hopes, desires, and political and social commentaries about their work in a "man's world," something that most self-employed women – those myriad laundresses and boarding-house keepers eking out a subsistence income – did not or perhaps could not take the time to document. I hope that some of the latter women's experiences can be glimpsed occasionally through the eyes of their more privileged middle-class contemporaries, who documented their club life and their experiences as entrepreneurs in the province. The story of entrepreneurship for women in British Columbia is thus told here, with multiple techniques and lenses. The story covers women in different towns, operating a variety of businesses, but in the end the faces of female self-employment are illuminated. The ways in which these entrepreneurs were defined, and defined themselves, provide some understanding of businesswomen in male-dominated work worlds.

2

The Marriage of Business and Women

FAMILY STATUS AND ENTREPRENEURSHIP IN BRITISH COLUMBIA

B efore the Second World War, wage-earning women in British Columbia and in the rest of the country were very likely to be single, less likely to be married, and even less likely to be widowed or divorced. In the first half of the century, relatively few women returned to wage-earning jobs after marrying and having children. Self-employed women, however, were more likely to be married or once-married (widowed or divorced) than single. Furthermore, the ages and marital situations of self-employed women made the presence of children likely. When marriages end, children remain: the needs of family form part of the story of women and self-employment.

The fact that age, marital status, and child-bearing affected women's job options in the first half of the century was not unique to British Columbia. Self-employed women across Canada were more likely to be older, married, and mothers than were wage-earning women. However, the experiences of self-employed women in the province were different from those in the rest of Canada. In British Columbia, women married in higher proportions, and they continued to work after marriage (and after marriages ended because of widowhood, abandonment, or divorce) in higher proportions than did women in the rest of the country. Despite the passage of provincial legislation, such as 1901's Deserted Wives' Maintenance Act, which was supposed to "compel maintenance from deserting husbands," maintenance orders were "difficult to obtain and enforce."[1] Many married women with husbands absent but children present turned to self-employment as a means of support.

Women in British Columbia were also more likely than women in the rest of Canada to be self-employed. Frontier characteristics of the province, such as a scarcity of women and more opportunities to commercialize some services, help explain this propensity for self-employment. Interestingly, frontier characteristics may also explain why men in the province were less likely to be self-employed than their Canadian counterparts: men came to British Columbia because there were lots of opportunities to work as wage earners in natural resource extraction. They chose these readily available jobs over self-employment, but they were considered men's, not women's, jobs.

Women's marital status and the needs of their families also explain their relatively high rates of self-employment in the province. The presence of comparatively few (white) women meant high rates of marriage but not necessarily lasting marriages. Women with children sometimes supported their families alone. Frontier conditions pulled, while economic and familial situations pushed, some women into entrepreneurship.

Many studies of women in the labour force have focused on "working girls,"[2] wage earners who accounted for the steady rise in women's labour force participation in the first half of the twentieth century. These young single girls captured historians' attention, and most conclusions about the age, marital status, type of occupation, and even geographic locale of gainfully employed women in the decades before the Second World War have been reached based on wage earners. This approach to the female labour force overlooks the less numerous self-employed. Self-employment was not the most common choice of women (or men) between the census years of 1901 and 1951. Considering that they were a minority among all working men, businessmen have received more attention than businesswomen as biographical subjects: their enterprises have also garnered more interest than have women's. As Wendy Gamber facetiously points out, "is not the history of business – of self-made men, robber barons, and men in gray flannel suits – necessarily a chronicle of masculine activity?"[3] Mary Yeager argues that "men have long controlled, dominated and defined the business world."[4] Historians of business and enterprise and historians of women and work have largely ignored, or avoided studying, businesswomen.

That women's self-employment was a small component of the entire female labour force should not deter us from examining businesswomen more closely. Understanding the patterns of women's employment in their entirety demands that we look beyond the cadres of female wage earners. Moreover, identifying the actions of the minority may shift our perspective on women at work and how their employment choices reflected their marital status, age, family situation, and locality. Recognizing the patterns specific to female entrepreneurs broadens our understanding of women at work and illustrates that not all women in the labour force exhibit the same characteristics as the working girls of the early twentieth century.

Men greatly outnumbered women in British Columbia at the beginning of the twentieth century, and women in British Columbia had higher rates of marriage than did women in the rest of Canada. It should be stressed that the gender imbalance in the province is often assumed to be an imbalance between white men and white women, although census data on overall population size and overall rates of marriage included First Nations people who were enumerated by census takers. It is known, however, that First Nations people were under-enumerated. The proportion of the province's population that the census lists as First Nations at the turn of the century may be incorrect, but we do know that it had certainly declined since first contact.[5] According to census records, "Indians" constituted 14 percent of the total population of the province in 1901.[6] Given the scarcity of data about indigenous women – particularly indigenous self-employed women – and the likelihood that the First Nations population size was not accurately recorded, most of what I argue can really only be confidently applied to white settlers in British Columbia. Thus, this study deals primarily with white women, even though some First Nations women were wage earners and entrepreneurs.

Despite their low numbers, the relatively small population of women in the province had similar rates of employment as women in the rest of Canada. There were fewer women in British Columbia overall, but they were as likely to work as their Canadian counterparts.[7] This is especially interesting given that women's employment is usually strongly associated with being single; in British Columbia, however, less of the female population was single. Women in the province married but they also worked: married, widowed, and divorced women had higher labour force participation rates in British Columbia than in the rest of the country. Women in the labour force were also more likely to be self-employed in British Columbia. The higher rates of both marriage and self-employment among women in the province provide an opportunity for a closer examination of the relationships between women, marriage, and work.

This chapter uses data from the published reports of the Census of Canada from 1901 to 1951, as well as data from the Canadian Families Project's 5 percent sample of the 1901 census. When I refer to the adult population, I am relying on census definitions of adulthood, which seem surprisingly young by today's standards. The ages chosen to represent adulthood changed over the century, from ten and over between 1901 and 1931 to fourteen and over for 1941 and 1951. The change has little impact on this discussion, for we would rarely find girls between the ages of ten and fourteen among the self-employed population or among the married population. But it is worth noting that my data does not include those defined by the census as children.

FRONTIER CHARACTERISTICS

Some archetypal frontier characteristics associated with early white settlement in the mid-1800s were still evident in the early decades of twentieth-century British Columbia and help to explain women's employment and marriage options. Representative elements of the frontier included the large number of single white males from various social classes and occupational backgrounds, a perception of rowdy and undisciplined masculinity, and a perception that the province was on the outskirts of civilization.[8] I speak here of the frontier as a metaphorical open space, a site of encounter where "persons willing to take a chance on the unknown had a greater possibility to achieve their goals."[9] The idea of the frontier as an unknown and more permissive space is useful, although the concept is less applicable to the First Nations who had been living in the land that we now call British Columbia for centuries. They would not have viewed it as unknown or unexplored. With the arrival of white settlers, they experienced less "possibility" and more oppression. Certainly, the concept of the frontier as an undiscovered wilderness is only relevant in relation to the arrival of white settlers.

In the following discussion, I refer to a broad set of demographic characteristics associated primarily with the relatively recent white settlement in the region. While the census data probably under-represented the turn-of-the-century First Nations population, it is nonetheless clear that disease and other side effects of contact reduced indigenous populations and diminished their economic and political influence in the region as it became first a colony and then a province. Furthermore, the records I use refer to a set of cultural characteristics that speak primarily of the white settler population, although I do not presume that white settlement marked the beginning of the province's history.

The newness of white settlement, the influx of mostly male miners during the gold rush of 1858, and the high immigration rate in the early 1900s of single males who worked in logging, fishing, mining, and road and railroad building all contributed to an overabundance of men in the province.[10] Work for men at the turn of the century was in primary resource extraction or in road and town building, in preparation for the imminent arrival of more white settlers. Even after settlers arrived, the province's economy still relied on primary resource extraction – and the province was still largely undeveloped. By 1930, the British Columbia government had replaced old dirt roads with new ones, yet the system "remained meagre."[11] Cole Harris points out that in 1930 most of British Columbia was still roadless, and the province still had resources "in the spaces beyond the transportation corridors, often high on mountains or tucked away in inaccessible valleys."[12] While British Columbia was modernized by the time the Second World War began, some frontier elements had not changed: men still worked in logging camps and canneries, immigrants built cabins in remote areas inaccessible by paved roads, and "packhorse trails and railways intersected."[13]

The role that distance and geography played in the slow pace of modernization in the province, the continued economic reliance on primary resource extraction, and the isolation of many settlers in remote and inaccessible parts of the province are imprints of British Columbia history left behind by a frontier mentality. These imprints were present in 1901 and remained at mid-century. Remnants of the pre-1901 white settlers' struggles to tame and inhabit their new environment, their struggles with the province's First Nations inhabitants, and the effects of a gender imbalance that took decades to even out were still present in the 1950s. Vestiges of what Harris termed the "struggle with distance" remained, as did the overwhelming dominance of resource extraction in the province's economy.[14]

The gender imbalance was significant and long lasting. In 1901, there were 44,094 adult women in British Columbia out of a total adult population of 136,590. This means that there were 48,402 *more* adult men than women, a ratio of 2.10 to 1. By 1921, the ratio of adult men to women had dropped to 1.34 to 1, but there were still 61,575 more men than women, with a total adult population of 420,551. By 1951, the gender imbalance had all but disappeared. There were 23,079 more men in the province than women, but the total adult population had more than doubled since 1921, making the difference between numbers of men and women relatively slight.[15]

The gender imbalance in British Columbia was not reflected in the rest of Canada. In 1901, when only 32 percent of the adult population of British Columbia was female, 49 percent of the adult population of the rest of Canada was female. In 1911, when the ratio of adult men to adult women was 2 to 1 in British Columbia, it was 1.14 to 1 in the rest of the country, and this difference continued to be negligible from 1921 to 1951 in the rest of Canada.[16]

In the early decades of the century, adult women in British Columbia would have found it relatively easy to marry, while adult men may have had difficulty finding a spouse. As Elizabeth Herr noted in a study of women in 1880 Colorado, gender imbalances meant that women had better choices and options in the marriage market.[17] In British Columbia, Adele Perry suggests a scarcity model, the idea that "women's experience improves commensurate with their rarity ... women's value and options soar when their numbers trail behind those of the male population."[18] British Columbians noticed the connection between a small female population and a potentially attractive marriage market. Byron Johnson noted in 1872 that "even the homely laundress was raised by the scarcity of her sex into a goddess for the nonce."[19]

Census data indicates that more women were married in British Columbia than in the rest of Canada between 1901 and 1951. In 1901, 59.3 percent of all adult women in the province were married, while 45 percent of adult women in the rest of Canada were married. The percentage was consistently higher in British Columbia than in the rest of Canada for the next fifty years.[20] Fewer adult women were single in the province than in the rest of the country, and the percentage of single women was consistently lower in the province than in the rest of Canada between 1901 and 1951.[21]

In addition to their worth as sexual beings and eligible brides, white women were also labourers. Colonial promoters wanted white women to aid British Columbia's transformation "from a rough, racially plural resource settlement into an orderly settler colony."[22] This could occur through marriage, but frontier conditions also gave women "greater possibilities for independent economic activity," as Peter Baskerville suggests was the case in Victoria in 1901.[23]

Thus, settler men outnumbered women, who had correspondingly high rates of marriage but also a variety of employment opportunities.[24] At first glance, women in British Columbia seem to have been less involved in the labour force than women in the rest of Canada: because there were fewer women than men in the province, there were also fewer women than men in the labour force in British Columbia. But if we look only at the female population, we gain a better understanding of women and work. Looking only at women – what I call a female universe – demonstrates the greater labour force activity of some women over others, indicates more clearly the kinds of work that women undertook, and tells us more about their marital status and their work options.

If we consider only the adult female population, we see that women in British Columbia worked for pay in approximately the same proportions as their Canadian counterparts. In 1911, the published census reported that 15 percent of all adult women in British Columbia worked for pay, compared to 13.9 percent in the rest of Canada. In 1931, the percentages were similar: 17.2 percent in British Columbia and 17 percent in the rest of Canada. By 1951, 23 percent of all adult women in British Columbia and 23.7 percent of all adult women elsewhere in Canada were in the labour force.[25] If we consider self-employment, something else becomes clear: a higher proportion of all employed women were entrepreneurs in British Columbia than in the rest of Canada. Table 1 demonstrates that self-employed women were a minority of all women in the workforce, and

TABLE 1   Self-employed adult women as a percentage of all gainfully employed adult women in British Columbia and Canada, 1901-51

	1901	1911	1921	1931	1941	1951
BC	27.4	N/A	13.4	12.8	11.1	6.6
Canada	19.5	N/A	13.1	11.0	8.1	4.7

NOTES AND SOURCES: 1901 data is from the Canadian Families Project 5 percent sample of the 1901 census of Canada. Data on employment status of women in 1911 is not available. In 1921, data on female employment status – whether women were employees or self-employed – was limited. The only figure for female self-employment rates was listed in a 1931 table, and it was for all of Canada in 1921 (see Canada, Dominion Bureau of Statistics, *Census of Canada 1931*, vol. 13, table 29, which lists female self-employment for 1921 at 10.5 percent). For the somewhat higher 1921 figures listed in Table 1, I estimated rates of female self-employment based on occupations that had routinely high self-employment in the period from 1901 to 1951. For 1921 employment data used to estimate this, see Canada, Dominion Bureau of Statistics, *Census of Canada 1931*, vol. 7, table 1; *Census of Canada 1941*, vol. 3, table 1; *Census of Canada 1951*, vol. 4, table 1. Data was more complete for the period from 1931 to 1951: see Canada, Dominion Bureau of Statistics, *Census of Canada 1931*, vol. 7, table 21; *Census of Canada 1941*, vol. 7, table 5; *Census of Canada 1951*, vol. 4, table 11. The term "self-employed" includes those who worked for themselves (also called "own account") and those who employed others (employers). In this table, I have removed British Columbia figures from Canadian totals.

it shows the declining importance of self-employment among employed women generally. But it also illustrates that a higher proportion of gainfully employed women were self-employed in British Columbia than in the rest of the country.

Interestingly, this was not the case for men in the province. The proportion of men who were self-employed declined between 1901 and 1951, as it did for women, but adult men had lower rates of self-employment in British Columbia than in the rest of the country between 1901 and 1951. This difference is also related to the frontier characteristics of the province.[26] Men's employment opportunities were in jobs that did not employ many entrepreneurial men or many wage-earning women. A variety of unskilled employment was available for men in the province in mining, building and construction, and in the sawmilling industry between 1871 and 1921.[27] What is more noticeable is the number of men who worked in female-dominated wage-earning jobs as housekeepers, nurses, servants, and boarding-house keepers. In 1921 in British Columbia, 41.5 percent of boarding-house keepers were men, while 16.9 percent of boarding-house keepers in the rest of the country were male. In British Columbia, 3.7 percent of nurses were men, compared to 0.8 percent in the rest of Canada; 19.4 percent of housekeepers and 27.7 percent of servants were men in British Columbia; in the rest of Canada just 3.1 percent of housekeepers and 5.8 percent of servants were men. While the differences lessened, the pattern was still visible at mid-century.[28]

There are a few explanations for this. First, fewer women in the province, particularly in the late 1800s and early 1900s, meant fewer women to take jobs in what were traditionally female domains. Second, race and gender were entwined in these occupations. British Columbia had a large Asian population: at the end of the nineteenth century, up to two-thirds of domestic positions (servants, cooks, housekeepers) in the province were filled by Chinese men.[29] That there were fewer women available to do low-paid work, and that non-white men were willing or forced to take low-paid work, may account for the high number of men in "feminine" jobs. It is also possible that if Chinese men filled some of these positions, women may have looked elsewhere for employment or they may have been more likely to turn to self-employment.

If wage-earning jobs in British Columbia were plentiful for men, the opposite was true for women. There were almost no labouring jobs in resource industries, with the exception of canneries. Women's employment in manufacturing was extremely limited, "in contrast to eastern Canada where industries that employed women – clothing and textiles, canning

TABLE 2   Marital status of gainfully employed adult women in British
Columbia and Canada, 1901-51

	Single (%)		Married (%)		Widowed or divorced (%)	
	BC	Canada	BC	Canada	BC	Canada
1901	60.1	78.5	24.6	9.3	15.3	12.2
1921	77.2	82.3	11.4	7.0	11.4	10.7
1931	76.5	81.0	13.6	9.8	9.9	9.2
1941	74.9	80.3	11.3	10.2	13.8	9.5
1951	49.8	63.3	39.3	29.1	10.9	7.6

NOTES AND SOURCES: Data for 1911 is not available. Data for 1901 is from the Canadian
Families Project database; all other data is from published censuses, 1921-71. See Canada,
Dominion Bureau of Statistics, *Census of Canada 1921*, vol. 2, table 24; *Census of Canada
1931*, vol. 1, table 17B, and vol. 7, tables 25-29; *Census of Canada 1941*, vol. 1, tables 20 and
63; vol. 3, table 7; and vol. 7, table 5; *Census of Canada 1951*, vol. 2, tables 1 and 2, and
vol. 4, table 11. For my figures, I have taken British Columbia data out of Canadian
totals in order to compare the province to the rest of the country.

and food processing, and tobacco – were more developed."[30] One result
of these characteristics of the province was high rates of self-employment
for women and low rates of self-employment for men.

Marital status is a key variable in understanding the difference between
self-employed women and wage-earning women. It also helps elucidate
the high rate of female self-employment in British Columbia. First, it is
clear that the majority of women in the labour force in the first half of the
twentieth century were wage earners, and many historians have demonstrated that women in the labour force were likely to be young and single.[31]
Census data also demonstrates that the percentage of the adult female
population that was single ranged from about 20 to 30 percent in both
British Columbia and Canada, but the percentage of the gainfully employed female population that was single was much higher (Table 2).

Table 2 also tells us something specific about British Columbia: just as
there were more married and fewer single women in British Columbia
than in the rest of Canada, there were also more married and fewer single
women in the labour force in British Columbia than in the rest of Canada.
Women in the province married in high numbers and worked in high
numbers. These two factors are connected to their high self-employment
rates; women who were not single and who were more likely to have children to support were also more likely to be self-employed than working

for wages. If wage earning was for single women, self-employment was the domain of married or once-married women.

This is not clear, of course, in data that does not distinguish the marital status of wage-earning women from that of self-employed women. To tease out the importance of marriage and family to self-employed women, we need to look at entrepreneurial occupations in the province. The Canadian Families Project's 5 percent sample of the 1901 census demonstrates that 73.5 percent of self-employed women in British Columbia were married, widowed, or divorced, while almost as many wage-earning women – 72.8 percent – were single. Published census data between 1901 and 1951 does not differentiate the marital status of all wage-earning women from that of all self-employed women. However, by selecting jobs with high rates of female self-employment – such as hotel and boarding-house keepers; farmers; and owners of retail stores, taverns, or restaurants – the pattern of high rates of marriage, widowhood, and divorce is evident. For example, 100 percent of female farmers and boarding-house keepers in the province in 1901 were married, widowed, or divorced. In 1931, 49 percent of women who worked in jobs with high rates of self-employment were married, widowed, or divorced.[32] Again, in jobs with almost total self-employment, the pattern is even more obvious: in 1931, 84 percent of female farmers and 91 percent of female boarding-house keepers were married, widowed, or divorced. The same pattern is evident in 1941 and 1951 census data.[33]

Jobs that featured high rates of entrepreneurship show us that self-employed women in British Columbia were far more likely to be married or once-married than single, unlike the majority of women in the workforce who were more likely to be single wage earners. City directories indicate that married women in the province ran a wide variety of businesses. Mrs. Hanes in Kelowna and Mrs. Clark in Cranbrook operated dairy farms in 1918, while married women in Vancouver ran grocery, tobacco, and confectionery stores; bakeries; tearooms; laundries; and women's clothing stores. Businesses normally operated by men could occasionally be avenues of entrepreneurship for married or once-married women in the province. Mrs. H. Couts, for example, operated the Seymour Street Auto Stand in Vancouver.[34]

Mrs. Couts may have been widowed or deserted. Regardless, it seems clear that she did not operate this business with a spouse. If she had, he would have been listed in the directory, given the type of business Couts operated. It is also unlikely that dairy farms run by husbands and wives would be listed in city directories under only the woman's name. It was unusual for a business run by a married couple to be listed solely as the woman's business, unless there was a legal reason to keep the business separate, such as to protect property from a husband's debts and liabilities. In fact, one benefit that accrued to men from the passage of married women's property laws in the late 1800s was that a married man could protect his property from creditors by putting it entirely in his wife's name. Beyond this, there was little reason for a married man to list his wife as the owner or co-owner of a business run by both spouses. This makes married women's entrepreneurship all the more interesting. Married women were actively engaging in self-employment and their actions suggest that if they were listed as sole proprietors, their husbands were either absent, deceased, or, less commonly, wage earners who were uninvolved in their wives' enterprises.

I am interested in businesses run solely by women rather than those run by husbands and wives together. Women's entrepreneurial status was often obscured if they were in partnership with their husbands. Furthermore, the question of property ownership is not always germane to the question of entrepreneurship: some women might have been property-less but self-employed, while other women owned property but were not entrepreneurs. However, it is the case that after the passage of married women's property laws, it was theoretically possible for women to own businesses with their husbands as well as independently of their husbands.[35]

Marriage and Entrepreneurship

The connections between marriage and entrepreneurship are clear in Canada, and they are especially clear in British Columbia. Beyond the fact that there were simply more married women in the province, they were also more likely to be out working.[36] The observation that a new frontier in Colorado had "loosened the constraints under which women lived in more established areas and offered them a variety of opportunities," may also apply to women in British Columbia.[37] The "relative scarcity of women" in the first half of the twentieth century indicated an "attractive marriage market," and this, combined with a demand for female labour, allowed women to both marry and work.[38] In British Columbia, women could arguably demand a higher wage for performing services that were usually provided by women because there were fewer women available to provide them, but they could also expect to marry eventually.

These trends were clear early in British Columbia's development as a resource frontier. Sylvia Van Kirk argues that during the Cariboo gold rush (1862-75), women (particularly wives) had a role to play and "an impact on the society out of all proportion to their numbers."[39] While the mining frontier "did not provide an opportunity for women to step out of traditional sex roles it did occasion rather exceptional opportunities to commercialize these by providing a range of services for a large male population."[40] In the Cariboo, many women married *and* opened businesses.[41] This continued to be the case throughout the first half of the twentieth century. The unique combination of the characteristics of the frontier, the scarcity of women, and the high rates of marriage, which Elizabeth Herr points to in Colorado, are also visible in British Columbia. These factors are linked to women's entrepreneurial endeavours in the province.

Herr argues that in Colorado the pull of a high wage attracted married women to the labour force. "Almost all women seemed to marry eventually ... but this did not preclude some women from participating in the labor force."[42] Charlene Porsild notes that such pull factors existed at the beginning of the twentieth century in the Klondike, another frontier with high ratios of women to men: enterprising women found that work was "plentiful and the demand for services was high."[43] In Dawson and other communities, Porsild notes that the demand for restaurants, saloons, and laundries ensured employment and business opportunities for many women. When women were scarce in the Klondike, female-typed work brought considerable wages.[44] The scarcity of women in British Columbia also led to a market demand for the types of services women typically provided, such as food preparation, cleaning, lodging and boarding establishments, nursing, and teaching. Married women may have been pulled into entrepreneurship in British Columbia, lured by the need for their services and by financial reward. Women such as Mrs. Koenig, listed in the 1905 British Columbia directory as widow of George and "proprietress" of the Shawnigan Lake Hotel in the small community of Koenig's Station, operated their businesses in isolated frontier regions.[45] They were motivated by the needs of male workers who were willing to pay handsomely for lodging, food, and drink. Married proprietors such as Mrs. Revesbeck, Mrs. Roberts, and Mrs. Allen operated hotels in Yale, Nelson, and Rossland, small outposts that existed only to provide services to men working on the resource frontier.[46] These businesses, set up to serve a larger industry, provided a niche for female entrepreneurs at the beginning of the twentieth century, but frontier conditions persisted in British Columbia until at least the 1950s.

Women also worked after marriage because of what might be called push factors, namely, when spouses did not provide adequate financial security. A higher proportion of self-employed married women in British Columbia than in Canada were living without a spouse and were listed in the census as heads of their households. The 5 percent sample of the 1901 census reveals that 53.8 percent of women in British Columbia who reported that they were married and self-employed (or employers) headed their households, which usually meant they were living without men. According to 1901 census instructions, men who were away temporarily were to be listed as head of the household if they normally lived there for part of the year. Female-headed households were described that way because there was no male present, and these women can be considered as separated or single. This helps explain the high percentage of married, self-employed women in British Columbia: many of them were effectively single and self-employed, but they did not have the means to state that they were separated. And by law they were married women. The instructions to enumerators for the 1901 census indicated that couples "separated as to bed and board will be described as married."[47]

In the rest of Canada, the percentage of married, self-employed women who were listed as heads of households, and presumably lived without a spouse, was 19 percent in 1901. Proportionately more married, self-employed women lived with a spouse outside of British Columbia. The percentage of married women who said they were heading their households decreased after 1901 but remained higher in British Columbia than in the rest of the country.[48]

We need to be careful not to make too many inferences about the reasons married women entered the labour force. Older arguments that suggested married women worked for pin money may not be justified if these women did not live with their husbands and had no income but their own. If marriage was a form of economic security for women, it is reasonable to infer that when husbands ceased to provide economic support, and when Deserted Wives' Maintenance legislation passed by the provincial government proved ineffective, married women were compelled to enter or return to the labour force. Self-employed housekeeper Maggie Yates of Rossland, British Columbia, whom the census listed as married but not living with her spouse, worked to support herself and her eight-year-old daughter in 1901. Marriage did not provide her with economic security. Self-employed washerwoman Minnie Mcleod of Slocan was in the same position and raising two children, ages five and seven.[49] Being legally married but having no spouse at home was in many ways the same as being single.

There are a few possible reasons for the high numbers of married women who lived without their husbands in the province. The pressure to marry may have been strong enough to sway even the faint of heart in British Columbia, but long-time bachelors may have been ill-prepared for the rigours of marriage. While they married quickly and excitedly, perhaps anticipating wedded bliss after months or years labouring with other single men, the reality of married life with women they hardly knew may have overwhelmed many men. George Seel, a trapper and prospector in north central British Columbia, married Else Lübcke in 1927, the day after she arrived from Germany in response to his advertisement for a bride. One week after they arrived at their home near Burns Lake, George left for two months of trapping and hunting.[50] While Seel occasionally returned home, he repeatedly left his family to pursue work.

Men like George Seel returned to the transient or seasonal work they had done before marriage. While the Seels remained married until George's death in 1950, his homecomings were sporadic. Some men never returned, leading wives to list themselves as household heads. Employment opportunities in remote resource areas may have lured men back into nomadic working lives. George Seel did not change his nomadic ways upon marriage. Elsie Lübcke Seel may have been one of those who listed herself as head of her household, given that her husband was rarely home.[51]

It is also possible that men and women who were living separately still saw each other throughout the year and supported each other emotionally or financially. The census cannot describe or explain what marriage meant to individual couples. Olive Fredrickson's first husband, Walter Reamer, whom she described as "afflicted with a fatal wanderlust," repeatedly left his wife and their three young children to wander, work, and trap.[52] She moved in 1928 with the children but without Reamer to a 600-acre homestead in northern British Columbia, which she purchased with her own earnings.[53] Yet she was still married and waited for her husband to join her. He never arrived at the homestead: he drowned in 1928 while on one of his long absences, and she was left a widow at the age of twenty-seven. While she clearly had not been able to depend on her husband for much of their married life, Olive Fredrickson lived sporadically with him, bore his children, and at the time of his death was anticipating his imminent return. Yet, given his many and prolonged absences, Frederickson may also have listed herself as a household head in the census prior to his death and was almost certainly listed as head of her household after her husband's death and before her remarriage.

Absence but also unreliability of a spouse factored into married women's decisions to work. The view that a married woman working outside of the home in the United States in 1900 provided a "clear and inescapable signal that her husband had failed to provide for his family" undoubtedly also applied in British Columbia at the turn of the century.[54] Not all married men were good providers. Susan Van Horn makes the point that the "pin money" designation did not fit these women either and represented "a humiliating degradation of both the value of their work and the import- ance of the money they brought home to their families."[55] Many married businesswomen whose husbands were employed intermittently or not at all were working because their income was needed. Mary Walker, a self- employed married dressmaker in Grand Forks in 1901, may have worked to supplement her husband's income. Marth Frenneth, listed in the 1901 census as a forty-three-year-old self-employed restaurant keeper in Ross- land, was raising ten children with her husband, who did not run the restaurant with his wife: he was a wage earner. Otto Freneth may even have been a good provider, but the family's size probably necessitated two incomes.

Rather than being deserted by their spouses, some women may have chosen to leave their marriages. Sylvia Van Kirk suggests that for women in the Cariboo, economic opportunities may have provided "a chance to escape from an unhappy marriage."[56] Whatever – or whoever – caused the marriages to falter, women who continued to state that they were married but who clearly headed their own households were more likely to be self- employed than employees.

WIDOWHOOD

In British Columbia, there were therefore a number of potential pull and push factors inflating the participation rate of married women in the labour force generally and in self-employment in particular. Some of these factors also applied to once-married women, those who were widowed or divorced. Widowed or divorced women participated in the labour force in higher rates in British Columbia than in the rest of Canada, and for the first half of the century they were also appreciably more involved in the labour force than were married women.[57]

These features seem irregular; one would think that the gender imbalance in the first half of the twentieth century, which led to high rates of marriage among women in the province, would have provided strong incentives for remarriage as well. Several factors help explain why many of these women worked. Widows in particular (for there were many more widows than divorcées for most of the period under study) were apt to be poor and vulnerable. Their survival strategies more frequently involved entering the workforce than remarrying. Bettina Bradbury states that in nineteenth-century Montreal, men whose wives had died remarried rapidly, essentially replacing one domestic worker with another, while women did not have the same opportunities for remarriage.[58] Widows often had children at home. The prospect of marrying an older woman with children, and with few financial assets, was likely not an attractive one to many men. Bradbury argues that "widows already experienced in motherhood should have appeared attractive spouses, but they competed in the marriage market with young, attractive, and not yet weary girls."[59] This was true even in British Columbia, where there were ostensibly fewer "not yet weary" girls available for marriage because of the gender imbalance.

A widow's age and the presence or absence of children were thus "critical factors in determining whether or not she would remain a widow."[60] Those who did remarry were apt to be under the age of forty and childless.[61] This was the case for widows in the late nineteenth century, but it also applied to women in early-twentieth-century British Columbia. However, it is difficult to study young widows since remarriage obviously altered their status. Anna Sprott, in her mid-thirties and with a young daughter, was a widow when she arrived in Vancouver in 1911. She remarried in 1918 and had a long career as a married businesswoman and city politician. Sprott's prominence makes her an exception to the rule that remarriages can be difficult to trace.[62] Nonetheless, it is clear from the census and from other sources that older widows with children were more likely to remain widows. Annie Gordon was a typical example: widowed in 1911, she found she was "kept busy with financial affairs," with her children, and with an expanding role in social reform and public service. Remarriage was either not wanted or not plausible for a woman in her mid-forties with three children.[63]

The relative scarcity of women in British Columbia may not have been enough incentive for widows to find a new spouse: their liabilities (age, financial vulnerability, and possibly dependents) outweighed their attributes.[64] Moreover, the frontier nature of the province provided pull factors for enterprising women that included higher wages and a market demand for women's services, factors that might have enticed widowed women more than the prospect of remarriage.

At the other end of the spectrum, some widows were financially secure enough that they may have been able to attract a new spouse but did not need or want one. Affluent widows "may have shunned a second marriage in order to maintain their financial independence."[65] Perhaps this was the case for forty-six-year-old newspaper publisher Rena Whitney. According to the 1901 census, her twenty-two-year-old son lived in Vancouver with Whitney; he was a printer, likely employed at his mother's newspaper. Whitney was listed in the British Columbia directory in 1901 as "Mrs. Rena Whitney, wid. Mayo, editor, Mt. Pleasant Advocate."[66] Widows such as Whitney often inherited the businesses that they had helped their husbands run, even if their roles were not acknowledged when their spouses were alive. They became the proprietors, a better option for many than remarriage. Inheriting a husband's business was therefore another reason for widows' high rate of self-employment. Bradbury also argues, in the case of late-nineteenth-century Montreal, that some widows had the "practical experience" and knowledge they needed to continue to operate the businesses after the death of their spouse.[67] Others chose to set up their own businesses rather than remarry.[68] If they received any pension or death benefit, opening a small business was an important survival strategy.[69]

It is also the case that wealthy widows more easily attracted new spouses than did poor widows. Peter Baskerville has noted that in 1901 Victoria widows remarried at relatively high rates, but he links this fact to the accompanying high rates of property ownership and investment activity. Widows with property had greater opportunities for remarriage. Women were gaining independence in economic activity through land ownership and investments – but they had full control over these investments and did not relinquish control when they remarried.[70]

Proprietorship, like other kinds of work, "potentially freed women from economic dependence on men."[71] The same factors that might have led to a high participation rate of widows and divorcées in the labour force generally – vulnerability or a desire to remain independent – may have also influenced their interest in self-employment.

Furthermore, widows may have been overrepresented in self-employment because they were, like married women, less likely than young single women to be hired in wage-earning occupations. Even though married and once-married women with no men to support them were not castigated for entering the labour force, they did not enter wage-earning occupations in large numbers, suggesting at least a societal barrier. Many women and men saw wage-earning jobs as the domain of men, particularly if they had families to support. Widowed and divorced women may have turned to self-employment because wage-earning jobs were not a viable option for married or once-married women. On the other hand, home earning was an "attractive alternative to public sphere employment" for women who were bound by home responsibilities.[72] Married or widowed women who had children and domestic work that tied them to their homes turned to home-based forms of self-employment, such as taking in boarders, sewing and laundry, and operating small shops.

Margaret Hobbs discovered outright hostility directed toward married women in the labour force in Canada during the 1930s. Many people expressed concern that wage-earning women were taking jobs away from men, and Ontario premier Mitchell Hepburn announced in 1936: "We take the position, as have all previous governments, that if a woman marries, her husband should keep her."[73] British Columbians expressed similar opinions. In 1939, Vancouver City Council considered denying employment to married women in stores, offices, and factories.[74] And as the Second World War ended, the *Prince Rupert Daily News* argued for women in industrial jobs returning to their homes. The newspaper suggested that one way to ensure this was "for some veteran to take a woman's job, then marry her and support her."[75]

Joan Sangster refers to a marriage bar that existed at least until the Second World War: employers who willingly hired women only employed single women. In her case study of Peterborough, Ontario, Sangster argues that the marriage bar was "linked in women's minds to the impermanent status of women in the workforce and to the family wage ideal."[76] Thus, the bar was real in many cases, but it was also imagined in the minds of the women. "In those days," one woman recalled, "your husband kept you. That's why you got married."[77]

With such limitations on married women's labour force participation in effect until the mid-twentieth century, married or once-married women may have felt freer to pursue self-employment than to seek out wage-earning jobs. Subject to policies such as that of the Manitoba government, which declared in the 1930s that for civil service jobs the "retirement of women is compulsory at marriage,"[78] they turned to self-employment instead. The six female founders of York House, a private school for girls that opened in 1932 in Vancouver, did just this: some of the women recalled that they "wanted to keep on working and were not allowed to teach in the public school because [they] were married."[79] The idea that married

women did not belong in wage-earning jobs may have continued to influence women who were widowed or divorced to turn to self-employment
until at least the 1950s, if not beyond.

THE FAMILY CLAIM

The most important reason why many married, widowed, and divorced
women ran businesses was the need to support their children. In *The Tale
of Benjamin Bunny*, a children's story written by Beatrix Potter in the
early twentieth century, we are introduced to Old Mrs. Rabbit, a widow
who "earned her living by knitting rabbit-wool mittens" and by selling
herbs, tea, and "rabbit-tobacco."[80] This widow was also the mother of
Flopsy, Mopsy, Cotton-tail, and Peter. Potter's story, first published in
1904, depicts a widowed mother working in a home-based business in
support of family. While Potter's widowed rabbit is a fanciful and fic-
tional character, the historical reality is that entrepreneurship was an
important source of income for older women with children. Self-employed
women in British Columbia and Canada were not only more likely to be
married or once-married, they were also older than their wage-earning
counterparts.[81] These facets of female self-employment elucidate the need
to consider family in women's decisions to enter, or re-enter, the labour
force. The claims of family had particular importance for self-employed
women, who were in a different stage of the life cycle than most wage-
earning women. The history of self-employment is closely tied to the
history of the family, as the image of Old Mrs. Rabbit, a mother and a
widow, confirms.

As has been noted, many self-employed women were married, but their
husbands were infirm, absent, or otherwise unable to work. They were
thus like single women, who worked because they were not financially
cared for by a male breadwinner, but they were unlike single women in
that they often had children. As historian Lisa Wilson has noted, when
families "suffered the loss of a father and husband, the woman left behind,
then as now, had to juggle financial and family responsibilities."[82]

The family's claims upon women influenced their decisions to enter the
labour force. Prominent American reformer Jane Addams argued that
women placed the family's needs before other considerations. She called
this "the family claim."[83] Historian Angel Kwolek-Folland also uses the term
and suggests that "women's involvement in business usually occurred in
the context of their families' needs rather than for personal autonomy or

individual satisfaction (although those things may have followed)."[84] While many women, regardless of their status as wage earners or as entrepreneurs, entered the labour force out of necessity, the majority of self-employed women were in a different stage of their life cycles than their wage-earning counterparts. The idea that the claims of family (particularly dependent children) led some women to enter the labour force is a useful concept for thinking about women who were self-employed. Of course, not all married women had children. But the chances were considerably greater that an older married or once-married woman would have children, compared to young, single, wage-earning women. Thus, the family claim is much more pertinent to self-employed women, who were older and more likely to be married, widowed, or divorced than their wage-earning counterparts. Family motivated women's employment and seems to have been a key to women's self-employment.

As Julie Matthaei has suggested, "jobs incompatible with active home-making were almost exclusively reserved for single women" in the early twentieth century, while occupations that could be viewed as an extension of homemaking but that also happened to be entrepreneurial — such as taking in sewing, laundry, or boarders or operating small enterprises out of the home — were undertaken by married or widowed women.[85] Lucy Eldersveld Murphy noted that in the American Midwest motherhood may have increased the desire for additional income and "promoted the choice of self-employment over other types of work because a proprietor could set her own hours and, when necessary, locate the work most advanta-geously relative to her children."[86] Women had to coordinate "enterprise with family responsibilities" in the mid- to late nineteenth century, and I suggest that this did not change drastically for twentieth-century women in British Columbia. A dressmaker from Grand Forks, Mary Walker, exemplified this pattern: working at home as a self-employed dressmaker undoubtedly made it easier for her to care for her two-year-old son while still earning an income.

For much of the twentieth century, women specifically exited the labour force because of pregnancy, child rearing, or marriage (although the latter reason became less of an obstacle for women after the Second World War). The critical difference between working men and women with families was not that women supported families when necessary by entering the labour force, since men also did this, but that the needs of their families shaped the kinds of work they undertook and dictated when and how they entered the labour force. Women's business interests were irrevocably tied to their familial interests. They went out to work or opened businesses when it was necessary for the survival of family, but their employment also had to fit around the tasks that they performed in the home. Those who chose to work "always had to find accommodation with the demands of marriage and family."[87] In contrast, men might be businessmen and also husbands and fathers, but the roles were not necessarily entwined, nor did the demands of caring for family members specifically dictate whether they opened businesses or worked as wage earners. Men entered the labour force to establish themselves as successful men and household heads, while women sought money to aid the family.[88]

The way we define female entrepreneurs must take into account those "who act not as individuals but ... for family prosperity and survival."[89] While more could be said regarding the sexual division of labour and the role of capitalism in enforcing gender roles,[90] what is important in this context is that in the first half of the twentieth century most married women did not work outside the home. Homemaking and child rearing were publicly lauded (but unpaid) feminized vocations. In turn, women's decisions to return to the labour force were frequently in support of that primary interest, identified as women's interest: family. More importantly, women who were at the stage of their life cycle in which they were more likely to have children and who were married or had been married were much more likely to choose self-employment than were their younger single female counterparts.

When women entered the labour force, society praised those who took in boarders or sold chickens to supplement family income.[91] Moreover, women specifically framed their entrepreneurial endeavours as a means of helping their families in order to justify their entry into business. If a woman "tried to do men's work for her own self-advancement, she would be shamed and ostracized; but if she undertook the work of men because her family's needs dictated it, her actions were ... praised."[92] The kind of work that married women did was often home-based, and it could be supplemental. But it was also often entrepreneurial. Married women taking in boarders were not working for wages: they were self-employed, even though they may not have considered themselves as such. There are many examples in the Canadian Families Project database of the 1901 census of women who were clearly working as boarding-house keepers or in their husbands' businesses but who were not listed as gainfully employed. David McCannell lived in Vancouver with his wife, Elisabeth, and their four daughters, one son-in-law, and one granddaughter. While Elisabeth was not listed as having an occupation and David's only listed occupation was as a wage-earning blacksmith, the family also had sixteen boarders living in their household. Elisabeth McCannell was most certainly occupied. We could make the case that she was a self-employed boarding-house keeper, despite the census record.

Many married women in 1901 British Columbia lived with their husbands and had boarders in the house, but census takers listed the men as having other jobs and the women as having no jobs: neither spouse was listed as a boarding-house keeper. Similarly, census takers did not list the vast numbers of "farmer's wives" as employed, even though they undoubtedly worked alongside their husbands on family farms. When women were married and their husbands were present and employed, there seems to have been reluctance on the part of census takers (and society more broadly) to recognize the wives as employed. This is noticeable in the case of occupations that might normally be seen as entrepreneurial. The work of women, particularly when they were secondary earners in the household and when their work took place in the home, was not well documented. The way the census recorded these women reflects a societal understanding that husbands were financially responsible for wives.

We can infer that the presence of children significantly affected why and where women worked. In this respect, marital status is a critical link between family and entrepreneurship. Self-employed married or once-married women were more likely than single women to be supporting, either partially or fully, dependent children. Deana Pike, a self-employed hotel keeper in Cumberland, British Columbia, had four children, ranging in age from eight to eighteen, living at home in 1901. She also housed thirteen lodgers. She was married, but she headed her household and her husband was absent. Minnie McLeod, Marth Frenneth, Mary Walker, and Maggie Yates were recorded in the 1901 census as married, self-employed mothers. As Murphy noted, self-employment provided such women with a "flexibility of schedule" that could accommodate child rearing to a certain extent.[93] Widowed dressmaker Maria Forester of Vancouver was fifty years old and supporting her eight-year-old son, Hector, in 1901. Another Vancouver widow recorded in the 1901 census, Alice Berry, supported her three sons — ages six, eight, and nine — by working as a self-employed music teacher.

These women were not unusual. Widows were also mothers, and many supported their children through self-employment. However, while Alice Berry may have been typical in 1901 as a young widow supporting children, her entrepreneurial life would become prominent and atypical in terms of the level of success she achieved. Berry founded World Printing and Publishing in 1905 and in 1911 purchased, with her father's help, the *Vancouver World* newspaper from Sara McLagan (another prominent female entrepreneur). Berry was the first woman to be a managing director of a Canadian daily newspaper. In 1916, she married Louis D. Taylor: a sometime newspaper publisher and one-time business partner of Berry, he served as mayor of Vancouver seven times between 1910 and 1934. Berry died in 1919, just three years after marrying Taylor; he survived until 1946.[94]

Berry was quite successful, but many other mothers probably found it difficult to support their children with the proceeds of their enterprises. Single mothers were an economically vulnerable group. Their financial success was not guaranteed, particularly because their businesses were usually very small and their income was irregular. Poverty and family breakups were common. Not all widows succeeded at supporting their families through self-employment – but the same was true of wage-earning women who struggled to provide for family members.[95]

Another factor influenced entrepreneurship: part-time work or occupations with flexible schedules were not common prior to 1950. Full-time hours, long workdays, and inflexible schedules were obstacles to some women's entry into wage-earning occupations until after 1950, when an "increase in part-time work made it possible for women with household responsibilities to enter and remain in the labour force."[96] With limitations on married or once-married women's labour force participation in effect until the mid-twentieth century in the form of general hostility, marriage bars, and a lack of flexibility in scheduling or in the number of hours worked, some pursued self-employment instead. If they did not inherit a husband's business, did not have a reliable or living spouse, did not wish to remarry, or could not find wage-earning work, they set up small businesses.

Some of the barriers to wage-earning occupations for women who were married or once-married lessened after the Second World War. This helps to explain a particularly steep decline in female self-employment between 1941 and 1951 (see Table 1). The wartime and postwar demand for labour, the increased availability of part-time work, and demographic changes that "reduced the supply of young female employees" while also increasing the supply of older married or widowed workers,[97] meant that wage earning became an option for married or once-married women. The postwar opening up of the labour force to women other than young single workers provided wage-earning alternatives to self-employment for married, widowed, and divorced women.

AGE AND ENTREPRENEURSHIP

Age is also an important factor in understanding women's participation in self-employment rather than wage-earning jobs. While not every published census reported the age of female workers in various occupations, the 1921 census provided a fairly detailed commentary on the age of female workers in Canada. Table 3 strikingly demonstrates the age differences between female workers in a selected group of predominantly wage-earning jobs, compared to those most likely to be self-employed.

The first five occupations listed had higher than average rates of self-employment between 1901 and 1951.[98] These jobs attracted older women. The last five occupations in the table were filled almost entirely by wage earners. In these occupations, in 1921, the distribution by age period

TABLE 3   Percentage distribution of female workers in selected occupations according to age, Canada, 1921

Occupation	Total/ Age group	10-17	18-19	20-24	25-34	35-49	50-64	65+
Boarding-house keepers	100.0	–	–	1.1	11.0	*37.5*	37.3	13.2
Dressmakers	100.0	–	5.3	14.8	25.5	*33.2*	17.4	3.8
Farmers and stock raisers	100.0	0.1	0.1	1.0	5.8	29.2	*43.2*	20.6
Merchants and dealers, retail	100.0	0.1	0.6	6.2	20.0	*41.4*	24.3	7.4
Milliners	100.0	–	12.4	32.5	*35.7*	15.9	3.3	0.2
Saleswomen	100.0	15.5	16.0	*30.4*	23.9	11.8	2.1	0.2
Servants	100.0	22.3	14.4	*22.6*	17.9	13.5	7.1	2.3
Telephone operators	100.0	17.2	22.6	*37.2*	18.8	3.7	0.5	0.1
Textile factory workers	100.0	*30.0*	17.6	25.4	14.8	8.8	2.7	0.7
Waitresses	100.0	15.2	17.1	*29.4*	25.0	11.2	1.8	0.3

NOTES AND SOURCE: Data is compiled from Canada, Dominion Bureau of Statistics, *Census of Canada 1921*, Vol. 4, table 29. In this table, Canadian data includes data for British Columbia. Numbers in italics represent the age group with the highest proportion of women in a given occupation. The age groups are reproduced here as they appeared in the published census. The figures have been rounded for clarity.

demonstrates a much younger workforce than among the occupations with high self-employment. The notes on age in the 1921 census mention that the presence of women in older age brackets "is considerably influenced by such classes as farmers, boarding and lodging-house keepers ... which include a large number of married women or widows."[99] There was a relationship between the age of female workers, their marital status, and their specific occupations.

The data for 1921 represents the whole country. In British Columbia, in 1931, women from twenty to thirty-four years of age made up over half of the female workforce.[100] However, similar to the 1921 data for all of Canada, the occupations with high rates of female self-employment reflected an older workforce: 31 percent of female farmers and stock raisers in British Columbia in 1931 were between forty-five and fifty-four years of age, and an additional 26 percent were fifty-five to sixty-four years of age. Only 1.2 percent of farmers and stock raisers were aged twenty to twenty-four. As a point of comparison, almost half of all female telephone operators in British Columbia, who were largely wage earners, were aged twenty to twenty-four, and just 1.2 percent were forty-five to fifty-four years of age.[101] These patterns persisted in the rest of Canada in 1931, and they persisted in 1941 and 1951 for the province and the country: women in jobs with high self-employment fell into older age brackets than women in wage-earning occupations.

For many married or once-married women who were also raising children, home-based businesses were sometimes the best option. Married women turned their homemaking skills into income-earning jobs or they turned their homes into businesses.[102] This was still common in the 1940s in the United States, as Debra Michals documents.[103] Women were "enticed to commercialize domestic skills as their entrée to private enterprise" and, by linking enterprise to domesticity, women could be "both in the economy and in the home at the same time. As such, women's businesses ... occupied a liminal space, simultaneously within the broader economy and outside it in a separate feminized realm."[104]

A similar picture emerges in British Columbia of married mothers who earned incomes as entrepreneurs working in small home-based businesses that revolved around domestic skills that they were already using. In a sense, such self-employed women turned their "two jobs" into one, combining home and business by opening home-based businesses and reconciling the often separate worlds of public and private life. Whether these women were successfully able to do both jobs is more difficult to ascertain. A 1928 article by Justine Mansfield, published in the Toronto-based publication

The Business Woman, asked whether two-job women (women who had paid jobs and who had the "job" of maintaining a home and a husband too!) could succeed in two worlds: "Can the two-job woman succeed at home and in business?" Part of the answer lies in the fact that the job of home and family sometimes necessitated a second job, running a business to support family. Mansfield primarily addressed wage-earning women in white-collar jobs. Moreover, she did not address child rearing except to suggest that in the 1920s women had "few babies to take care of."[105] It was therefore not too difficult for her to conclude that the working woman brought a "greater efficiency into her home through her broad business interests," and that the "business girl" was "more systematic in her house-keeping tasks." She concluded that "a capable, strong, modern girl can quite easily run both these jobs and run them well at the same time."[106]

DEFINING SUCCESS

While Mansfield referred primarily to wage-earning women in business and professional jobs, she suggested that married women worked out of a sense of freedom and choice and worked because they wanted to and not because they had to. Certainly, some women sought opportunity and independence in self-employment, and for them the decision to open a business was more freely made: it may have been a choice rather than a necessity. Some sought a particular kind of independence and wealth in entrepreneurship, prized themselves on their business acumen, and succeeded financially to a degree that many businesswomen never achieved.

In British Columbia, some of these exceptional entrepreneurial women were breaking new ground in various ways. Between her arrival in Vancouver in 1889 and her death in Kelowna in 1955, Alice Elizabeth Jowett was at various times a bakery owner, hotel keeper, and prospector. She had left England for Vancouver as a widowed mother of four children. While her later endeavours were riskier and perhaps ultimately more financially ambitious, she operated a bakery in Vancouver for seven years while her children were young.[107] Rosemary Neering, author of a popular history of the "wild" women of British Columbia, suggests the business did not hold the "adventure she was seeking," and Jowett moved to the mining town of Trout Lake City, where she operated two hotels between 1896 and 1945. Jowett also became an avid prospector in the region. A photograph of Jowett with a group of friends, taken around 1915, indicates something of her adventurous personality. Moreover, the fact that all the women are

FIGURE 1 Mrs. W.A. Jowett (second from front) and friends, circa 1915 | Photograph courtesy of the Columbia Basin Image Bank, 0119.0085

dressed in men's suits may mark their awareness of gender difference and of the ways in which some women challenged notions of female propriety.[108] "Wild" women recognized that they sat on the boundary of what was expected, appropriate, respectable behaviour: sometimes they demonstrated their difference in their work and business decisions, and sometimes it came through in humorous photographs.

Significantly, Jowett's more adventurous enterprises in the province occurred after her children's needs were met. Indeed, most of the stories that have survived of adventurous female entrepreneurs document women who did not have families to consider. Their exceptional stories were just that: exceptions to the more ordinary kinds of work that most entrepreneurial women in the province undertook. Neering's profiles of female travellers, adventurers, and rebels are fascinating and demonstrate the wide variety of businesses operated by women in the province, but they represent a very small minority of entrepreneurial women in terms of their occupational choices and their family situations.

Neering notes that many of the women she profiles were single, widowed, divorced, or of "uncertain status."[109] Some of the enterprising miners, writers, hotel keepers, and farmers she uncovered never married, or they were married women and widows who never had children. Female miner Nellie Cashman operated a variety of businesses in the United States and in British Columbia, including hotels, boarding houses, restaurants, and grocery stores, and in the process achieved an unusual degree of freedom. Cashman arrived in Victoria in 1875, prospected on the west coast of the United States and Canada, and died in Victoria in 1925. She remained single and childless. Although she did take charge of five nieces and nephews upon the death of her sister in 1883, no mention of the children is made in any of the stories of her adventures. [110] She seems to have been relatively free to move when and where she liked, and her other enterprises – running boarding houses and restaurants – supported her love of prospecting but were not necessary as a means of familial support. [111] Ella Frye ran her own trapline in the North Thompson Valley in British Columbia from 1933 to 1975, had no children, and did not marry until she was in her seventies. [112] Artist Emily Carr, another exceptionally adventurous woman, supported herself through painting and running a boarding house. She never married, never had children, and shocked the staid citizens of Victoria and Vancouver with her atypical lifestyle. [113]

These women were not typical, as Neering herself points out. [114] And while such women existed, the great majority of female proprietors in British Columbia were not risk takers to quite the same degree. They were exceptional on some level simply in their decision to run their own businesses, and that they were self-employed at all demonstrates a level of independence and competence that should not be forgotten. But most female business owners were not self-employed because they were rebellious: they needed to work, they had families to consider, and even if they were married, their spouses were often absent, dead, or unable to earn a breadwinner wage. Economic necessity, rather than individual ambition, led them to self-employment.

It is dangerous to assume that women who ran small businesses in support of family, and who did not became entrepreneurial "successes" of the type modelled by successful male entrepreneurs who acquired wealth and property, were somehow less entrepreneurial or less successful. Susan Ingalls Lewis notes that it may be necessary to "problematize the concept of ... entrepreneurial 'success' based on male models." [115] She proposes that we look "beyond gendered assumptions about what constitutes a successful business, to discover the ways in which women used businesses within the scope of their particular needs and life cycles." [116] Businesses provided women with a form of survival and security and a way to support their children. Managing to do so can be considered a form of business success. Their accomplishments were small by conventional standards of financial success or individual ambition, but they succeeded at the two jobs of "home" and "business" if they managed to keep the former afloat with the latter, no matter how small the enterprise.

The constraints (real or perceived, external or internal) that prevented women from remaining in the labour force after marriage seem to have been less influential in British Columbia than in the rest of Canada. I suggest, as Herr does, that the nature of the frontier environment, society, and economy meant that particular female-typed tasks were in high demand. When women were outnumbered by men, they were in demand as marriage partners and as workers in feminine-typed occupations: their opportunities for marriage were high but so were their opportunities to enter the labour force. The relatively high rate of female entrepreneurship and the high rate of marriage in British Columbia's adult female population were not isolated variables. Self-owned and self-operated businesses such as sewing and dressmaking, boarding and lodging houses, restaurants or other food preparation, and cleaning or laundry establishments were traditionally female occupations. Women were often occupied doing these tasks as wives, and the work was unpaid. In British Columbia, married women could and did offer these same services, but many offered them for a fee to the abundant population of unmarried (or married, spouse absent) men.

The demand for these services pulled more women into the labour force and into self-employment despite the fact that many were married, and it provided certain freedoms that were not available to them as employees. But the ending or financial insecurity of marriages also sometimes pushed women in British Columbia into the labour force and into self-employment in particular. Self-employment was not something that many women undertook *in place of* marriage or family, nor was it a form of employment to enter only *before* marrying. Female proprietors did not fit the prescribed pattern of the female labour force, that of young single women who worked before marriage. Female entrepreneurship was more closely tied to the family claim than was wage-earning work, and it is not readily apparent that the majority of female-owned businesses were tied to notions of personal autonomy. Self-employment should not be viewed as an opportunity to break out of feminine-typed occupations or even to pursue a larger financial gain. Rather, it provided women, who in many cases worked out of necessity, with the opportunity to work in the home, set their own hours of work, and manage children and households simultaneously.

Data on the province and the rest of the country demonstrates that women's ages, families, and marriages are integral to understanding their employment options. For women in British Columbia, entrepreneurship and marital status were tightly connected. Frontier characteristics inflated their rates of self-employment in the first half of the twentieth century. The kinds of businesses self-employed women opened are the subject of the next chapter, which considers the enterprises run by women in British Columbia and the degree to which businesswomen were segregated in what were deemed womanly trades.

3

Careers for Women

SEX SEGREGATION IN SELF-EMPLOYMENT

There are many occupations, such as carpenter or black-
smith, which women usually do not follow. Therefore, if
you are told that a woman follows an occupation which is
peculiar or unusual for a woman, verify the statement.

– *"Selected Instructions to Enumerators,"*
in Census of Canada 1931, *Volume 7*

This chapter examines the kinds of jobs most businesswomen in
British Columbia could be found in between 1901 and 1951. Gender
was a determining factor in the limited occupational categories,
and in the specific occupations, open to women workers. The labour force
in British Columbia and in the rest of Canada was gendered in that certain
occupations were open to women *because* they were women, while others
were closed to them, again, *because* they were women.

Wage-earning and self-employed women were similarly clustered in a
narrow range of occupational categories, or groups. Although they were
similar in terms of the kinds of work they did, which determined the occupational categories in which we find them, their specific jobs were different. Furthermore, self-employed women were not sex-typed by
occupation to the same degree as wage earners. While wage-earning women
worked almost entirely in jobs dominated by women in what some historians have defined as a female work culture, self-employed women were
more often found in male-dominated professions, working alongside men
rather than other women.[1] Self-employed women, by virtue of being a
small proportion of all employed women and all business owners, were
operating in a male-dominated environment. Gender forms an important
part of the story of working women in the first half of the twentieth century, but gender mattered in different ways for entrepreneurial women
compared to wage-earning women. Even when businesswomen participated in womanly trades and capitalized on what were deemed feminine

skills, they were working in a predominantly male work world. Self-employment connoted independence and manliness; broadly speaking, businesswomen thus challenged women's place in the working world.

Data presented here on specific occupations buttresses the points made in Chapter 2 about the nature of British Columbia: women worked in relatively high numbers in a province with a high ratio of men to women and were more willing to pursue entrepreneurship in general, in male-dominated professions in particular, than were their counterparts in the rest of Canada. Furthermore, members of the business and professional women's (BPW) clubs, discussed in Chapters 4 and 5, engaged in many of the entrepreneurial occupations discussed in this chapter. While women's self-employment was limited to a small list of specific occupations in the province, women in British Columbia made the most of those restrained possibilities, as both quantitative census data and qualitative records illustrate.

Occupational Groups, Women, and the Census

The occupational categories, or groups, used by the census shifted in small ways that make comparisons across decades difficult because, as the 1941 census pointed out, there was no "uniform scheme of classification of occupations."[2] In addition, changes took place in "the nature of the work performed in many occupations" with the introduction of machines.[3] As more women and men entered clerical and other professional white-collar jobs, the occupational groupings changed to reflect the new workforce. However, examining broad groups illustrates differences between women's and men's jobs and between British Columbia and the rest of the country.

In 1901, the census used the following main groups to organize individual occupations: agriculture; logging; fishing, hunting and trapping; mining and quarrying; manufactures; building trades (construction); transportation; trade; finance; and service (professional and personal). Most of the groups continued to be used throughout the first half of the twentieth century, although there were a few changes. The clerical occupational group first appeared in 1931, and the transportation occupational group became "transportation and communication" in 1931. By 1931, occupations such as telegraph and telephone operators had become more prominent across Canada. And while there were clerical workers in Canada and in British Columbia before 1931, they were scattered across other occupational groups.

The new clerical category was largely filled with "stenographers and typists" in 1931.[4]

The service occupational group encompassed personal, professional, and recreational service jobs from 1901 to 1941. Occupations that had previously appeared in the service group under the subheading "Professional Service," such as accountants, architects, dentists, physicians, and teachers, appeared in their own "professional" occupational group in 1951. The creation of this group occurred as professional service jobs became more important in the labour force – a reflection of an increasingly bureaucratic and white-collar work environment in which office skills were becoming more valuable than manual skills, and a further extension of the clerical category that had been introduced twenty years earlier.

The distribution of workers certainly changed in the first fifty years of the twentieth century: specific jobs came and went as the labour force changed and grew.[5] Despite these shifts, one aspect of the labour force remained the same. Women were not evenly distributed across occupational groups, nor were they found in very many groups, and this situation did not change perceptibly between 1901 and 1951. In 1901, some gendered patterns emerged in the occupational groups that were still present at mid-century. First, most women worked in the same four occupational groups in every census year between 1901 and 1951. At the beginning of the twentieth century, over 90 percent of the female labour force in British Columbia and in the rest of Canada worked in four groups: manufacturing/mechanical; trade/finance (the two were combined from 1911 on); service (personal, professional, and other); and clerical.[6] In 1901, 20 percent of all women in the labour force in British Columbia, and 30 percent in the rest of Canada, worked in manufacturing occupations, while 65 percent of working women in British Columbia, and 57 percent in the rest of Canada, worked in service occupations.[7]

The distribution across these groups changed over time – more employed women were found in the clerical and trade/finance groups as the century progressed, while manufacturing lessened in importance – but the same four groups continued to employ most of the female labour force. At mid-century, the same percentage of the female labour force worked in the same four occupational groups as in 1901.[8] The combined service occupational groups continued to hold large numbers of women. In 1931, 53 percent of employed women in British Columbia worked in the combined service occupational groups; these groups still employed a considerable 39 percent of the female workforce in the province in 1951. When combined, the clerical and trade/finance groups employed 31.4 percent of British Columbia's female workforce in 1931 and 45.3 percent in 1951. Women's specific jobs may have changed, but they remained clustered in the same occupational groups. They were very heavily concentrated in service jobs and, increasingly, in clerical jobs.

The differences between British Columbia and the rest of Canada remained constant between 1901 and 1951. Proportionately more women worked in service, trade/finance, and clerical occupational groups, and fewer women worked in Manufacturing groups, in British Columbia than in the rest of the country. By 1951, just 8 percent of the female labour force in the province worked in manufacturing, but a still-high 19 percent of employed women in the rest of Canada could be found in this occupational group.[9] There were not many manufacturing occupations open to women in British Columbia in the first half of the twentieth century. Most worked as domestic servants, cooks, waitresses, teachers and nurses, all service occupations; others turned to entrepreneurial activities, such as boarding-house keeping, in which they capitalized on domestic skills that were in demand in a province filled with labouring, often-single males.[10] These occupations were in trade and service, not in manufacturing – with the exception of dressmaking and related occupations, which employed high numbers of women in both British Columbia and in the rest of the country.

Women in the rest of Canada also worked in service occupations, but they had more opportunities in manufacturing than did women in British Columbia. Women in central Canada found manufacturing jobs in food processing, garment and textile factories, boot and shoe factories, and the tobacco industry; in British Columbia, there were some jobs in food processing (confectioneries, bakeries, salmon canneries, and other fish processing). Some women worked in textiles and laundries, but despite fairly rapid industrialization, "there weren't as many factory jobs for women in manufacturing in the West as in the East."[11] In the early twentieth century, British Columbia's economy was based heavily on primary resource extraction, particularly on what Robert McDonald calls "forest wealth."[12] In 1911, more than twice as many Vancouver workers, compared to Toronto workers, were employed in wood and lumber manufacturing, while "a Toronto worker was three times as likely to labour in clothing and related industries and twice as likely to find employment in metal manufacturing firms ... industrial jobs in Toronto and Montreal exceeded manufacturing work in Vancouver by a ratio of almost two to one."[13] And even after 1911, when the manufacturing sector grew more rapidly in the province, "the leading manufacturing industries were still based on lumber, fishing, and smelting, just as in 1911."[14]

British Columbia's manufacturing diversified, but the processing of fish and timber continued to employ more than half of those in manufacturing jobs. This emphasis partly explains the high number of wage-earning jobs for men and also the correspondingly low number of wage-earning jobs for women: women were not clustered in natural resource extraction industries. Such differences indicate industrial differences between British Columbia and the rest of Canada but also explain the higher rate of self-employment for women in British Columbia. More entrepreneurs worked in the occupational groups of service and trade than in manufacturing, and proportionately more women worked in those two occupational groups in British Columbia than in the rest of Canada.

By 1951, the white-collar workforce – "the professionals, the managers, the clerks and the salesmen" – formed the "largest single occupational sector of the working population" in Canada.[15] This shift in the entire labour force was also clear in the female labour force. Even though the combined service categories still encompassed more of the female labour force than did any other occupational category, more and more women were entering wage-earning jobs as sales clerks, telephone operators, secretaries, and stenographers. In the "post-1900 economic boom, firms grew along bureaucratic lines, offices were restructured, and the clerical labour force grew and shifted in sex composition from mostly male to mostly female clerical workers."[16]

Despite such shifts, women in 1951 remained in low-paying occupations within the same four occupational groups that they were found in at the beginning of the century. Their concentration in "traditionally female" jobs showed a "disturbing continuity."[17] The sex-typing of occupations as particularly feminine or masculine is clear in the limited array of occupations and occupational groups in which we find women, but it was also made explicit in the published census notes that accompanied the tabular data. The 1921 census stated that "the increase in the proportion of employed females synchronizes with the more general introduction of typewriters and other mechanical office appliances, in the operation of which women have shown marked ability."[18] It is difficult to assess whether women entered these jobs because they were particularly skilled at operating mechanical appliances in the office as opposed to mechanical appliances on factory lines, or whether office jobs happened to be the only ones that were open to women. The argument tends to be circular: the jobs women get are the jobs that are open to them, which are then described as the only jobs that they can competently perform. The census takers did not interrogate how or why women's abilities were tied to assumptions about gender. Women's "marked ability" was, perhaps not coincidentally, attached to jobs that had already been labelled feminine and were usually low paid.

The census commentary implies that women chose low-paid clerical work because they were naturally good at such tasks. The problem with this assumption has been acknowledged by historians such as Joan Sangster, Shirley Tillotson, and Graham Lowe, all of whom have argued that gender is the locus of "power and inequality" within the workplace.[19] Lowe maintains that "stereotypes of women as manually dexterous, patient, ineffectual supervisors, and secondary wage earners ... have provided strong rationale for their restricted employment at the bottom of the occupational hierarchy."[20] Sangster concurs that sex segregation in the workplace is "grounded in the historical and material structures imposed by advanced capitalism; but these structures were in turn fostered by social practices established in family life and by an ideology of female difference, dependency and subordination," an interweaving, she suggests, of "material necessity and patriarchal ideology."[21] This can be said of work in a variety of jobs deemed feminine: office work, cooking, cleaning, food preparation, and other domestic and personal service occupations. Moreover, sex-specific pay has accompanied occupational segregation, and women have consistently entered occupations with very low pay.[22] A clear division of labour based on sex existed (and still exists) in the Canadian economy. Women "are segregated into particular sectors ... and within these sectors they perform a limited number of low-skilled and/or low-paid jobs."[23]

Census data corroborates that women in the labour force have been clustered in a very few occupations and occupational groups. Women were not branching out into new occupational groups, and the only real change by mid-century was a shift from domestic service work to clerical work. Furthermore, "not only are men not concentrated in the same occupations as women, they are not concentrated in any small number of occupations at all."[24] Women's work was clearly not the same as men's work in the Canadian labour market.

The census occupational categories give little indication of class or income. Knowing that a woman was employed in manufacturing is not a helpful indicator of her status or her class position: whether she worked in a bakery or owned a bakery is not indicated by these broad categories, and whether she owned a large profitable bakery or a small bakery run out of her home is also unclear. Broad occupational groups are imperfect in their categorization of women and men and do not illuminate class or economic differences between women. However, while the data might place all women employed in manufacturing in one broad category, more detailed census tables allow us to examine the rates of self-employment within occupations.

SELF-EMPLOYMENT AND SEX SEGREGATION

There were a limited number of occupations in which most businesswomen were found from 1901 to 1951. Many self-employed women in British Columbia and elsewhere in Canada, much like female wage earners, did not stray from the realm of acceptable women's work. Self-employed women were concentrated in work involving housekeeping, food preparation, sewing, and personal care, jobs that were in the service and manufacturing occupational groups; a significant number were also farmers (Table 4).

Self-employed women were clustered in three of the main occupational groups that wage-earning women were also clustered in throughout the first half of the twentieth century: manufacturing, trade/finance, and service (professional and personal). Self-employed female farmers were also found in high proportions in agriculture, an occupational group that did not employ a high percentage of wage-earning women. The clerical category was the one group that employed a lot of wage-earning women but not many self-employed women.

For the most part, the jobs in which self-employed women were "ghettoized," to borrow the term used by Armstrong and Armstrong, were in the same occupational groups as those in which we usually find wage-earning women. Sex segregation, the "unwritten set of rules that distinguished 'masculine' from 'feminine' pursuits, proved as salient for female entrepreneurs as for their wage-earning counterparts."[25] Wendy Gamber points out that women "were not evenly distributed within the universe of entrepreneurial occupations; rather, they congregated in particular types of businesses."[26] In *The Female Economy: The Millinery and Dressmaking Trades, 1860-1930*, she argues that women safeguarded their entrepreneurial positions as milliners and dressmakers by defending the femininity of their trades.[27]

Women may have chosen to work in feminized trades, a choice constrained by the limitations and ghettoization of women's work. However, concern for preserving femininity did not necessarily limit women's business success. Femininity could, as Kathy Peiss argues, become an advantage and a source of power in consumer advertising and marketing, the business industry, and local small businesses.[28] Some businesses, particularly in the beauty industry, opened opportunities for women "by aligning commercial enterprise with the very ideals of femininity and beauty that had long justified women's exclusion from most lines of work."[29] The sex segregation that pushed women into a limited selection of businesses became the tool for their success in those businesses.

Gamber and Peiss are referring to American women. However, some entrepreneurial occupations were indisputably women's work. The gendered division of labour, which resulted in gendered divisions of occupational groups and of specific occupations, was reinforced in the Canadian context by Gabrielle Carrière's 1946 publication *Careers for Women in Canada: A Practical Guide*. Carrière stated that careers open to women were strongly associated with feminine abilities and attributes – because, she intimated, women's careers involved selling women's goods. Her book was not limited to entrepreneurship, but many of the proposed careers were entrepreneurial. Chapters separate women's options into categories that include "On the Farm," "Feeding Folk," and "Dressing People." Carrière steered women toward certain types of proprietorship: "Many lines of trade are particularly suited to women ... and while some of these may be carried on by men, women are practically always engaged to serve the clientele." She suggested "women's lingerie, babies' wear, women's dresses, hats and coats, novelties and smallwares, laces, linens and knitted goods."[30] Potential female entrepreneurs were coached about what kinds of businesses were suitable for women and were therefore prey to a similar kind of occupational sex-typing as that faced by wage-earning women. Carrière suggested that some lines of trade were as well suited to women as men, such as groceries, restaurants, gift shops, bookstores, and flower shops, but most of the work that she recommended in 1946 was in female-typed occupations and occupational categories.[31]

Gamber cautions that the reason for sex-segregation among self-employed women was not necessarily that it allowed them to capitalize on their domestic (and already sex-typed) skills, such as cooking, cleaning, washing, and housekeeping.[32] However, women entrepreneurs have long clustered in these occupations. "More than 80 percent of the women listed in the business pages of the *Boston Directory* of 1876 prepared food, made clothing, or offered lodging."[33] The same pattern appears in Carrière's 1946 Canadian publication: the image of the enterprising woman was associated with domestic, feminized trades.

TABLE 4 Self-employment rates (provided as number self-employed and as percent of total employed) among gainfully employed adult women in selected occupations in British Columbia and Canada, 1901, 1931, and 1951

Occupational category	Occupation		1901 (#)	(%)	1931 (#)	(%)	1951 (#)	(%)
Agriculture	Farmers	BC	11	91.7	880	100.0	644	100.0
		Canada	718	98.6	18,287	100.0	7,519	100.0
Manufacturing	Dressmakers and sewers	BC	15	53.6	453	53.0	260	22.9
		Canada	447	35.6	6,449	50.7	4,234	32.3
Transportation/communication	Chauffeurs, taxi drivers	BC	0	0	4	80.0	11	16.7
		Canada	0	0	2	28.6	61	29.2
Trade/finance	Retail store owners[a]	BC	2	100.0	639	93.4	1,803	82.3
		Canada	95	80.5	5,420	90.0	12,754	81.4
	Real estate agents	BC	0	0	33	78.6	109	52.4
		Canada	1	100.0	64	61.5	203	49.9
Service (personal)	Lodging-house keepers	BC	11	100.0	1,419	100.0	864	100.0
		Canada	102	98.1	17,288	100.0	5,429	100.0
	Hotel keepers	BC	4	100.0	79	78.2	919	77.4
		Canada	235	98.3	518	84.9	6,272	81.2

Barbers, hairdressers	BC	1	100.0	315	48.0	437	48.2
	Canada	2	33.3	2,906	50.9	4,973	50.0
Service (professional)							
Musicians, music teachers	BC	1	25.0	343	79.8	328	70.9
	Canada	69	67.0	2,816	66.9	1,787	43.2
Total							
Selected occupations	BC	45	72.6	4,165	82.1	5,375	70.2
	Canada	1,669	65.3	53,750	82.7	43,232	67.4
All occupations	BC	68	27.4	5,585	12.8	6,472	6.6
	Canada	2,395	19.5	68,102	11.0	50,250	4.7

a   Managers and dealers are included with store owners in the published census data; this explains why the category "Retail store owner" is not entirely composed of the self-employed, as store managers could be wage earners.

NOTES: Data provided for Canada does not include British Columbia figures. For brevity's sake, and because the data is very consistent across every published census (with the exception of 1911, for which the data is incomplete), the table shows only the years 1901, 1931, and 1951. The occupations selected are those with high rates of female self-employment *and* with high numbers of self-employed women. The only exceptions: first, I included chauffeurs/taxi drivers and real estate agents, despite their low numbers, because of their unusual prominence in British Columbia compared to the rest of Canada; second, 1901 data does not include *all* self-employed women as it is based on a 5 percent sample of the population, so the numbers of businesswomen appear very low. However, in British Columbia these occupations employed forty-five of the sixty-eight self-employed women captured by the 5 percent sample. A high percentage of self-employed women worked in these occupations in both the province and the rest of the country.

SOURCES: Data for 1901 is taken from the Canadian Families Project 5 percent sample of the 1901 census. Other data for this table is from Canada, Dominion Bureau of Statistics, *Census of Canada 1931*, vol. 7, tables 50, 53, and 54; and *Census of Canada 1951*, vol. 4, table 11.

Some businesswomen in British Columbia pursued the recommended lines of trade. Business directories show women selling ladies' and children's wear and operating bakeries, tearooms, and dressmaking shops. In 1918, Mrs. Butler operated the Kelowna Steam Laundry, Mrs. St. Clair ran a millinery shop in Kamloops, and Miss J. Lattrass was listed as "proprietress" of the Allendale Lunch and Tea Room in Victoria.[34] In the 1920s, Mima Brown ran a florist's shop in Vancouver, and in 1948 Mrs. Margaret Bell, corsetière, operated in Victoria.[35] These businesswomen capitalized on traditionally feminine tasks. Most of their clientele was also female. They also had a relatively high profile in the community, as evidenced by their activities with the BPW clubs (described in Chapter 4).

While Carrière did not suggest it, another avenue of female entrepreneurship was operating a school. In Duncan, Miss Norah Denny opened Queen Margaret's School for Girls in 1921 in partnership with Miss Dorothy Geoghegan, and Miss Jessie Gordon founded Crofton House in 1901 in Vancouver.[36] Other notable female-run schools in the province included Strathcona Lodge School on Shawnigan Lake, opened in 1927 by Minna Gildea, who ran the school until her death in 1950. York House was a joint venture, opened in 1932 by six women. There was also Athlone School, a boys' school founded in 1940 by a widow, Violet Dryvynsyde.[37] As Jean Barman has noted, operating a school was a "woman-like" occupation because it "encouraged the nurturing attributes which young women were perceived to need in order to be good wives and mothers." And for the female headmistresses, the qualities of "refinement and gentility and deference associated with being a woman" could be utilized in running a school for girls: their success in business did not compromise their success as proper women. Barman also suggests that the qualities necessary for women's success as private school owners were the antithesis of the crafty business strategies associated with male entrepreneurship.[38] And yet, these women also had to employ crafty strategies: success depended on appearing deferential and gentle, while simultaneously aggressively seeking out funding to keep the schools in operation.

Female owners of nursing homes and private hospitals and self-employed midwives also capitalized on what was acceptable womanly work. Lying-in hospitals dedicated to childbirth were run by women in the early twentieth century but had almost disappeared by the Second World War. Midwives also lost prominence in the early decades of the century to the increasingly male-dominated spheres of medicine and childbirth. However, some persisted: between 1925 and 1929, Vancouver recorded 1,743 deliveries by midwives out of a total of 19,730 births.[39]

Perhaps the more important point is that even though self-employed women capitalized on domestic skills and participated in womanly trades such as sewing clothing or keeping house, they were in business. As David Burley discusses in his work on self-employment and social mobility, self-employment represented independence and was valued as a "masculine" condition.[40] His book is a case study of one Ontario town in the mid-1800s, but the link between self-employment and manliness did not disappear in the twentieth century. Women participated to a large degree in womanly trades and, for many, operating a business meant capitalizing on skills deemed womanly. Businessmen vastly outnumbered business-women in all but a few occupations; even businesswomen in feminized trades were working in a predominantly male work world. Gamber also observes that female proprietors "defied imperatives of gender." That they were self-employed at all was a form of independence usually reserved for men.[41] Female entrepreneurs challenged "woman's place," even if they did so within the confines of a feminized enterprise.[42]

Some businesswomen challenged woman's place doubly, by being in business at all *and* by being in types of business that men dominated. While many self-employed women worked in particularly feminine oc-cupations, they were far more likely to work in occupations dominated by men than were wage-earning women. Many entrepreneurial women worked in male-dominated business worlds rather than female-dominated work worlds. Some, such as Wendy McDonald, successfully ran businesses not at all associated with femininity. Widowed in 1950, she took over owner-ship of B.C. Bearings, her husband's company. She remarried but was widowed two more times by 1967. With ten children from her three marriages, McDonald continued to operate the bearings company until 1998.[43] Other widows also took over their husbands' businesses: Wanda Ziegler continued to run Ziegler Chocolate Shops after her husband's 1923 death and expanded the chain from three to eleven stores. She retired in 1956.[44] Selling chocolates was not a particularly masculine job, but the expansion and prominence of the business was unusual for a female entrepreneur. And McDonald was exceptional for her prominence in a male-dominated field.

Their inclusion in encyclopaedias about community leaders suggests that Ziegler and McDonald were also economically successful, and they were probably considered members of a middle- or upper-class business elite. While being an entrepreneurial woman might indicate a level of independence, were women who ran businesses always in the middle or upper class? City directories and census data cannot illuminate the class position of most entrepreneurial women in the province, but type of business and associations within the community can: most businesswomen ran small operations, did not have distinctive community profiles, and were not members of the upper class. It was a different, but not necessarily an upwardly mobile, choice of occupation compared to wage earning.

However, the size and the type of business occasionally indicated a more privileged status. Barman's descriptions of refined and respectable headmistresses illustrate that the perceptions of an enterprising woman's social status and personal qualities, as well as the type of business she operated, could be more important indicators of social standing and class position than her economic profile. Women's choice of business (girls' school versus home-based laundry, for instance), their associations, their community profile, and even their membership in things like BPW clubs were better markers of class status than incomes or business sizes, as will be seen in Chapters 4 and 5.

WOMEN'S WORK IN A MAN'S WORLD?
BUSINESSWOMEN'S PROMINENCE IN SELECTED OCCUPATIONS

While there were exceptions, more than half of all businesswomen were consistently found in just six entrepreneurial occupations from 1901 to 1951 in British Columbia and Canada. While some occupations gained or lost prominence as entrepreneurial pursuits over the first half of the twentieth century, 60 to 80 percent of all self-employed women worked as farmers, seamstresses/dressmakers, retail store owners, lodging-house keepers, barbers/hairdressers, or musicians/music teachers (Table 5).[45]

Dressmaking and keeping a lodging house were the only entrepreneurial occupations of the six that were distinctly feminine: the proportion of women employed in these two occupations was greater than that of men.[46] Of the other four, the ratio of men to women in the occupation of musician/music teacher was almost even. Barbers and hairdressers were far more likely to be male than female in the first half of the twentieth century, although this was changing by mid-century, when about half of all barbers/hairdressers were female.[47] The two jobs were listed together in census data. This masks whether the difference was because both jobs were dominated by men and both came to be dominated by women, or whether the shift to a more feminine cast in this occupation was due to an increase in women cutting women's hair. The 1961 census notes suggest a "faster rate of increase of female hairdressers rather than the entry of

TABLE 5   Self-employed adult women in selected occupations as a
percentage of total female self-employment in British Columbia and
Canada, 1901, 1931, and 1951

Occupational category	Occupation		1901 (%)	1931 (%)	1951 (%)
Agriculture	Farmers	BC	16.2	15.8	10.0
		Canada	28.3	26.9	15.0
Manufacturing	Dressmakers, sewers	BC	22.1	8.1	4.0
		Canada	17.6	9.5	8.4
Trade/finance	Retail store owners	BC	2.9	11.4	27.9
		Canada	3.8	8	25.4
Service (personal)	Lodging-house keepers	BC	16.2	25.4	13.3
		Canada	4.0	25.4	10.8
	Barber, hairdressers	BC	1.5	5.6	6.8
		Canada	0.1	4.3	9.9
Service (professional)	Music teachers	BC	1.5	6.1	5.1
		Canada	2.7	4.1	3.6
Total	Selected occupations	BC	60.3	72.4	67.1
		Canada	56.6	78.2	73.1

NOTES: Data for Canada does not include British Columbia figures. For brevity's sake,
I did not include every census year in this table: the published data is unavailable or
incomplete for 1911 and 1921, but the pattern of high female self-employment shown
here was clear in the limited data available for 1921, and the 1941 data showed the same
pattern as that shown in 1931 and 1951.
SOURCES: Data for 1901 is taken from the Canadian Families Project 5 percent sample
of the 1901 census. Other data for this table is from Canada, Dominion Bureau of
Statistics, *Census of Canada 1931*, vol. 7, tables 50, 53, and 54; and *Census of Canada 1951*,
vol. 4, table 11.

females into the occupation of barber."[48] The field of hair cutting (regardless of the gender of the customer) was clearly an occupation that was
attracting more female workers. However, men dominated the farming
and retail enterprises, occupations that nonetheless employed significant
proportions of all entrepreneurial women in British Columbia and in
Canada. A closer look at these jobs, including those that appear to have
high numbers of women working in feminine occupations, demonstrates

that businesswomen worked in a man's world. My discussion of farmers and boarding-house keepers is particularly detailed because these jobs employed very high proportions of all female entrepreneurs throughout the first half of the twentieth century.

Farmers

The percentage of all female entrepreneurs who were farmers declined between 1901 and 1951, but farming was the only occupation in the agriculture group in which women were found, and 90 to 100 percent of female farmers were self-employed. Despite the fact that men have always dominated the occupation, farming employed significant numbers of female entrepreneurs, both in British Columbia and in the rest of Canada from 1901 to 1951. Less than 5 percent of all farmers were women in either the province or the rest of the country in this period,[49] but as Table 5 illustrates, a high proportion of self-employed women worked as farmers.

Much of the work performed on farms was sex-typed, and a wide range of literature dealing with women's work on farms documents that women's and men's farm labour was frequently delineated by gender.[50] Many women listed in the census as unemployed were in fact farmers' wives or other unpaid family workers in farm families. Until 1951, census instructions were explicit: married wives of farmers were not to be listed as farmers, but as farmers' wives. Their work was sex-typed as "feminine": farmers' wives cooked, cleaned house, laundered, and sometimes oversaw egg, butter, and milk production, while male farmers were responsible for all other outdoor farm labour.[51] It is tempting to argue that women's work in certain elements of farm production – the "butter and egg business" – formed a rural enterprise in its own right.[52] Women were often responsible for tending poultry and for selling butter, eggs, and other farm produce that they churned, bred, or cultivated themselves. Sometimes they kept that income separate from household income. However, even if we wanted to include these women as entrepreneurs, the census did not. They appeared in the census as farmers' wives.

Whether those who were called farmers actually farmed is another question. Many received assistance from hired help or from sons and daughters to perform the labour associated with farming, but it is difficult to know exactly which tasks may have been performed by female farm owners. The 1901 census tells us that Elizabeth Milne was a thirty-nine-year-old widow living near Vernon in 1901 with her two young children. She reported that she was a self-employed rancher, and while nobody else

FIGURE 2 Two "lady farmers" running their own farm near Terrace, British Columbia, in the 1920s | *Source:* H. Glynn-Ward, *The Glamour of British Columbia* (New York: Century, 1926). H. Glynn-Ward is a pseudonym for Hilda Howard, the author of the book and the photographer.

lived in her household, she may have hired labourers. Kate Hoffman, a forty-eight-year-old widowed rancher in the Kootenays, had five children living at home. Her twenty-four-year-old son was also listed as a rancher, and her other children, ranging in age from ten to twenty, probably helped out as well.[53]

Sometimes, we are given a more detailed glimpse of the work that female farmers did. In a travel guide about British Columbia, author and photographer Hilda Howard describes two "lady" farmers living and working near Terrace, British Columbia, in the early 1900s. Howard comments that the farm belonged to and was run entirely by two women who "had been music mistresses in the Old Country. They have developed the place from virtually nothing and do every scrap of the work themselves, except the plowing – and even take a hand in that when labour is short."[54] Farmer Elizabeth O'Keefe was widowed in 1919, and her daily journals and correspondence indicate her active role in running the family ranch in Vernon, British Columbia. O'Keefe's son was just twelve when his father died, but by 1924 her diaries frequently mention his help with the farm. O'Keefe also refers to employees and to a ranch foreman.[55]

Elizabeth O'Keefe and women like her may not have done all their own farm labour, but they controlled the daily operations of their businesses. O'Keefe's diaries note when she hired help. Her detailed accounting indicates that she controlled the farm finances. She also kept track of the land she rented out and collected rent from her tenants. She provided pocket money to her son, clothing and tobacco to her foreman, and in 1924 she listed all the bulls, cows, and calves that had died the previous year.[56] Her correspondence demonstrates that female farmers asserted their independence through their self-employment in an occupation that was notably masculine. Female farmers challenged "woman's place" by their status as businesswomen and by the nature of their stated occupation.

Widowhood was the most common marital status of female farmers in the first half of the twentieth century. Unlike male farmers, of whom less than 6 percent were widowed or divorced in the first half of the twentieth century, well over half of all female farmers were widowed or divorced.[57] Some were single – about 10 to 20 percent, depending on the census year. Similar percentages of female farmers (more in British Columbia than in the rest of Canada) reported that they were married, but those who were generally headed their own households and lived without their spouse.[58] In some ways, these married women were much like their single or widowed counterparts who operated on their own. Sometimes the spouse might even have been present but incapacitated: the wife of one veteran, who had returned from the First World War "suffering from a form of creeping paralysis," operated a forty-acre fruit ranch herself until it was sold in 1935.[59]

While it is the case that widowed women in rural areas had few other options if they wanted to enter the labour force, widowed farmers nonetheless chose self-employment over remarriage, relocating into urban areas to find work or moving into their children's homes as dependents. Widows could only maintain their status as farmers if they did not remarry; those who did would have reverted to being the farmers' wives of their new spouses. There were other reasons not to remarry. Thelma Mercer farmed with her husband near Quesnel in the 1930s. Widowed while pregnant with her seventh child, she decided not to remarry because she "didn't want any other man bossing them [her children] around."[60] Mercer ran the farm on her own for fourteen years while raising her children. She eventually remarried and farmed with her new husband, but like many other widowed farmers, she first operated her own farm to support her family.

Farming was overwhelmingly male-dominated, but women were more prominent in certain kinds of farming. In 1913, the *Victoria Colonist* newspaper complained when Miss Binnie-Clark (a British promoter of female emigration) claimed that a woman with five hundred dollars could buy five acres of land near Victoria, raise fruit and vegetables, keep cows, and develop substantial capital over twenty years of farming. According to the *Colonist,* land could not be purchased for that price, and a woman would need additional capital to build a house and farm buildings. The article did not deny, however, that women could potentially farm independently.[61] This may have been because small mixed-farming operations, fruit and vegetable farms, and poultry and horticulture operations were more acceptable rural enterprises for women. City directories between 1901 and 1920 illustrate women's prominence in beekeeping and poultry and dairy farming. Female-run cattle ranches and large mixed operations were less prominent, although there were exceptions, such as female ranchers in the Okanagan and large fruit farms in the Kootenay region.[62] Mrs. Kemball, a war widow, operated a Kootenay fruit ranch with her two daughters and "whatever casual help might be available" until she sold it in 1927. Edith Attree, also widowed during the First World War, successfully managed her Kootenay ranch and orchards with the help of her sons.[63]

Widowed women may have had little choice but to continue to run family farms of all types and sizes, but when women had a choice, they turned to small mixed farms or poultry and horticulture operations. Helena Gutteridge started a poultry farm in 1921 outside Vancouver, while Estella Hartt became a herb farmer in 1928 in the Arrow Lakes region, growing goldenseal and ginseng.[64] At the time they were farming, these women did not have spouses or children.

Female farmers may have been somewhat segregated into butter and egg operations, and a great many farmed without recognition, being recorded as unpaid farmers' wives with no paid vocation. However, the small number of women who were self-employed as farmers operated in a male-dominated occupation. Whether they farmed alone or with help, farmed fruit or cattle, or had small or large operations, they represent a segment of entrepreneurship that disproves the notion of a female work culture.

Dressmakers and Sewers

Dressmakers, seamstresses, and sewers were the only categories in the manufacturing occupation group with high rates of female self-employment. It can be said that self-employed women in these occupations worked in a woman's world because of the feminized nature of the trade, although as business owners, dressmakers would have worked alongside male retailers of all kinds in an average town or city. Dressmaking and most other sewing jobs were indisputably sex-typed as feminine work, whether the women were wage earners or self-employed.[65] While women dominated all other sewing occupations, men dominated the occupation of tailor, which was sex-typed as masculine. Tailors sewed men's clothes, while many other sewing occupations involved sewing for other women. Sewing occupations were clearly demarcated by gendered ideas of women's work and men's work.[66] The relative importance of sewing occupations for women in the labour force declined over the twentieth century. The entrepreneurial nature of these occupations declined as well, because of an increase in ready-made clothing, mostly manufactured elsewhere.

Retail Store Owners

In the trade and finance group, the percentage of women entrepreneurs who owned retail stores increased over the first half of the twentieth century. In 1951, a greater proportion of all self-employed women worked in retail than in any other type of occupation in British Columbia. While female retailers were significant in number as a proportion of female entrepreneurs, shopkeeping was a profession dominated by male retailers. Women shopkeepers worked in a male-dominated field, but their individual stores were in trades that were sex-typed as feminine. As David Monod points out, women operated stores in areas in which "women's domestic role was thought to have given them a certain 'natural' proclivity: groceries and women's and children's clothing. It was the constricting influence of the normative that kept all but a few women from moving beyond their accepted sphere."[67] Despite women's increased participation in shopkeeping as the twentieth century advanced, they "remained occupationally sex-typed, accepted as, and accepting of, a presence in trades geared to relatively low-cost frivolities – hairdressing, stationery, millinery, and fancy goods – yet all but barred from such big-ticket items as furniture or such sensitive ones as drugs."[68] This gender segregation is evident in British Columbia business directories of the early twentieth century: Mrs. Vigor's "Fancy Goods" shop in 1901 Victoria and Mrs. Clark's crockery and glassware business in Vancouver were typical examples of female-run businesses, while hardware stores and large retail operations were dominated by men.[69] Women were largely to be found running gift and hat shops and women's clothing stores.

In 1921, the only stores with more than a few female owners were women's clothing, dry goods, grocery, confectionery (bread and pastry), and general stores. By contrast, men operated more than twenty-five types of stores, including drug, men's clothing, hardware, jewellery, livestock, lumber, and feed stores. Even in the more female-friendly grocery, dry goods, confectionery, and general stores, there were more male than female owners. The only operation with more female than male retail owners was women's clothing stores.[70] In 1931, 44 percent of all female proprietors in British Columbia retail stores worked with food, most in either confectionery or grocery stores. The only retail operations with more female than male proprietors in 1931 were women's clothing, millinery, and children's clothing stores, and tearooms.[71] The situation was the same elsewhere in Canada, and it was the same in 1941 in British Columbia and the rest of the country.[72]

However, women in business were enough of a rarity that even if they sold women's goods to a chiefly female clientele, they could not help but be surrounded by businessmen. In that sense, just by choosing entrepreneurship they had moved beyond what Monod calls their "accepted sphere" or what Gamber refers to as the "female economy."[73] Although her clientele could be entirely female, a businesswoman in a town of any size would have been physically surrounded by other businesspeople – mostly men. Self-employed women selling "low-cost frivolities" or other items that had come to be associated with women were, nonetheless, more likely to be working alongside other businesspeople than alongside wage-earning women or other self-employed women. Gender was a determining factor in what kinds of occupations were open to women who sought self-employment, but self-employed women and men were not segregated by occupation in quite the same manner as were wage-earning women and men. It was impossible for businesswomen who owned retail stores to operate in an entirely feminine work culture, if only because self-employed women were a relative rarity in the labour force. This sense of isolation may be one reason why women joined clubs such as the business and professional women's clubs, described in the next chapter.

Lodging-House Keepers

From 1901 to 1951, self-employed women were also consistently found in the service category. The occupation of lodging- or boarding-house keeper fell into the subcategory of personal service. Lodging houses provided rooms only, while boarding houses also provided food. Since they share many characteristics, in this and subsequent discussions the two terms are used interchangeably (and were sometimes used interchangeably in census data).

Almost all lodging-house keepers were entrepreneurs. The enterprise was sex-typed as feminine, incorporating domestic tasks such as doing laundry, cleaning, and cooking. While many women operated boarding houses, they worked in isolation rather than in a female work culture. Boarding-house keepers did not spend their time in a workplace or factory, surrounded by other women. They worked alone; if anyone else was around, it was likely to be their children or their customers – male lodgers and boarders. It was an easy business for women to enter because it was run out of the home and required manual labour and extra room(s) but little financial investment. Women could also run a lodging house while looking after children.[74]

The proportion of all self-employed women who operated lodging houses was high in the early twentieth century (Table 5). The 1931 census notes mention the "marked growth" in the number of lodging-house keepers in Canada between 1921 and 1931 and account for it in two ways. First, a "considerable number of ... women were forced into the ranks of the gainfully employed through economic necessity, their husbands being unemployed."[75] In particular, wives "whose husbands' earnings had been greatly reduced owing to prolonged unemployment ... probably were forced by household ties to take up occupations that could be carried on in the home."[76] The Depression led to increased female employment in certain occupations. As lodging-house keepers, women continued to do the same domestic tasks they had done as unpaid wives and mothers, but more of them started to provide domestic services for paying lodgers as well. In times of high male unemployment, women's unpaid work could become paid work.

The second reason for the steep increase in the number of lodging-house keepers between 1921 and 1931 was a "change made in the 1931 Census in the definition of the class 'lodging and boarding house keepers.'"[77] The manner in which lodging- and boarding-house keepers were defined and counted in the census was somewhat variable, which had some effect on the published census numbers. It is still clear that the job occupied a lot of female entrepreneurs in the first half of the twentieth century.[78] In fact, during the first four decades of the century, one-third to one-half of all women in British Columbia who claimed in the census that they were entrepreneurs were either farmers or boarding-house keepers. Female lodging or boarding-house keepers are thus a significant part of the story of female entrepreneurship.

Unlike female farmers, who were likely to be widowed, female boarding-house keepers were likely to be married: in British Columbia, more boarding-house keepers were married than widowed in the first half of the century.[79] However, they did not all live with their spouses. Like widowed farmers, many headed their own households. In 1901, none of the married boarding-house keepers in the 5 percent sample of British Columbia census data lived with their spouses; all of them headed their households. Forty-eight-year-old Elizabeth Clarke of Nelson was married, but her husband was not present and she headed her household. She had two daughters, eleven lodgers, and four servants living in her home; her operation was quite large compared to the many female-run boarding houses in the province and may well have been run as a hotel. Elizabeth Elliott, also a mother, ran a boarding house in Nelson in 1901 that contained two boarders. She too was married, but her husband was absent, and she headed the household. The marital status of boarding-house keepers is not coincidental. It is linked to their family status as mothers and household heads. In both the province and the rest of the country, jobs with high rates of female self-employment also had high numbers of married, widowed, and divorced women. In the case of a marriage ending in death, separation, divorce, or abandonment, self-employed boarding-house keepers could continue to provide for dependent family members.

Interestingly, there were some married women in the 1901 sample who lived with spouses and had lodgers or boarders in their households, but they did not report any occupation, and their husbands were usually employed elsewhere. Much like the farmers' wives who worked but declared no paying occupation, these wives with lodgers were not considered entrepreneurs, despite the work they appeared to be doing.

While many boarding-house keepers were mothers, not all of them lived with their children. In 1901, 66 percent of female boarding-house keepers did not report any children in their household. That there were no children in a home is no indication that a woman was not also a mother. Self-employed women were older than their wage-earning counterparts and thus more likely to have children, even if those children had left the nest. Half of the boarding-house keepers in the 5 percent sample of the 1901 census were aged forty-five or older. Their children likely lived elsewhere, although their enterprises may have been used, during an earlier stage of their lives, to support those children. In 1921, boarding-house keepers across Canada were most likely to be between thirty-five and forty-nine years of age, while a still-considerable 13 percent were over age sixty-five. Only one woman was under twenty-five. This pattern continued in later years. At mid-century, the average age listed in the census for employed women in British Columbia was thirty-eight, while the average age for female boarding-house keepers was fifty-one. As the 1921 census stated, "the fact that most boarding and lodging-house keepers are married or widowed accounts for the greater number in the older ages."[80] This occupation further corroborates the links between self-employment, motherhood, and family obligations. The high rates of abandonment combined with the older ages of the women – who were far more likely than single women to have children – suggest that boarding-house keepers worked to support themselves and their children and that self-employment was attractive to women with families. The ability to work from home, combined with the lack of wage-earning opportunities for older or married women or the death or desertion of a spouse, pushed some women into running boarding houses.

Hairdressers

The occupations of hairdresser and barber were combined in the published census data. The different titles generally referred to the gender of the hairdresser: women were hairdressers, dressing or cutting women's hair, while men were barbers, cutting men's hair. Less than 3 percent of female entrepreneurs worked as hairdressers in the first three decades of the twentieth century. Nevertheless, unlike other entrepreneurial occupations that declined in significance over the twentieth century, the job captured an increasing share of total female self-employment in British Columbia and in the rest of Canada over the course of the twentieth century. Moreover, self-employment rates within the occupation of hairdresser remained very high for most of the period under study, and the number of self-employed hairdressers as a proportion of all self-employed women in the labour force actually rose. The 1941 census of Canada noted the phenomenal growth in the number of hairdressers between 1921 and 1941.[81] A steady increase also occurred in the percentage of all self-employed women who worked as hairdressers in Canada between 1901 and 1951. In this profession, women were more likely to find themselves in a female work culture, although few women's enterprises were large enough to employ staff. Hairdressers were, by being in business at all, a relative rarity.

Music Teachers

The occupation of musician or music teacher (they were listed as one occupation in the census) was categorized as a professional service and was not seen as particularly feminine or masculine. If the two jobs had been listed separately in the census, a gender difference might have appeared, but it is not possible to compare the number of male to female music teachers or the number of male to female musicians because the data does not list the proportion of musicians to music teachers. We can surmise that music teachers dominated the category in the early years of the twentieth century, when there would have been a limited demand for professional musicians in the fledgling province.

An examination of newspaper advertisements in British Columbia suggests that single women dominated the occupation of music teacher. A typical example was Miss Margaret Marshall of Vancouver, who advertised in 1912 that she was a "teacher of piano; young pupils a specialty."[82] Miss Hazel Kirk offered instruction in piano and violin in 1920.[83] Single women placed most of the classified advertisements offering musical instruction in Vancouver and Victoria newspapers, and the advertisements were most plentiful between 1901 and 1920. By 1940, fewer women, single or otherwise, were seeking students through classified advertisements. Women were also less inclined to state their marital status in advertisements by the 1940s. In Victoria's *Daily Colonist* in 1945, two women – Florence Gunn and Catherine Brown – offered music lessons in the classified columns, but neither stated their marital status.[84]

Some men – although not as many men as women – advertised as music teachers in the classified columns. Their marital status is impossible to ascertain. It is also possible that women and men worked in roughly equal numbers as both musicians and music teachers but that proportionately more women than men placed advertisements as a way to seek out pupils. The classified columns do not accurately portray the number or gender of musicians or music teachers in the province, and the census' combining of the two occupations makes this difficult to unravel. But British Columbia directories provide numerous examples of women working as music

and voice teachers and almost no examples of male music teachers. The
occupation was female-dominated.

Summary

As this discussion of specific occupations makes clear, female entrepreneurs
were as likely to work alongside male entrepreneurs as they were to work
alongside other women. In some years, as many as 70 percent of female
entrepreneurs were in "male" work cultures. Even when they performed
tasks that were sex-typed as feminine (such as shopkeeping or hairdressing),
worked in domains that were sex-segregated in terms of specific types of
stores, and sold goods and services to a largely female clientele, they were
working in a business environment dominated by men. In most decades,
30 to 50 percent of female businesswomen found themselves in a female-
dominated profession, but almost all of them were seamstresses and
lodging-house keepers who were more likely to be working at home and
also less likely to employ staff. Hana Murata, a self-employed dressmaker
with a store in Vancouver in the 1920s, described herself as a "woman
working alone."[85]
    Jobs with high rates of female self-employment, such as the six just
described, were not the jobs that employed most wage-earning women in
the country. Much of the extant literature on women's labour force participation in the early twentieth century illustrates the precepts that a
women's work culture is identifiable and that separate female preserves of
labour existed. While these precepts may be clear among women in the
labour force working in occupations dominated by wage-earning women,
neither holds true for large numbers of female entrepreneurs. Self-employed
women were, however, clustered in the same small selection of occupations
and occupational groups in 1901 as in 1951 – a situation akin to that of
wage-earning women. The top six entrepreneurial opportunities for women
in 1901 were still the most prominent choices at mid-century, employing
well over half of all self-employed women. As Carrière stated in 1946, women
were employed on the farm, feeding folk, and dressing people. Countless
women entrepreneurs could be so described: they were farmers, shopkeepers, lodging-house keepers, and dressmakers. Women entrepreneurs often
worked among men, and self-employment had the potential to provide
some freedoms and potential rewards (financial, social, and otherwise).
But the barriers that *all* women encountered when they entered the labour
force, largely due to gender, should not be forgotten.

BUSINESSWOMEN IN BRITISH COLUMBIA VERSUS CANADA

The scarcity of women in British Columbia in the first half of the twentieth century meant that the proportion of the labour force that was female was lower than in the rest of the country. It seems plausible that with fewer women in the labour force, some men might have taken the opportunity to open businesses in fields traditionally dominated by women. While this was the case in wage-earning occupations such as nursing and domestic service, it occurred in only one of the occupations marked by high rates of female self-employment: lodging-house keeping attracted more men in the province than elsewhere in Canada, despite its status as an occupation dominated by women.[86]

Many individual occupations notable for high rates of self-employment confirm the conclusion reached in Chapter 2: despite the smaller female population in the province, between 1901 and 1951 women who entered the labour force in British Columbia were more likely to choose self-employment than women entering the labour force elsewhere in Canada. This is borne out by the statistics for a number of jobs with high self-employment rates, although not necessarily high numbers of businesswomen. Women consistently worked in higher proportions in British Columbia than in the rest of Canada as real estate agents, farmers, chauffeurs/taxi drivers, hotel keepers, and barbers/hairdressers (and, after 1921, as retail shopkeepers). In other words, the female share of total employment in these jobs was higher in the province than in the rest of the country.[87] All of these occupations were marked by high rates of male and female self-employment, but they were sex-typed as men's work; women formed a minority of the total employed.[88]

The occupations of chauffeur or taxi driver, real estate agent, and hotel keeper did not employ very many women, but they employed proportionately more women in British Columbia than in the rest of Canada. All three occupations were masculine: more than 80 percent of real estate agents, chauffeurs/taxi drivers, and hotel keepers were male, in British Columbia and in the rest of the country. Looking at businesswomen in these three occupations highlights some of the characteristics of entrepreneurs in British Columbia.

An article published in *The Business and Professional Woman* titled "Women CAN Sell Real Estate" profiled three women who opened Triangle Realty in 1957, "the only all-woman real estate firm in the city of

Vancouver."[89] The women felt that large real estate firms "tended to squelch the enthusiasm of the woman agent," so they left wage-earning jobs as real estate agents to open their own business. One of the owners, Mrs. Marianne Linnell, considered real estate "an ideal field for a woman with responsibilities, because her time is her own, and she can arrange appointments to fit in with her other responsibilities." The implication that a woman with a family might find a career in real estate flexible enough to suit her needs may explain the growth of the occupation among women between 1921 and 1951. This growth may also simply reflect the economic development of urban British Columbia. Robert McDonald documents the "speculative ethos" that accompanied rapid population growth in the city of Vancouver before the First World War. At the core of the city's boom period was "the belief that riches could be had quickly through the buying and selling of land and other natural resources."[90]

With many people wanting to invest in land, it makes sense that there were a lot of realtors in the province. Female realtors had high rates of self-employment, and real estate jobs attracted proportionately more women in the province than in the rest of the country. In 1921, there were twenty-three female real estate agents in British Columbia alone, and just forty-nine in the rest of the country: in other words, 32 percent of *all* female real estate agents in Canada worked in British Columbia. But if real estate was a booming field in the province in 1921, it seems to have been especially so for women. Only 16 percent of all male agents in Canada were working in British Columbia in the same year. By 1951, the number of female (and male) agents in both regions had increased, and the number of female agents working in British Columbia was still very high. There were 208 female agents in the province and only 407 in the rest of the country. Of all female real estate agents in the country (again, *including* the province), 34 percent were employed in British Columbia.[91] Female real estate agents were also more likely to be self-employed in the province than in the rest of Canada, as Table 4 illustrates.

Like real estate, the occupation of taxi driver remained male-dominated, but the share of women in the occupation increased by mid-century (when more women entered the labour force in general). British Columbia also attracted proportionately more female taxi drivers than did the rest of the country. There were no female drivers in 1921 in British Columbia. Although taxi drivers were overwhelmingly male, women made up 1.5 percent of all taxi drivers in British Columbia by 1941, and 4.5 percent in 1951. By contrast, in the rest of Canada, women taxi drivers only accounted for 0.5 percent of all taxi drivers in 1941, and 1.1 percent in 1951.

Running a hotel was a masculine pursuit, but in 1941, 18.5 percent of hotel keepers in British Columbia were women. Women in British Columbia were again more involved in a male-dominated occupation than were their counterparts in the rest of Canada, where, in the same year, 13.4 percent of hotel keepers were women.[92] Like driving a taxi, hotel keeping remained an occupation with high rates of self-employment. More than three-quarters of female hotel keepers were self-employed in 1901, 1931, and 1951, as Table 4 shows.

It is important to note that hotel keeping involved much the same work as keeping a lodging house, yet the former was an overwhelmingly masculine-typed occupation, while the latter was predominantly feminine. The difference can be explained as an issue of professionalism as well as perception. Lodging houses were small operations, run mainly by women out of their own homes. Many female lodging-house keepers had just one or two lodgers at a time. Hotels were often larger operations, serving a different need and a different clientele. Some people lived there permanently, but hotels also catered to temporary residents. Hotels were more likely to have employees than lodging houses, and they were not usually run out of owners' homes. They also required more capital, something not available to many women. By the 1920s, hotels that were large enough to obtain a liquor licence could also serve alcohol: operating a bar further differentiated hotels from boarding houses.[93] Thus hotels were larger businesses, not solely for sleeping and eating. They were considered to be a more refined business option, run by middle-class or upper-class proprietors – a perception not necessarily reflected in the amount of profit realized. Hotel keeping was viewed as a profession, while lodging-house keeping was viewed as a way to bring in a second income or to make ends meet. In what was a fairly common experience, one female boarding-house keeper in post-Second World War Vancouver explained that taking in boarders provided financial security for her family, since her husband's work in construction was low paid and intermittent.[94]

Many female boarding-house keepers were perceived as housewives with a heavier workload, in contrast to the more businesslike hotel keepers. But the work should not be seen as less businesslike or less labour-intensive than that of hotel keepers. Many women operated lodging or boarding houses as a primary way of earning an income and as sole supporters of their families. The perception of lodging-house keeping as an extension of domestic work, and of hotel keeping as a legitimate business endeavour, evolved out of conventional understandings of women's and men's work. But the actual work performed for both occupations was very similar.

The ownership of hotels is not always clear, and the Canadian Families Project's sample of the 1901 census records far more boarding-house keepers than hotel keepers.[95] The ownership is known in the case of the Island Hall Hotel, opened in Parkesville in 1917 by Miss Joan Foster and Miss Winifred Philpott. The two women had started up a poultry farm then a confectionery business (both of which failed) before becoming successful hotel owners. That Foster and Philpott were single and supported only themselves is telling. Married women with dependents were far more likely to own boarding houses, but these two women entered into business free of encumbrances. In this they were arguably more like male entrepreneurs. The women's partnership ended in 1927 with Philpott's marriage, something that would not have ended a male-run enterprise. Interestingly, in 1946 the hotel was again run by two women, Mary Sutherland and Eileen Allwood.[96]

While the distinctive features of women's work in British Columbia – the disproportionate labour force participation of married women and the high rates of female self-employment, even in masculine occupations – seem surprising given the scarcity of women in the province, the data is in keeping with what we know about businesswomen in the province. Female entrepreneurship in British Columbia was related to the particular characteristics of the frontier environment. Women capitalized on a set of opportunities not available elsewhere in Canada. The data presented here on specific occupations between 1901 and 1951 strengthens the more general observation made in Chapter 2. Although women's work was still clearly sex-segregated in the province, and although women were contained within a relatively small number of occupational groups and specific occupations, they made the most of those restrained possibilities and in some cases made inroads into professions that were indisputably male-dominated.

A variety of unskilled employment was available for men in the province in mining, building and construction, and the sawmilling industry between 1871 and 1921.[97] Women had fewer options. Wage-earning work could be found in nursing, teaching, or domestic service, but these jobs were limited in the early decades of the twentieth century when single transient males were a more characteristic population feature than established families in need of servants and teachers. Much of the work open to women on the frontier was entrepreneurial: running hotels and lodging houses or taking in sewing and washing, all jobs with a large male customer base.

DECLINING SELF-EMPLOYMENT

Self-employment was a more likely choice for both women and men at the beginning of the century than at mid-century. Table 1 in Chapter 2 shows how self-employment declined as the decades passed. The decline seems particularly sharp between 1901 and 1931, although this may be related to how census data has been compiled and published. Published census data on self-employment is woefully incomplete from 1901 to 1921. In contrast, the Canadian Families Project's sample of the 1901 census is both detailed and malleable: the user can examine individuals and their employment status and can even include women who answered the census in unusual or incomplete ways.[98] Regardless of the difficulties comparing women across census decades, it is still the case that self-employment declined in British Columbia and in the rest of Canada throughout the period of study. It is worth considering why the drop might have been particularly steep between 1901 and 1931. One way to understand the decline is to look to changes within occupations. Although more and more women were entering the labour force between 1901 and 1931, they were entering wage-earning jobs, not self-employment. Sylvia Ostry discuss occupational trends between 1901 and 1961 in a labour force study for the Dominion Bureau of Statistics. She suggests that gains in the wage-earner share of the labour force that occurred over time for both men and women reflected changes in occupational structure. As the century progressed, the importance of white-collar work increased, while the importance of occupations with high self-employment, such as farming, was greatly reduced.[99] The declining importance of entrepreneurial occupations in farming, fishing, and skilled crafts, "as well as shifts to wage earning status *within* most occupations,"[100] had occurred by mid-century.

In the first three decades of the century, women's rate of labour force participation increased. Their segregation into "the least attractive and lowest paid jobs" also increased, while their rate of self-employment decreased.[101] Clerical occupations, chiefly wage-earning occupations that came to employ large numbers of women, proliferated. In addition, fewer firms came to account for "a larger and larger share of the country's production of goods."[102] This ultimately meant fewer proprietors but more managers within large firms and within government.

Certain clerical white-collar occupations – for example, stenography or telegraph and telephone operating – became women's work, in part because women's entry into the labour force coincided with the de-skilling of white-collar work. The availability of work in what were becoming low-pay, low-status occupations was connected to the increase of women in the labour force. Since so few women were in the labour force at all in the first few decades of the twentieth century, they formed "a vast reserve supply of labour able to fill the sudden growth in clerical openings."[103] Ultimately, women's rising participation in the labour force before the Second World War was marked by entry into low-paid wage-earning occupations. This occurred at the expense of female self-employment. The improvement in women's participation rates was not matched by a growth in the types of occupations open to women, nor did it lead to the growth of new entrepreneurial endeavours.

Another factor that explains the dramatic decline in women's self-employment in the first three decades of the twentieth century was the decrease, as the 1941 census of Canada pointed out, "in the number of dressmakers, milliners, and tailoresses since 1911."[104] Manufacturing occupations in sewing had provided opportunities for female employment in general and female self-employment in particular, but these occupations were becoming less lucrative. Wendy Gamber argues, in an American context, that the early twentieth century was marked by "the triumph of mass production and large-scale retailing" and that by 1930 the dressmaking and millinery trades "had been all but supplanted by the ladies' garment trade," a field of unskilled wage-earning work.[105] The factory "claimed an undisputed victory over the custom shop."[106]

The steep decline in self-employment among women that occurred between 1901 and 1931 was greater in British Columbia than in Canada. Again, British Columbia demonstrated regional distinction. In 1901, the number of wage-earning jobs available for women in the province as limited. By 1931, a higher percentage of women in the province had entered the labour force, and wage-earning occupations accounted for much of the increase. The extremely high female self-employment rate in British Columbia in 1901 was thus related to a lack of manufacturing wage-earning jobs for women but also to a demand for female-provided services. Businesses providing beds, food, and laundry services for men living without female companions were not as needed by 1931. The entrepreneurial occupations that had provided such services declined as the gender ratio evened out.

Gender clearly affected the number of women in the labour force and the kinds of work that women did in British Columbia and Canada between 1901 and 1951. Wage-earning *and* self-employed women were limited to a narrow range of occupational groups and occupations. Despite being hindered by similar limitations in terms of work options, and despite a host of popular assumptions about what kinds of work were suitable for women, businesswomen challenged the idea of what constituted acceptable women's work simply by choosing self-employment in the first place. Women in British Columbia challenged traditional assumptions even further: they chose self-employment more often than did other working women in the country, and they entered male-dominated entrepreneurial occupations in higher rates than did women in the rest of Canada. Women in British Columbia and elsewhere in Canada who owned businesses were a minority within the female labour force in the twentieth century (even at their strongest point, in 1901), and they formed an even smaller proportion of the entire labour force. Yet they did exist, and they provide an opportunity to re-examine our ideas about women's work.

Within the entrepreneurial arena, some women capitalized on preconceived ideas about women's work and opened businesses that either catered to a female clientele or incorporated tasks long associated with women, such as cleaning, teaching, cooking, and doing laundry. Despite the gendered nature of their work, these businesswomen challenged gender stereotypes by owning their establishments, however small the establishments and no matter what type of business they ran. Some challenged other stereotypes too: Blanche Macdonald, of First Nations ancestry and married with two children, opened a modelling agency and self-improvement school in Vancouver in 1960. She went on to launch a journalism program for First Nations students and continued to champion "native causes and feminist ideals."[107] Macdonald operated in a recognizably feminine field. Businesswomen who ran enterprises that did not seem to fall under the category of women's work, such as taxi drivers and hotel keepers, also pushed the concept of women's work cultures: they were a minority in that they owned businesses at all but even more so in their choice of business.

Their presence, particularly noticeable in British Columbia, suggests that we need to consider the gendered nature of businesswomen's occupations differently from the ways we have considered the gendering of the wage-earning labour force. Businesswomen affiliated themselves, variously, with other women who worked, with other people (men) who were in business, and with other wives and mothers. The ways they navigated between private and public life and between their identities as women and as businesspeople are addressed in the next two chapters.

4
"They are quick, alert, clear-eyed business girls"

THE BUSINESS AND PROFESSIONAL
WOMEN'S CLUBS OF BRITISH COLUMBIA

The Vancouver Business and Professional Women's Club
Is a club of good standing in the town.
Its women are the best you could find in any land,
And smart women cannot be kept down.
Some are holding big positions, some are holding bigger ones,
From the least unto the greatest they are fine.
They are quick, alert, clear-eyed business girls,
And they know how to have a good time.
CHORUS:
You will never find them slumbering,
No-No-No-No;
Never find them grumbling,
No-No-No-No.
For at work or play,
They're just the same
The Vancouver Business Women's Club.

— "*Club Songs,*" Vancouver Business Woman
5, 6 (November 1927), Add Mss 799,
588-A-3, City of Vancouver Archives

his chapter looks at the relationship between gender and business
by examining the first two business and professional women's
(BPW) clubs formed in British Columbia. The following discussion traces the early history of the Victoria and Vancouver BPW clubs and
their relationship to the Canadian Federation of Business and Professional Women's Clubs (CFBPWC). The charities that the clubs supported,
the political causes they championed, their efforts in the arena of female

employment conditions, and their social activities indicate how club members in British Columbia understood their own roles in the business world.[1]

In her history of American businesswomen and American BPW clubs, Candace Kanes discusses the ways in which businesswomen seemed to be simultaneously conservative and radical. Their identities as women in business meant a "radical" departure from traditional womanhood, but many club members were not interested in being seen as troublemakers. They were cautious about "appearing too feminist, too radical, or too independent of men."[2] Kanes neatly summarizes how businesswomen dealt with these conflicting identities, arguing that they developed an "inside-outside mode of coping with many of the claims of womanhood: marriage, children, domesticity and appropriate modes of behavior, dress, and attitude."[3] Inside their club meetings, women could and did critique the claims of womanhood, but outside the confines of the club rooms, the women were more likely to acknowledge the "importance of society's views of womanhood."[4] Kanes concludes that while American business-women "could not step outside of sex and gender dichotomies, they often disrupted the categories, paying public homage" to the claims of woman-hood while "privately critiquing such expectations."[5]

Much like their American predecessors, Canadian BPW club members were an odd amalgam of progressive political action and social conserva-tism, and they also adopted an "inside-outside" mode of coping with competing influences on their behaviour. The Canadian clubwomen were conservative in many ways. Like their American counterparts, the clubs in British Columbia publicly praised the conventional roles and societal expectations of women. The outside image of the club was respectable, and the Vancouver and Victoria clubs were relatively cautious in the reforms they proposed. Their public conservatism meant that their forms of pub-lic protest consisted of passing strongly worded motions or sending letters to governmental bodies. These methods of public protest were valuable. Their conservatism was not an inappropriate or ineffective tool for prompt-ing change. However, BPW clubs did not deviate from conventional perceptions of womanhood in their public activities, and the clubwomen were not on the fringes of mainstream society.

In her examination of the Victoria BPW club, Deidre Brocklehurst suggests that the club provided women with an opportunity to "assume a public life without too deeply challenging traditional gender roles."[6] A 1927 article printed in the Vancouver club's bulletin, *Vancouver Business Woman,* asserted that "the Canadian woman has proved her ability to take her share in the public and domestic life of the Dominion, while still maintaining her original place in the home."[7] While clubwomen supported equality in the work world, they did not, especially in the 1920s and 1930s, suggest a radical overhaul of society. They supported the rights of women in numerous ways, particularly through the use of the franchise and through their support for legislation that pertained to women in the workforce. But they did not suggest that women replace men in the labour force – indeed, at times during the Depression era, they even argued that men should replace women in the labour force.

As I will demonstrate, BPW club members in British Columbia generally supported fair treatment for women working for or alongside men in the labour force. There were some progressive aspects to the clubs and to the women who joined them. Moreover, a more detailed look at club records shows that while they maintained a respectable outside image and could be considered conservative, some elements of inside club life were devoted to criticizing and overturning the more obvious signs of inequality that the women dealt with in their daily working lives. BPW clubs provided an outlet for women's frustrations with the economic arena in which they made their livings. Business and professional women were aware, and at times critical, of the gender conventions that bound their enterprises. The records of the Vancouver and Victoria BPW clubs demonstrate business and professional women's ritual parody of male-dominated business traditions in satirical news articles, mock debates, and mock weddings. Most of these events occurred under the auspices of the club's social activities, but they indicate that even in lighter social moments, club members were constantly aware of the gendered world that shaped – and limited – their working lives. And while the critiques were usually kept inside the club meetings, they could sometimes spill out into the club's public activities. In the press, in some of their proposed reforms, and in the privacy of the club's meetings, a more radical and less conventional side of the BPW clubs existed.

It could perhaps be argued that the experiences and activities of BPW club members do not represent the experiences of most self-employed women in the province. However, their actions and their interests reflect the concerns of working women and, in some cases, the specific concerns of self-employed women. The jobs they held and the businesses they owned were also not always representative. As Chapter 3 demonstrates, many self-employed women in the province were farmers, boarding-house keepers, and seamstresses, while clubwomen were more likely to operate retail businesses and hotels. Despite differences in scale, status, and business type, some of their concerns were very similar. Moreover, while many penny capitalists in British Columbia were unaware of, and probably uninterested in, the social lives of the relatively privileged group of women who participated in club life, the activities of the privileged hold resonance. The BPW clubwomen questioned their status and participated in public discourses on the subjects of business and appropriately feminine work. They walked many fine lines – between motherhood and self-employment, between marriage and work, and between masculine and feminine business types – just as their lower-class contemporaries did. Furthermore, these concerns were relevant to all businesswomen, but the majority of working-class business owners in the province did not have the time or the inclination to grapple with these questions. Those who did left no record of their opinions. The BPW clubwomen had the time and inclination to grapple and to record, and their commentaries illuminate a narrow but very relevant part of the story of gender, business, and family in British Columbia.

Businesswomen or Women in Business: Definitions

To begin, an examination of the historical use of the term "businesswoman" and its changing definition over time is warranted. Gender and business historian Angel Kwolek-Folland argues that female business owners were more likely to be defined as penny capitalists than as entrepreneurs, if they were identified at all.[8] This definitional issue also involves class: small businesses run by working-class men and women were more likely to be defined as forms of penny capitalism, rather than as businesses in the more corporate sense. Women's businesses were frequently smaller than men's. They were often created out of the labour that women already did on the domestic front, meaning that in the eyes of many they barely registered as businesses. This helps explain the lack of recognition afforded to women who were technically self-employed and working as laundresses, washer-women, or prostitutes, working-class occupations that depended on the owner's labour rather than on the buying or selling of products.

By the early twentieth century, the prospect that women could be businesspeople in their own right seemed more plausible. In addition to the masculine terminology of the businessman, the terms "businesswoman" and "business girl" came into use. But they did not indicate that women and men were on equal footing in terms of entrepreneurial endeavours, or even that women in various types of business were viewed in the same way. Mary Yeager states that distinctions arose between business girls, "the young single women who worked as part of the clerical force in corporations dominated by men," and women who were "viewed as independent proprietors or 'women in business.'"[9]

Kwolek-Folland notes the same trend, also in an American context, and suggests that the distinctions were important in understanding how business was gendered: "After the advent of female professionalism around 1900 and continuing at least to 1930, female office workers stressed the feminine qualities of the business or office girl and the masculine qualities of the businesswoman."[10] Business girls were not entrepreneurs, but they were feminine. Self-employed businesswomen, however, were entrepreneurs and therefore "manly." According to Kwolek-Folland, one female secretary stated, "I really feel that the business world rubs the bloom from a woman."[11]

In terms of acceptable gender conventions, self-employed women were more likely to be called businesswomen after 1900, but even though the term was woman-specific, it was sometimes associated with masculine qualities. A businesswoman "has to take hold of [her] work as a man does, make the sacrifices a man does," according to a short story written in 1915 for the *Saturday Evening Post*.[12] By contrast, wage-earning business girls were appropriately feminine and posed no threat to gender conventions because the work the "girls" did was associated with women's work. Female office workers (who were often secretaries for men) did not challenge gender hierarchies. They were younger and less educated than male office workers and were subordinate to male managers, becoming "office wives" in what Kwolek-Folland has termed an ideology of "corporate domesticity."[13]

A further complication arose after 1900 in the definition of the terms "businessmen" and "businesswomen," which could include all people working outside the home (usually in white-collar occupations). The term "businessman" would not be applied to a labourer but could be applied to an office clerk or a bank manager, just as the term "businesswoman" was not used to describe domestic servants but could indicate female sales clerks or women who worked as stenographers and typists. These women were conducting business, but they were not self-employed. They worked for someone else. This broadening of the definition occurred among men and women. Kanes notes that as companies "grew in complexity and separated ownership from management in the late nineteenth and early twentieth centuries, 'business' began taking on new meanings." Even among men, the term "businessman" was not limited to the self-employed:

it also included managers.[14] Being in business meant working in the world of business, whether as a wage earner or a business owner. In this respect, it implied much more about one's class position than about one's gender.

In some ways, the twentieth-century use of the term "businesswoman" was too broad, encompassing a wide variety of wage-earning and self-employed women in the labour force; in other ways, it was extremely narrow, limited to middle- and upper-class women who ran businesses that were bigger and more successful than those of the penny capitalists. The BPW clubs that became prominent in the 1920s and 1930s in Canada and the United States reflected both of these definitional difficulties. Clubs included both wage-earning and self-employed women as businesswomen. Because they did not always clearly distinguish between women who worked in business and women who owned businesses, membership lists for British Columbia cannot easily be broken down into entrepreneurs and employees. The bylaws set out in 1925 for the Victoria club stated that any woman "engaged in business in the district of Victoria" was eligible, and the membership included women in a variety of occupations, many of whom were employees.[15] The constitution and bylaws of the CFBPWC, which also applied to the Victoria club since it was a member of the Canadian federation, were more specific. "'Business Woman' means any self-supporting woman in receipt of an income earned by herself, whether such income be received as salary, fee, or commission, as head or member of a firm, executive, employer, or employee."[16] I use the term "businesswoman" to refer to self-employed entrepreneurs, despite its use in the early twentieth century to refer to women in a variety of occupational situations. I also use more specific terms, such as self-employed, entrepreneur, or proprietor, to clearly distinguish wage-earning from self-employed "businesswomen" when such a distinction is necessary.

Wage-earning women engaged in white-collar office work or in other professional occupations were more prominent in BPW clubs in the province than were business owners. This is partly a reflection of the female labour force: the self-employed made up a small proportion of all working women in British Columbia. In fact, given the low rate of female self-employment in the labour force, self-employed women were well represented in the Victoria BPW club. According to census data, 12.8 percent of the female labour force in British Columbia was self-employed in 1931. In the same year, an estimated 22.1 percent of the Victoria BPW club members were self-employed. In 1948, an estimated 21.5 percent of the Victoria club members were self-employed, while in 1951, the closest census year, just 6.6 percent of the female labour force in the province was self-employed.[17] Even though the club had more wage-earning than self-employed members in the two years for which complete membership lists exist, a disproportionate number of self-employed women, compared to their proportion of the female labour force, joined the club (Table 6).

Table 6 was created based on the Victoria BPW club membership lists. Whether club members were self-employed was not specified. To estimate the rates of self-employment in the table, I placed members in categories according to their likely employment status, relying on the specific occupation they listed in the club records. When it was too difficult to determine a woman's status from her job title, I used the "other" (status unknown) category. There are weaknesses in this method: not all milliners were self-employed, but I included them in the self-employed category because those who joined a club for professional women were far more likely to be self-employed than to be wage earners. Other decisions were easier: most photographers were self-employed in the early to mid-twentieth century, just as almost all stenographers or clerks in the same period were wage earners. By making conservative inferences, I can estimate levels of entrepreneurship amongst members in 1931 and 1948 because the lists, with occupational descriptions, exist. This is useful, especially because information about club members can be compared to other information

TABLE 6   Victoria Business and Professional Women's Club membership, 1931 and 1948

	1931		1948	
Occupational category	Total (n)	(%)*	Total (n)	(%)*
Clerical (wage earners)	30	34.9	38	35.5
Professional (wage earners)	19	22.1	21	19.6
Retail workers (wage earners)	5	5.8	11	10.3
Self-employed	19	21.1	23	21.5
Other (status unknown)	13	15.1	14	13.1
Total, all categories	86	100.0	107	100.0

NOTES: For the complete list of individual 1931 and 1948 BPW club members, with names, stated marital status, and occupations, see Appendices 2 and 3. The figures in this table have been rounded for clarity.
*   As percentage of total BPW club membership
SOURCES: "Membership List, Victoria Business and Professional Women's Club, 1931," Attendance and Registration Book, BPW Club Records, 89-1386-3, BC Archives; "Membership List, Victoria Business and Professional Women's Club, 1948," BPW Club Records, 89-1386-2, BCA.

about businesswomen in British Columbia in the first half of the twentieth century.

As membership information and club bylaws illustrate, a businesswoman
was broadly defined as any woman who worked to support herself, but
the club catered to those in professional or middle-class occupations.
However, the overall aims of the clubs served the interests of all women
in business and in the professions. Club projects appealed to self-employed
women, who had no other space in which to network with like-minded
women – that is, with other women who worked outside the home and
who encountered challenges in their workplaces that were related to their
gender. There were some other clubs that catered to women in business
and the professions, such as Soroptimist International, which had branches in Victoria and the Lower Mainland. The oldest was established in 1926.
While the Soroptimists attracted women who might also have been interested in the BPW clubs, they were service-oriented, formed to "foster the
ideals of service and improve the quality of life for all people."[18] The Zonta
Club, another international women's club, had branches in Vancouver but
was never very big. It catered to professional women and focused on
women's legal, political, economic, and professional status.[19] Businesswomen would undoubtedly have found fellowship in these clubs, but the
BPW clubs were specifically focused on women's employment. While club
members also performed service work, employment issues were primary.
In this respect the BPW clubs provide a unique window on issues of gender,
employment, and self-employment. Club records provide a representative
sample of some of the issues that were pertinent to women in business for
themselves or for others. All of the women worked for pay and encountered
the peculiar gendering of their work experiences.

That the BPW clubs included self-employed and wage-earning women
reinforces the distinct lack of networking associations available to self-
employed women. Their marginality in the labour force is reflected in the
fact that the BPW clubs were really the only space within which self-
employed women could meet with other female entrepreneurs. BPW clubs
are therefore extremely important in the study of female self-employment.

The Victoria and Vancouver BPW Clubs

The business and professional women's clubs of Canada were modelled
after similar clubs in the United States. The American model was one of
local community BPW clubs tied together by the National Federation of

Business and Professional Women's Clubs. Formed in 1919, the federation brought American businesswomen's clubs together to lobby state and federal governments on concerns common to all women in business and the professions.[20] The federation was also interested in furthering the gains women had made during the war. Like the local clubs, the federation focused on women and their "innate ethical and behavioural differences from men."[21]

While they acknowledged their members' differences from men, the American and Canadian clubs were inspired by men's organizations. In the United States, businessmen joined clubs in the interests of fellowship and civic improvement and to generally boost their communities. Organizations such as the Rotary Club, which began in 1905, the Kiwanis Club, formed in 1915, and the Lions Club, formed in 1917, were exclusively male.[22] Their refusal to admit women might have prompted the women to form similar clubs. The men's groups of the early twentieth century evolved out of ideas about the growing importance of business and the professions.

Although women's clubs were modelled on men's clubs, they were "less concerned with reforming the image of business or with boosting the business community ... than with finding a place for women in that venue."[23] The national federation in the United States provided strength in numbers, a way for business and professional women to address issues common to all club members.

The Canadian clubs looked to their American counterparts for inspiration. The goals of the American and Canadian clubs were similar. It is clear from the friendships between women in the Victoria club and neighbouring US clubs that their American neighbours influenced the British Columbia clubs, among the first established in Canada. In May 1921, the Seattle Business and Professional Women's Club invited the newly formed Kumtuks Club (which would become the Victoria Business and Professional Women's Club in 1930) to send representatives to its meeting.[24] In 1923, Lottie Bowron, founder of the Victoria club, clasped hands with Lulu Fairbanks, of the Seattle BPW club, "across an imaginary border-line at Blaine, Wash. and pledged friendship and loyalty between the Business & Professional Women of the two countries."[25] Bowron also attended a convention of American clubs in Portland, Oregon, in 1924,[26] and the Victoria club later helped to organize a BPW club in Port Angeles, Washington.[27]

In Canada, local clubs formed first and later helped to create a national federation. The Victoria club formed in 1921 as the Kumtuks Club, and the Vancouver Business and Professional Women's Club was established in 1923. Josephine Dauphinee, a nurse, teacher, and supervisor of special needs education classes – and a supporter of eugenics – was one of the Vancouver club founders.[28] She was president of the club in 1928, when a committee of Victoria and Vancouver club members suggested that the two work toward forming a Canadian federation.[29] This idea was clearly a result of the close contact between the British Columbia clubs and their American neighbours. Canadian representatives attended the biennial convention of the United States federation on Mackinac Island in July 1929. With help from the American clubwomen, they drafted a constitution for a Canadian federation. "In between sessions they went over the draft constitution and by-laws for the proposed Canadian Federation and returned to Canada fired with enthusiasm to get a national Federation under way."[30]

The Vancouver club adopted and approved the clauses and constitution of the Canadian federation at its November 1929 meeting.[31] The first convention for the CFBPWC was held in Winnipeg in the summer of 1930 and included representatives from clubs in Montreal, Hamilton, Toronto, Winnipeg, Vancouver, and Victoria.[32] Mrs. Madge Hall attended as the delegate for Victoria. When she returned, she informed Kumtuks Club members that if they wanted to be included in the CFBPWC, the club had to bear the name "Business and Professional Women's Club."[33] They changed the name to the Victoria Business and Professional Women's Club in September 1930.

In its early years, the CFBPWC thrived. Additional clubs quickly sprang up across the country. At the time of the federation's third annual convention, held in Vancouver and Victoria in 1932, there were nineteen BPW clubs in Canada. Delegates attended from six British Columbian clubs: New Westminster, Vernon, Kamloops, Nanaimo, Victoria, and Vancouver.[34] British Columbia's clubs made up a significant proportion of all the clubs in the country in 1932. Their prominence at the national level is evident in their involvement with the national federation's executive and even with the publications put out by the CFBPWC.[35]

That British Columbia club members were an important force in terms of the total number of clubs in the national federation at its inception seems fitting, since women in British Columbia were very active in the labour force and were proportionately more likely to be self-employed than women elsewhere in the country. Their involvement in entrepreneurship in the province was noticeable in historical census data, but the qualitative records also demonstrate this. The prominence of the Vancouver and Victoria clubs in the early years of the Canadian federation may reflect the distinct attributes of the female labour force in the province. It is therefore worth examining the formation of these two clubs in more detail.

Miss Lottie Bowron was the founder and first president of the Kumtuks Club of Victoria. She was the daughter of John Bowron, one of the original settlers in the Cariboo gold rush town of Barkerville. She worked for Conservative premier Richard McBride from 1904 until he stepped down in 1915. Bowron was apparently disappointed that the new government did not offer her a job, and she left for England, returning in 1918. In 1921, Bowron was in her forties and working in British Columbia as a public stenographer.[36] Finding herself somewhat isolated and bereft of her old occupation and associations might have prompted her to form the Kumtuks Club, although she highlighted other public political issues as influencing her decision:

> As founder of the Club, I feel I may be allowed to express, unmistakeably [sic], what was the chief reason for its being, – to educate us in public affairs, so that we, as intelligent women with the vote, might know how to properly play our part in the life of Canada ... An organ of our own was a necessity, where we could express our views, learn to speak, to give and take, enlarge our public activities – a place of preparation for our larger work of community service.[37]

Bowron's concept was thus of a serious club with a political purpose. She clearly believed that an "organ" (probably her short form for organization) solely for women, was much needed. But she also remembered that she had envisioned a place where businesswomen could, "like the Rotarians," meet for lunch. She was very interested in "what women could do, what the future of our sex must be, what its responsibilities and priveleges [sic] would entail, and the great need of preparation for this future," but she also wanted a club where women could meet for social reasons.[38]

Bowron began what was the first business and professional women's club in western Canada with a luncheon on 17 January 1921 in Victoria.[39] There were twenty-four founding members: nine were married, and fifteen were single. Another forty-two members joined throughout 1921, eleven of whom were married.[40] Bowron's vision encapsulated the many functions of the BPW clubs that would later form across Canada: the clubs would be serious and political and chiefly concerned with using women's franchise. An informal history of the Kumtuks Club stressed that the "exercise of the franchise" was "one of the essential qualifications of membership."[41] Women were encouraged to vote (for women whenever possible) and even to run for public office. But the clubs were also intended to be social networks. A member of the Winnipeg BPW club recollected in 1946 that the members' main objective had been "to have a Club where we tired business and professional women might relax and get away from all the worries of our every-day life."[42]

A group of women proposed organizing a Vancouver Business and Professional Women's Club at a luncheon in November 1922, and the women elected their first executive on 19 January 1923. The first official club luncheon, held on 20 February 1923, attracted eighty-two women. Newly elected president Mabel Ingram told them that the club "must have been formed at the [right] psychological moment, as so many women had responded." Ingram continued, "There are women in all branches of business and the professions today, we are shut out of nothing, and the men are recognizing more and more that we are in the business world to stay and to shoulder our share of the big things of the world."[43]

BPW CLUB ACTIVITIES

According to Article 3 of the Vancouver club's constitution, its "Aims and Objects" included "to promote the interests of business and professional women, to stimulate social intercourse and further the educational development of its members. To elevate the standards for women in business and professional life, and to take such action on social and economic questions and such other matters as the club may deem advisable."[44]

Much like the Kumtuks Club, the ideals of the Vancouver BPW club were more ambitious than simply providing a place to socialize, although the success of their many luncheons indicates that socializing and networking were key aspects of the club. More importantly, the women who formed BPW clubs in British Columbia in the early 1920s were aware that if they wanted to achieve parity with men in the "business world," they needed their own space. The formation of the clubs was a response to the gendered world in which the women worked. Had women perceived their work worlds as "gender-neutral," they would have had no need for a separate social space. Moreover, they needed more than a social space, as the minutes of the Victoria and Vancouver clubs indicate: the clubs helped women embrace the franchise and learn how to use it to better their own and other women's working lives.

Like the American BPW clubs, those in British Columbia imitated men's clubs to some degree. It is clear that Bowron had the Rotarians in mind as a model when she formed the Kumtuks Club, particularly in the area of community service.[45] But it is important to note that women's business clubs also sought specific recognition for women in the working world. They strove to "create a community of women who could support and encourage one another in ventures into uncharted territory."[46] This is a key difference between businessmen's clubs, which provided an organizational model, and businesswomen's clubs. Men in business were not at a threshold. They were not starting into a new field or into uncharted territory, even though their twentieth-century business clubs may have been a new form of expression for businessmen. BPW clubs were an important marker of a changing world for women in the labour force, and it is significant that women saw a need to create a female club space. Even if that space was in some ways modelled after the clubs started by men, the issues women dealt with in their clubs differed from those of men, precisely because of gender.

The BPW clubs took their community work seriously, beginning with small acts of generosity directed toward other women and children in their community. In 1923, club members donated money to needy children and provided mugs and oranges to an orphanage. Club member Miss Bay Wigley became a member of the board of the Children's Aid, an appointment that pleased Kumtuks members keen to keep up liaison work with other service organizations in Victoria.[47] This indicates an early association with issues related to children and families.

While the minute books for the Victoria club in the early 1930s recorded many social activities and continuing service-oriented activities, the club also took on a variety of issues that highlighted women's inequality in the labour force. Brocklehurst argues that the club began with a commitment to community service and philanthropic work but, over time, made women's work-related issues its primary focus. Club members defended women's right to work. Between 1920 and 1961 they became more outspoken on employment issues such as wage equity, the rights of married women to work, the vulnerability of older women workers, and the status of domestic workers.[48]

These issues became more important with the onset of the Depression. The Vancouver BPW club addressed rising unemployment in the city and its effect on women by contributing to the Women's Committee for Unemployment Relief in 1931, giving "the use of their club rooms daily as a sewing room for unemployed women."[49] Following Vancouver's lead, the Victoria club opened a similar room in 1932: women on the "work roll" worked four hours a day and were paid twenty cents per hour to remodel clothes. Bay Wigley reported that it was "a source of great pleasure to Victoria to know how much good that room has done in the way of helping these women who otherwise must have applied for relief and in that way have lowered their own morale."[50] While Wigley suggested that these women did not have to apply for relief, their work in the sewing room was not billed as full employment but as relief work. The project did not create permanent jobs for women.

In January 1934, Miss Nettie Foxall, owner of a photographic studio, moved the following resolution:

> Be it resolved that this Victoria B and P W Club ... strongly deprecates any tendency on the part of employers, in any class of employment, to exploit women and girls who, in many cases, are driven almost to desperation by [their] need to accept wages which are incompatible with decent standards of living.[51]

The motion, which passed, was clearly motivated by Depression-era working conditions. But it was not until May 1936 that the club appointed a committee to look at the unemployment situation for women in Victoria.[52]

In 1935, an insightful editorial published in *The Business and Professional Woman,* the national federation's newsletter, addressed the unemployment issues faced by women. Titled "A Momentous Time," the author pointed out that "the girl of today, standing on the threshold of the business world, views a very different prospect to the girl of ten years ago. 'How can I get a job?' is the question on her lips; not, as it was ten years ago, 'what career should I choose?'"[53] The editorial urged businesswomen of Canada to face the "slump" and "the immediate future with clear eyes ... to be prepared to ask for, and fight for, reasonable treatment in every channel of business and the professions, and to adapt themselves to changing conditions." Business and professional women recognized that they would need to fight for "reasonable treatment" given that the Depression led to layoffs.

The onset of the Second World War brought new issues. An article in *The Business and Professional Woman* in May 1941 noted that there was a "danger of becoming so immersed in the routine of war work ... that we lose sight of the real issues involved and the part educated business and professional women can play."[54] Despite the warning, the Canadian federation focused on "war interests" during the July 1941 convention. British Columbia clubs also focused on wartime aid rather than political questions during the 1940s. An article in the November 1940 issue of *The Business and Professional Woman,* titled "All Clubs Put Emphasis on War Work," reported that the New Westminster club had "adopted" two soldiers. The Victoria Club had a Red Cross Group and imposed a monthly levy on their members that was put into a war emergency fund, while the Fanoba (Vancouver) club was knitting and collecting funds.[55]

While political and social justice issues may have been placed on hold during the war, the BPW clubs returned to them as the war came to a close. In 1944, at a regional conference in the Vancouver BPW club rooms, Mrs. Lillian Smith of Victoria spoke on full employment and on the role business and professional women could expect to play in the postwar world. She repeated the same goals for club women in 1944 that Lottie Bowron had stressed in her explanation of what the Kumtuks Club sought to do more than twenty years earlier. Smith drew attention to issues such as the equality of men and women and the "right of married women to work." She also proposed that women in business should "employ women wherever possible" and vote for women and specifically for business or professional women.[56] Hiring and voting for women were two tangible steps that club members were urged to take. These were serious political and economic messages for women in business and professional life.

The right of married women to work was a persistent issue for BPW clubs during the Depression and postwar years. In 1930, the Victoria Chamber of Commerce advised the Victoria BPW club that it had "appointed a committee to consider and make a special study of the unemployment question." The Chamber planned to urge employers to "employ unmarried women who are obliged to earn their own living or work in support of others in the place of married women who are now employed and whose husbands are also working."[57] The Chamber of Commerce clearly saw this as a strategy to deal with mounting unemployment during the Depression but sought support from a club composed of both married and single women, all of whom worked.

Unfortunately, the club's response to the Chamber was not noted in the minutes. In the 1930s, married women did not work in huge numbers, and self-employed women were more likely to be married than were wage-earning women. Thus, the issue might not have aroused much debate at the time because the Victoria club had relatively few married members who worked as wage earners. But it is also possible that the membership agreed with a policy that barred married women from working during times of massive unemployment. Brocklehurst found evidence that the Victoria club felt that employment of married women was only justified when the family depended on that income for survival. This was a very limited endorsement of the right of married women to work, and Brockle-hurst notes that even though the CFBPWC maintained throughout the Depression that it "officially supported the right of married women to work," the Victoria BPW club's support wavered.[58]

Married, self-employed women were not in danger of losing their jobs as a result of the Chamber of Commerce proposal, although that danger may have been one of the reasons why married women chose self-employment over wage-earning work. While the majority of wage earners in the BPW clubs were single, many of the self-employed women in the Vancouver and Victoria clubs were married, widowed, or divorced.[59] By combing the records of the two clubs, recording every mention of self-employed women and comparing these mentions with existing full or partial membership lists that indicated women's occupations, I obtained a better profile of entrepreneurial club members. While not all entrepreneurs in the clubs could be captured this way, this form of data collection confirms the link between marriage and female self-employment that was also evident amongst other entrepreneurial women in the province. Of the clubwomen with entrepreneurial occupations listed between the 1920s and the 1950s, 59 percent were married or once-married.[60] Married women found it harder to obtain wage-earning work than did single women, but they may also have had trouble keeping their jobs if they were at risk of being replaced by men or by single women whenever the economy was in decline. Although it held many other financial perils, self-employment put married women in a position where they could not lose their source of income solely because of their marital status.

In later years, the Victoria club clarified its position and defended the rights of married women in the labour force. During the Second World War, many married women had gone to work; after the war, they were encouraged to return to the home.[61] In 1947, the federal government announced that it planned to terminate the employment of married women to provide jobs for, primarily, male war veterans. In response, on 18 February 1947, the Victoria BPW club sent the following telegram to the House of Commons: "The Business and Professional Women's Club of Victoria is deeply perturbed at the action taken by the Dominion Government in dismissing all married women in its employ as of March 31st 1947. On behalf of all employed women of Greater Victoria we would ask you to protest this policy with utmost vigour."[62]

That the Victoria club became more active on behalf of married workers after the war is not surprising. In 1931, just 32.6 percent of the entire club membership was married; in 1948, the only other year for which a complete membership list is available, 53.3 percent of the membership was married.[63] The percentage of clerical and professional wage-earning members who were married more than doubled, from 20 percent in 1931 to 41 percent in 1948, so policies that affected married workers had a more significant impact on Victoria club members in 1947 and 1948 than in 1931.[64]

Married government employees' right to work became a province-wide (and also a national) issue in the late 1940s. In 1948, although individual clubs continued to meet, a larger provincial body for business and professional women was formed in British Columbia. Delegates from twelve of the province's nineteen clubs attended the first meeting of the new provincial BPW club.[65] The provincial organization was meant to provide small clubs with stronger representation at the national level and to tackle issues of interest to members across the province. At a meeting of provincial delegates in September 1949, one of the issues on the agenda was married women in the civil service. Delegates were angered that married female employees had been asked to keep an open resignation on file "until the time comes when they can be replaced [by men]," according to Hilda Cryderman. British Columbia's Civil Service Commission had asked married women in the civil service to hand in "advance resignations" when they were hired, so they could be replaced in the event of a depression (or, presumably, for any other reason).[66] An official of the Civil Service Commission stated, "We don't want them (married women who are civil servants) to get the idea that they are firmly implanted in their jobs."[67]

Headed by its first provincial president, Minnie Beveridge (owner of a millinery shop in Victoria), the provincial organization responded by sending a telegram to British Columbia premier Byron Johnson:

> Representatives of 650 members of the British Columbia Business and Professional Women's Clubs in conference strongly protest discrimination against married women by British Columbia Civil Service Commission as reported in daily press of August and urge immediate reconsideration of this policy.[68]

In 1952, the Victoria BPW club again raised the issue of the employment of married women, noting that one of the tenets of the Canadian federation was "the right of all women to be gainfully employed regardless of race, colour, creed or marital status." Club members supported the tenet and accordingly congratulated Saanich municipal council on its decision to base further appointments of women on merit only.[69]

However, the Victoria club's support for the right of married women to work would again waver. In 1960, at a time of mounting unemployment statistics, club members conceded that every woman should have the right to work, whether married or single, "but a married woman with young children should not work unless she is the breadwinner of a family."[70] In this case, clubwomen may have been more concerned about the welfare of children than about married women's right to work. But they still ultimately proposed that in some cases married women ought to stay in the home, something that was never advocated for married men or for fathers. The Victoria club seemed to be returning to the policy proposed by the Chamber of Commerce in 1930, a more conservative stance than that endorsed at the federal level by the CFBPWC. This conservatism might have been influenced by the white, middle-class membership of the club. Women who did not need to work for financial reasons and who had high-earning spouses perhaps promoted the ideal of the stay-at-home mother. But many mothers who were not club members worked because their families needed their income, even if they were not the family's main "breadwinner."

The British Columbia clubs did defend women's right to work in support of family. They linked women with the family claim, just as earlier commentators had done. In an 1889 article on the "incapacity of business-women," Marion Harland stated that while business was a lifetime occupation and preoccupation for men, for women work was simply work. A woman's lifetime occupation was her marriage and her children.[71] What Harland did not say was that a preoccupation with marriage and children could be the reason for women to return to the business world. Sometimes spouses died or wives were abandoned. Other women simply needed to supplement their husbands' incomes. What remained constant for businesswomen was "the link between their participation in the economy and their role in the family."[72] But business and professional women also stressed that family came first. Despite the fact that Vancouver and Victoria BPW club members worked for pay outside the home, they also provided support to women who did unpaid work in the home. They recognized that many people regarded the home as the site of women's primary responsibilities: both men and women regarded women's labour force participation as a necessary evil. Therefore, the clubs were careful to praise women who worked in the home in support of family while simultaneously promoting the interests of women working outside the home for pay.

Pearl (Eaton) Steen, Vancouver BPW club president in 1936 and 1937, spoke to the National Council of Women of Canada some years after her presidency of the club ended, stating that the "highest role for women is still that of wife and mother – no higher calling, secondly – women in business and the professions, the aunts, sisters and daughters, many of whom help to support families and parents [sic]."[73] Steen was careful to praise wives and mothers who did unpaid work in the home but who did not work outside the home (and who therefore were not eligible for membership in BPW clubs). Even her reference to working women referred to their support of their families.

The BPW club records for Victoria and Vancouver frequently noted that a woman's most important role was as a worker within the family, doing the unpaid work of wife and mother. This might have been because some club members had families as well as paid jobs, a situation that would become more common after the Second World War: clubwomen juggled paid and unpaid labour. But the clubs also supported the rights of "housewives" in many of their appeals for legislative change. In 1944, at a one-day regional conference in Vancouver, British Columbia, club members stressed (albeit somewhat vaguely) their support for all "laws and legislation affecting women and children."[74] And in 1951, the British Columbia clubs recommended sending a petition asking the federal government "to permit the sale of colored margarine in Canada." Their reasoning was that the "pale and insipid color" of margarine was unappetizing, and adding colour to it entailed "unnecessary work for the house-wife."[75] This seems to be a minor issue, particularly for a club devoted to employment issues. But it demonstrates that BPW club members attempted to address the concerns of women who were involved in that "higher calling," staying home and caring for family.

The president of the Kingscrest branch of the Vancouver BPW club, Mrs. Olivia Rose Fry, wrote a letter to the *Vancouver Sun* in the 1950s in response to an earlier column written by *Sun* columnist Jack Scott, who had criticized married women's entry into the labour force.[76] While Fry was defending women's right to work, the title given to her letter – probably by the newspaper – was "Homemaking a Career," and Fry herself was careful to laud the roles of women in the home even as she defended married women's employment. As she stated,

> Those clubs which are working to promote women's status and exercise their franchise, which want equal pay for equal work, have no intention of ever encouraging women to leave their homes and turn the "diapers over to daddy" while they are proving themselves a better man than he is, as Mr. Scott put it ... It is not our aim to bring women out of their secure home

life into a business or professional field ... We are aware that to be a good wife, a good mother and home-maker is an art, a career by itself, therefore these women deserve acknowledgement and full partnership as well as business or professional women. When a woman, either married or single, finds it necessary to work and proves her equality on the job, she most certainly deserves equal pay for equal work and also equal opportunities for promotion. I am glad I live in an age where we are considered as advanced, progressive, intelligent, thinking women and not in the age where a woman danced to the crack of a whip of her master.[77]

Fry was perhaps optimistic in her assessment of the 1950s as an age in which women were considered equal to men. But she was clearly making a point about what women ought reasonably to expect and how they deserved to be treated and about the foolishness of opinions such as those held by the less progressive Mr. Scott. She was also quick to praise women who stayed in the home and careful to point out that advocating equal rights was not the same as pushing women into the labour force. Fry maintained that women only worked when it was necessary. Moreover, she reassured Mr. Scott (and probably others) that supporting women's rights did not mean abandoning children to the care of their fathers.

In this she was prescient. Despite continued assurances that career wives were, like housewives, important, competent, and focused on family, the fear that women might not be able to juggle paid work with families did not dissipate after the 1950s. Even as the BPW clubs and many other women's organizations petitioned for changes in government and society that would recognize women's rights to have families and careers, the full recognition of women's successes as career women and as married mothers would be very long in coming. Moreover, the fear that women were facing a difficult balancing act was justified, given that female entrepreneurs were rarely relieved of their family responsibilities when they started up their businesses. In surveys of British Columbia businesswomen in the 1980s, women continued to point to their difficulties juggling business, household, and family demands. One businesswoman stated, "I wanted to stay at home to raise my family but separated, I needed a full-time income to support us."[78] Another noted that trying to arrange a schedule that would accommodate young children was difficult, while a third woman stated that finding good childcare on a "part-time irregular hour basis" was a barrier to self-employment.[79] Self-employment might have provided flexibility for working moms, but late-twentieth-century businesswomen in the province worried about the needs of their families, just as their counterparts in the early twentieth century had done. Besides, after "putting in a full day ... in their own business, women often put in a second shift at home to ensure that their family is properly cared for."[80] Women workers continue to carry a "significant double burden," as Paul Phillips and Erin Phillips note in *Women and Work: Inequality in the Canadian Labour Market*. Studies of housework indicate that "most men do not significantly increase their household work to compensate for their wives' participation in the labour market."[81] As Fry noted at mid-century, diapers were still not being turned over to daddy.

The self-employed housekeepers, washerwomen, and boarding-house keepers documented in Chapter 2 and listed in the census and city directories in the early decades of the twentieth century were often heading their households and supporting families – often precariously. BPW clubwomen, who were more financially stable and who may have had high-earning husbands at home, still experienced the double burden of combining paid and unpaid work (given that women did more unpaid domestic work than their spouses). Although their needs were different and not all of them lived without a male breadwinner, the BPW clubwomen's work and home lives also undoubtedly collided at times.

The British Columbia clubs seemed unclear about how exactly they would support married women's rights. They were careful to stress that family came first, but in other areas their stance on women's equality in the workplace was forward-looking. In 1951, Victoria club members held a round-table discussion on how to acquire "equal standing with men in the business and professional world." Two main strategies were discussed: the group agreed that women should "use their vote" and that women had a "responsibility in backing up women in authority and at all times cooperating with other women."[82] The club took these strategies to heart. In 1951 and 1952, the Victoria BPW club's programs included "Business Women at Work" – talks by various members about their professions – and "Equal Pay for Equal Work," a study of this issue. These topics indicate that the club was working toward improving the status of women in the workplace, while also acknowledging that women did not have equity with men at work. Gender still mattered for business and professional women. Club records indicate women's responses to gender inequities.

Another function of the Victoria club was to prepare young women for their professional working lives. The club held a series of career previews to "acquaint students with the wide fields of opportunity for women today."[83] Female entrepreneurs ran the sessions. Mrs. Vera Wade, owner of

Lyle's Dress Shop, gave a talk on "selling." Mrs. Olive Henderson, owner of Olive's Beauty Salon, spoke about beauty parlour work. Another proposed career was working as a waitress, presented by Mrs. Lydia Arsens, proprietor of a health food shop and the Majorette coffee shop.[84] While all the presenters owned their businesses, none seem to have recommended entrepreneurship as an occupation. The previews focused on traditionally female wage-earning jobs, despite the club's desire to broaden the horizons of girls and women. That the choices portrayed stayed within the realm of acceptable (and, arguably, limited) fields of women's work further indicates that despite the BPW clubs' efforts to push for working women's equality, they still maintained a fairly conventional position. That club members were generally "white, and by occupation, respectably white collar," and that they were middle-class and Anglo-Celtic, influenced their interpretation of the issues and legislation that pertained to working women in the province. These factors also influenced the sorts of career previews put on by the club.[85]

Despite a conservatism that went hand in hand with the membership's class and race biases, the club challenged entrenched beliefs regarding the social position of women. Even if their challenges were sometimes limited to helping working women decide between work as a hairdresser or a waitress, they nonetheless defended women's right to work and demanded wage and employment equity for working women.[86] Still, existing membership lists show overwhelmingly middle-class women in white-collar occupations, and class and race biases are evident in club records. From 1921 to 1929, the Victoria club bylaws specifically excluded "persons of Asiatic birth or extraction" from membership. In January 1925, Lottie Bowron presented a motion to remove the part of the bylaw that excluded Asian women from joining the club. Her motion failed, and although she continued to present it, it did not carry until January 1929.[87] That this bylaw was so difficult to change makes evident that membership was not open to all working women. Brocklehurst notes that processes were in place "to ensure that only 'desirable' candidates were admitted to the club." Prospective members needed the support of two club members in good standing, and certain levels of "conduct" were expected of club members. If a member's behaviour was "detrimental to the interests of the club," she could be expelled.[88]

In September 1930, the Victoria club heard that the Victoria Chamber of Commerce was asking all citizens to "employ white labour wherever possible in the place of oriental labour," a request that did not appear to offend any of the club members present.[89] Two months later, a member of the Maple Leaf association was the guest speaker at the Victoria club meeting. Mr. Carey "explained that the principal aim of his association, was to eliminate the oriental, or at least stop immigration of more orientals to Canada." He concluded by asking the BPW club for support. "Miss Clay, on behalf of the club, thanked Mr. Carey ... adding that she was sure we all realize that this is a problem which requires our most careful attention."[90]

In 1948, the question of nationality of club members came up during the meeting of the provincial association of BPW clubs. While the national constitution for the CFBPWC stated that clubwomen "must be British subjects," provincial delegates agreed that women of other nationalities could be "associate members" of BPW clubs, but they should "be urged to take immediate steps to become Canadian citizens before being accepted into full membership into our clubs."[91]

That most club members were middle-class undoubtedly influenced their ideas about what constituted "respectable" women's work and hampered their progressiveness on some issues. It is possible to critique the clubs' policies on the basis that they only illuminated the experiences of a select group of mostly white-collar (and white) professional Christian women. Given these limitations, it is difficult to view club members in a completely progressive light. While they worked on behalf of working women, they did not let many working-class women into the club. They did not appear to support the rights of non-white working women at all, at least up until the 1940s.[92] However, the projects they took on and their responses to the business worlds in which they worked provide an important context for developing a better understanding of women's workplaces in British Columbia. It is clear that working-class entrepreneurial women, the penny capitalists of Chapters 2 and 3, did not join the clubs, and we cannot know if they paid any attention to the club activities. But the club's public profile and commentaries about women, marital status, work, and respectability highlight aspects of women's work in the province that would otherwise have gone unnoticed. Moreover, the actions of the BPW clubs played a role in slowly shifting provincial attitudes toward business and professional women, including those who were self-employed. Club members' voices reflect privilege, but they also reflect discontent with the prevailing system and with gender inequities, as well as a desire to speak out against those inequities in the work world.

Conflicting Aims

Exercising one's right to vote was essential to membership in all BPW clubs, and club activities focused on women's rights, stemming from the right to vote but extending into other arenas as demonstrated. Clubs also provided an outlet for women to socialize, free of the traditions of the male-dominated business world, and many club meetings and events served a purely social purpose. Members enjoyed the social activities and possibly also needed the company of other women because in their work lives they were surrounded by men. This was particularly true of self-employed women, but even wage-earning professionals (who may have worked in offices with other women) worked for male bosses. There were far fewer women than men in the labour force for all decades under study here. And while some female entrepreneurs, such as hairdressers, saw female clients, the BPW club could be a place to meet like-minded businesswomen rather than customers. The social elements of the club offered a valuable opportunity for women to network and socialize. Moreover, the BPW clubs provided a space where women were free of the restrictions they faced in their working lives. Club members pointed out that simply having a space where women could speak about issues was noteworthy. Pearl Eaton, president of the Vancouver club in 1936 and 1937, noted that the clubs "have done much to develop initiative in our own members, and taught them not to fear the sound of their own voice. In our own Club meetings many a once timid business girl has found her feet and her ability to speak."[93] If the clubs did not always achieve all of their more political objectives, which some members suggested were probably too many and too varied, they did provide an important social space for women.

The social aspects of the Victoria BPW club were well recorded in the first decade of its existence. The minutes refer to numerous picnics and parties. Miss Stead and Miss Thornley, who lived together, hosted numerous gatherings, including a "delightful supper served in the gardens of Miss Stead's home on Cook Street" in August 1930.[94] Club activities included, at various points, the formation of a glee club and orchestra, a drama group, and a reading club.[95]

As early as September 1923, President Mabel Ingram expressed concern that the Vancouver club's social events were better attended than business meetings.[96] Indeed, many members joined for recreational reasons rather than to promote economic and political reform. That the BPW clubs served more than one purpose continued to be recognized and even debated by club members. In 1932, at the Canadian federation's third annual convention, club members held a round table on club purposes. It is clear from the comments made that the women were not sure where to best place their energies. Miss Hazel Taylor, a Montreal member, had analyzed the constitutions of sixteen of the nineteen BPW clubs in Canada. She felt that many of the clubs had not clearly stated the aim that she felt was most important, that of "developing a closer relationship and sorority."[97] But she also recorded an additional thirteen aims and objectives that most of the clubs outlined in their constitutions, including promoting the interests of business and professional women, education, involvement in civic affairs, elevation of the standards of women, community service, and the encouragement of female leadership.

These were a great many functions for one club, and Miss Murray of Vancouver thought clubwomen "should consider very carefully the point that they (the women of the club) were disseminating their energies in too many directions." Rather than doing social service work, she felt that women should have club rooms in which they could "think and talk over the problems of the day as the men of our generation are doing, and not waste our energies in these minor activities." Miss Murray believed that businesswomen's sole purpose should be to "open every field of progress" for the better businesswoman and for the better business world. "She felt that until business women achieved a greater measure of economic independence, they would never arrive at a point where they would have the leisure to think of or to solve the vital problems which were affecting the progress of women."[98]

Murray clearly identified the club's main role as the fight for women's equality. Madge Hall of Victoria agreed and suggested that any club would "justify its existence ... even if it only produced one woman who was capable of taking her stand in world affairs on an equality with men." Others disagreed. Miss Burroughs of Vancouver said that "a great many of the members really looked to the Club for recreation ... mental recreation as well as physical."[99] With up to thirteen different purposes stated in many BPW club constitutions – and the members' various visions of what ought to be the clubs' purposes – the risk that Murray identified of sending their energy in too many directions was a very real one. These early concerns arguably foreshadowed some of the reasons for the club's eventual demise. By attempting to provide recreation as well as undertaking community service and philanthropic work, and by addressing issues pertaining to women in the workplace, the clubs were overextended even when they were at their most vibrant.

The issue of balancing the various purposes of the club was prominent in 1932. Victoria BPW club president Margaret Clay mentioned the dif-. ficulty in the same year. She noted that the two most important objects of the club were "to promote social intercourse and the educational development of our members. The social side of our club life has not received the emphasis that, in the minds of some, it should have ... For our sins of omission we beg your pardon but ... we are all extremely busy women."[100]

It seems that some clubs could not live up to the many expectations laid out in their constitutions: trying to be social *and* political was sometimes too much. Moreover, women who were "extremely busy" in 1932 did not become less busy in later years. Declining attendance was evident in club minutes over the next few decades. The Victoria BPW club recorded ninety-six members in 1933, but in 1955 there were just eighty members. And the membership continued to decline. The Vancouver club's membership also dropped, from 167 members in 1930 to just 89 in 1965. Many factors contributed to the decline. The BPW clubs' advocacy on behalf of married women's right to work was no longer as necessary after 1950, when married women and women with children began to enter the workplace in ever-increasing numbers. Single professional women were no longer the majority in the labour force. A club focused largely on them was perhaps less warranted. The club's efforts to provide social spaces were somewhat outdated after mid-century, when women were much more likely to encounter other women in their workplaces. Furthermore, busy wives and mothers were having enough trouble finding time for work and family: club activities ceased to be a priority.

Finally, the relevance of a club that had stronger ties to first-wave than second-wave feminism waned. Women's rights to be in the workplace, or to vote, had been established and were not the primary concerns of emergent feminist organizations in the 1960s and 1970s. In 1974, British Columbia president Lorraine McLarty actually blamed feminism for the BPW clubs' declining membership: "Over the past few years we seem to have let the new feminist groups drive us underground. It is time we were back in the forefront – living and working within the aims of our Federation."[101] These aims – to develop and train women in business and to improve economic, employment, and social conditions for women – could easily be those of feminist organizations. But the BPW clubs did not want to be thought of as feminist, at least not in their understanding of second-wave feminism. They did not see a place for their club's aims in feminist organizations of the 1960s and 1970s. "We don't believe in burning our bras," the coordinator of the 1974 Vancouver convention tersely stated.[102] Ultimately, the feminist movement was pushing women's organizations in new directions. The clubs were not willing to follow along.

The Vancouver and Victoria BPW clubs clearly pushed for change and demonstrated a commitment to women's equality over the years, although the clubs' antipathy to feminism is one indicator of what Brocklehurst refers to as a "backdrop of social conservatism."[103] Their membership was mainstream, their public image was respectable, and they were not prone to extremism: rather, they were committed to change through official channels. But there were also occasions when BPW club members brought a more critical and even satirical eye to the issues of their day. Some of the articles, editorials, and social functions of business and professional women in British Columbia and Canada suggest that even in their lighter moments, the women were aware of larger social and political issues. Even in jest, they made comments that reflected a deep awareness of women's unequal position in society. Some of these critiques were made publicly, but the majority of them were made within the confines of club walls or in the internal minutes and records of the club.

In 1927, Anna Sprott was the president of the Vancouver BPW club. She invited members to an evening party at her home, "adding that any husbands ... were also welcome as there would be plenty of room for them in the basement with her own husband; from which the members were encouraged to believe that married business and professional women at least are at last beginning to enjoy some rights."[104] Sprott was more of a socialite and clubwoman when she headed the Vancouver club, but she became a prominent entrepreneur and politician. As a young widow, she had attended the Sprott-Shaw business school in Vancouver, and in 1918 she had married its founder, Robert Sprott, the man who was relegated to the basement during his wife's party. Upon his death in 1943, she took over the burgeoning Sprott-Shaw schools, along with the radio station started by her husband. In 1949, she ran for Vancouver City Council, marketing herself as a "successful business woman." She won, served on city council for ten years, and in 1951 became the first woman to serve as acting mayor of Vancouver. She was still president of the Sprott-Shaw business school at the time of her death in 1961, at the age of eighty-two.[105]

PARODIES: DEBATES, "WEDDINGS," PAGEANTS, AND PARTIES

Wry comments such as Sprott's pepper the records of the Victoria and Vancouver BPW clubs. While clubwomen sometimes appeared extremely conventional and projected a conservative and serious image as they fought to improve the status of women through appropriate public channels, they also expressed the need for change through satire and parody. Obviously frustrated by the accommodation provided to men in business and the lack of recognition afforded to women in business, Miss Hilda Hesson of Winnipeg wrote a humorous but pointed article titled "T.B.W." It was printed in 1951 in *The Business and Professional Woman*, the national newsletter for members of the CFBPWC. As Hesson lamented,

> For years we have heard of the TIRED BUSINESS MAN ... tired of what? Of sitting in offices ... furnished with mahogany desks ... tired of pressing buttons that are answered by smart, efficient, well-dressed secretaries ...? Of business meetings on the golf course ...? ... The TIRED BUSINESS· MAN – He has become a national institution and a national menace. But, has anyone ever heard of or catered to the TIRED BUSINESS WOMAN? ... She who wearily and with tongue in cheek plans the entertainment for the T.B.M. The TIRED BUSINESS WOMAN – after hours, do sketchily clad males cavort for her delight? ... Far from it – the average T.B.W. goes home to, at least, supervise, more probably to get, the evening meal – to plan next morning's breakfast, to straighten up her house or flat or room.[106]

The article is significant for its sardonic portrayal of the self-satisfied businessman. Many women likely recognized their own employers or managers in this image. While her tone and choice of words might have provoked a knowing chuckle from many, Hesson also pinpointed some of the ways that women's work was different from men's work. She articulated the struggles that "tired business women" encountered in the workplace as well as the work they encountered when they got home. In fact, she suggested that women were the unrecognized helpmeets to men in the office. While she clearly believed that women deserved recognition for their hard work, she stopped short of suggesting that it should be women sitting behind the mahogany desks. She intimated that women should be recognized for the work they do as assistants to businessmen, rather than suggesting an overhaul of the system in which men became assistants while women ran the office.

Other satirical discussions among business and professional women pushed the point more forcefully. During meetings for the 1954 biennial convention of the CFBPWC, a panel of women "considered such questions as whether a man can successfully combine marriage and a career, and whether a man is really a person."[107] The tone of the discussion was satirical. The panel took the opportunity to reverse stereotypes, taking statements that were commonly directed toward many working women and addressing them to men. More importantly, the debate pointed out through mockery the very real stereotypes affecting women. The fact that this panel was a source of amusement demonstrates that women faced serious barriers to advancement in the labour force. Moreover, the BPW clubs were aware of the problems experienced by many working women, from issues such as pressure to dress a certain way to the pressures on married women to stay home. The *Globe and Mail's* report on the panel's debate demonstrates that the "joke" was a serious reflection on women's roles in the workplace:

> On the question of whether men should be allowed to enter public life, the women conclude that men are "too emotional to take an active part in public life," as their "feelings are too easily hurt." As for careers, the women decided that while a working father "seemed in many ways a degradation of fatherhood," some men did "surprisingly well in certain types of work – even in work which seems to be particularly a woman's field." The panel also considered "the problem of what is man's most important asset for success. Personality was ruled out as being too dangerous ... This left appearance and influence to be evaluated. Since all the men who travel transcontinental airlines appear to be snappy dressers, it was the considered opinion of the panel that all a man really needs to advance is natty appearance." On the topic of higher education for men, the panel's disapproval "hinged around the fact that studying the problems of nuclear fission would undoubtedly completely unfit him for the more pressing problems of fitting a new washer on the kitchen sink ... women were warned to exercise extreme caution before so daring a project as higher education for men was undertaken." On the question of whether women preferred beauty or brains in a man: "It was generally conceded that a certain amount of brain power was almost a necessity, but when it exceeded certain limits, it was felt that a man would be very wise to decently hide it."

But when asked, "should a man dress to please his wife?" panel members found it "debatable whether men dress to please women or to annoy other men."[108]

BPW club members were aware of gender issues that at times impeded their careers. The panel, set up to judge men in the same way women were judged, pointed out the idiocy of certain conventional opinions about what women were capable of doing. This is a very different approach from the conventional one that club members took. Most clubs *did* concern themselves with businesswomen's appearance and with appropriate dress codes. They held fashion shows and incorporated information on the importance of hair, dress, and general appearance into their various public events. However, the debate suggests that women were aware of stereotypes and were not altogether satisfied with the status quo. Gender affected the ways they were evaluated in their workplaces. Even though they continued to dress and behave appropriately in their jobs, the convention provided a place where they could critique established rules that distinguished workers by the perceived limits of their gender. The debate allowed the women to have a little fun at the expense of men.

Importantly, the debate occurred at what was supposedly the height of the postwar construction of an ideal domesticity. Valerie Korinek discusses this issue in an examination of *Chatelaine* magazine's yearly contest, begun in 1960, to find the ideal representative of the Canadian housewife and crown her "Mrs. Chatelaine." Korinek suggests that the contest illustrated underlying discontent about the ideology of domesticity in Canada at the time.[109] Some readers of the magazine actively criticized the portraits of apparently conventional, ideal, middle-class women, and they "derived pleasure from parodying, subverting or criticising the contest."[110] In letters to the editor, critics of *Chatelaine*'s contest mocked the ideal of a stay-at-home wife. These responses to the contest demonstrated that mid-century society was not so homogenous after all. The "emphasis on home, family and established gender roles" that mainstream Canadian society presented in the 1950s "masked considerable discontent" on the part of some women.[111]

Despite broad currents in postwar Canadian society that championed stay-at-home wives and mothers and advocated images of smartly dressed business girls who kept quiet and knew their place, there were undercurrents of dissatisfaction. Business and professional clubwomen found themselves the target of similar conservatism in the 1950s and 1960s and voiced their disapproval. The mock debate at the CFBPWC's 1954 convention allowed them to state their opinions without raising the ire of other members of society. Much like Hesson's "T.B.W." article, the discussion did not actually propose that women ought to take over from men. Presenting their opinions as a joke allowed club members the freedom to suggest that maybe women really *were* equal to men or that women could combine marriage and a career.

Other questions tackled by the panel included "Should boys be encouraged to train for both marriage and a career?" and "Should men receive as much money as women for the same job?" The panel was even asked if there was room for "male glamor in business." And while the women professed to "hate men who exhibit their muscles and calves too much," they agreed that "a certain amount of window dressing ... will help the man who has gone to pot."[112] The panel's approach revealed a thinly concealed resentment at women's treatment in the workplace. In this case, an "inside" critique of the status quo, expressed during a members' convention, illustrated another side to the BPW clubs. It also became part of their outside image when it was reprinted in a national newspaper.

Another form of mockery was BPW club pageants, "weddings," and parties at which some of the women dressed as men. Photographs of a Kumtuks Club party held in September 1925 show women dressed as men, on bended knee and kissing the hands of women. All the "men" and women are costumed as though acting out a medieval story. The party is not mentioned in any written records, but the set-up of the photographs seems to be a purposeful parody of women receiving marriage proposals.[113]

A series of photographs from the Vancouver club depicts a mock wedding. The undated photographs, titled "The Wedding at the Clubroom, 736 Granville," are in a scrapbook of Vancouver club member Pearl (Eaton) Steen's clippings and photographs from the early 1940s.[114] The women are evidently enjoying themselves and the visual gag, but no written records explain this event. The photographs show a "groom" – a woman in top hat and tuxedo – and a bride who towers over her groom by close to a foot.[115] One of the best men, also a woman, wears a fake beard and moustache.

Other authors have found evidence of ritualistic events such as mock weddings being acted out by all-women "casts." Lisa Fine found business and professional women acting out similar rituals in Chicago. Fine describes young, independent, white-collar women who called themselves "business women" and lived together in residential clubs or boarding houses opened for girls who came to work in the city in the early decades of the twentieth century.[116] While the BPW club members in Vancouver did not all live together, many would have fit Fine's description of the

FIGURE 3   The "Wedding" at the Clubroom, 736 Granville, Vancouver, British
Columbia | Photograph courtesy of the City of Vancouver Archives 272, 517-C-4, file 3,
temp no. 2

Chicago business girls. It is important to note that unlike the Chicago
girls, who resided together and were primarily young, single wage-earners,
the Vancouver women were from all walks of life and were not necessarily
young and single. They were united, however, by their club affiliations.
Fine found three main rituals acted out by the Chicago women: mock
weddings, funerals, and parties called man, kid, old maid, or spinster parties. For old maid and spinster parties, the young women dressed as old
women, while for kid parties they dressed as children and babies. These
events often marked ritualistic occasions such as wedding showers, holidays,
or birthdays. Sometimes the parties involved women dressing as widowers
or bachelors. But it was in descriptions of mock weddings that Fine typically found women dressing as men and representing "stereotypical images
of manhood."[117]
    Fine suggests that the parties were a form of ritualistic behaviour that
marked the particular place of young women in the business world of the
early twentieth century. The women recognized that they were important
transitional figures between a traditional world – in which many women

had stayed home and worked in the home – and a changing world in which women had more freedoms and more opportunities in the labour force.[118] Figure 1, in Chapter 2 of this book (which shows a group of women dressed in men's business suits in 1915), also seems to fit this theory. Alice Jowett and her friends, like the clubwomen in the Vancouver mock wedding, seem to be laughing at the visual gag that they know is being recorded. While the photograph of Jowett does not indicate a party, Fine's descriptions of Chicago women cross-dressing during social events are similar to the images of the Vancouver clubwomen's mock wedding. Female residences provided women with the "social space in which to enact these rituals," and the Chicago boarding houses, which provided independence to young women, motivated the activity.[119] This may also have been the case for Vancouver BPW clubwomen, who had relative freedom within their club rooms to socialize with other women and to privately mock the strictures of public gender conventions. Mock weddings indicate the women's ambivalence about marriage. While businesswomen might have considered marriage a happy occasion, they might also have viewed it as a loss of independence: the Chicago women "described marriage and success in a career as mutually exclusive."[120]

Finally, Fine argues that the rituals played out by women in residences in Chicago "suggest how women saw themselves historically as women." They mocked "old-fashioned" women and traditional values such as marriage.[121] The rituals were a source of amusement. They also helped the women to "negotiate between the world of work and marriage, and to make sense of the changing role of women in society. Even if these women ultimately abandoned work and an independent life for marriage, we now know that they did not do so unthinkingly."[122]

What seems most critical about the gender reversals in the Vancouver wedding photographs is that, regardless of the frivolity of the events, the women's actions demonstrate that they were aware of how they were perceived. They were aware, as the Chicago girls were aware twenty years earlier, that they were mocking tradition. The decision to have a tall woman play the bride next to a very short woman in drag seems calculated to mock the traditional wedding as much as possible. Like the young women in residence together in Chicago, the women of the Vancouver BPW club were twisting conventional societal rituals: their actions were not "unthinking." But this was a mockery and a critique of sorts that was carried out inside the club. It was not a part of their outside image as an organization of respectable, feminine, middle-class businesswomen.

Perhaps boarding-house keepers and other female entrepreneurs who were not in the clubs would have had little knowledge of or interest in these events. While they can be viewed as a frivolity for women with leisure time, and not something that the majority of the female workforce would participate in, mock weddings were not only the domain of the middle classes. Joy Parr found evidence of similar working-class rituals taking place in the knitting mills in Paris, Ontario, in the 1920s and 1930s. She suggests that the rituals "ridiculed conventions of patriarchal hierarchy within marriage."[123] While the Chicago and Vancouver weddings involved only women, in Paris, women and men who worked in the factories together took part in the weddings together. Sex and age roles were reversed, "the bride being a senior male skilled worker or foreman, the clergyman a young girl, the groom an older married woman." Parr argues that the weddings were "raucous parodies of domestic life."[124]

In the knitting mills, where men and women worked alongside each other – and where, sometimes, women did what was considered men's work and men did women's work – the "inversion of the mock wedding played upon the suppleness of gender boundaries."[125] The degree to which gender boundaries were supple is an important aspect of rituals that involved women dressed as men. That there were in fact gender boundaries, and that women were pushing the edges of those boundaries in certain types of occupations, is laughingly addressed by the ritualistic role reversals in the BPW club records. In their workplaces, business and professional women were encroaching upon what had long been recognized as male space. Clubwomen were aware of the importance of gender in all aspects of society. Their social events parodied the conventional roles of men and women.

Women who participated in mock weddings might also have been mocking traditional sexual roles more directly; some authors have argued that "imitations of marriage" may represent romantic lesbian relationships.[126] Martha Vicinus has studied single women's erotic friendships in all-female communities and argues that relationships between women could and often did emulate heterosexual relationships. Many women referred to their relationships with other women as "marriages," and their diaries and letters indicate "sexual passion, if not physical sexuality."[127] In the late nineteenth century, according to Lillian Faderman, the term "Boston marriage" referred to long-term monogamous relationships between two "otherwise unmarried women."[128] Whether these relationships included sex is not known, but some women formed lifelong ties akin to marriage. Moreover, that there was a language to describe them indicates that the relationships were not unusual. Faderman also notes that women in such partnerships were usually financially "independent of men, either through inheritance or because of a career."[129]

Whether the clubwomen's friendships – and marriage rituals – represent romantic or sexual relationships cannot be ascertained from photographs. Many women shared accommodations for economic reasons. However, it is worth recognizing that women who lived, worked, or socialized together may also have chosen to be in romantic and/or sexual partnerships and that these "Boston marriages" were relatively acceptable partnerships, particularly between middle-class professional women. We "must be prepared to assert that certain women were involved in relationships which have some relationship to lesbianism, even though in any historical period before the 1920s we are likely to have difficulty locating women who would be recognizably" defined as lesbians.[130]

This is the case in the BPW club records in British Columbia. There is evidence that some clubwomen resided together, but the nature of their relationships is not obvious. Lottie Bowron's scrapbook indicates that she "went into residence" with two other women, Miss Paul and Miss Mason, in the 1920s, but no other information about the arrangement is provided.[131] Miss Stead and Miss Thornley, members of the Victoria club, also resided together. Their home is described, variously, as their home and as the home of Miss Stead. They may have been roommates or romantic partners, but references to their home cannot entirely illuminate the nature of their relationship. In July 1931, the women cancelled a party "promised in their garden during that month" because they were on holiday, the only reference that hints at a relationship beyond a boarding arrangement.[132]

That there is, in the records of BPW clubwomen even after 1920, no explicit discussion of same-sex partnerships is no reason to assume that such relationships did not exist. If the concept of Boston marriages had been articulated and lived by women in the late 1800s, it is entirely possible that clubwomen in British Columbia in the early 1900s had no need to specifically explain the nature of such relationships. And while the presence of photographs of mock weddings or references to living arrangements cannot be taken alone as a statement of the presence of same-sex desire, they urge us to consider the prospect. Moreover, even female friendships that were not specifically sexual might have been unions that resembled marriages in most other ways.

Dress-up parties tackled political issues as well. The 1952 minutes for the Victoria BPW club mention that club members performed "The

Challenge," a historical pageant about women's suffrage.[133] Members had always been strongly urged to exercise their voting rights, and the pageant presented the history of an important political issue – but in this case the message was "performed" as a social event. The women approached the subject in a lighthearted way, acting out the history of suffrage for their own and others' amusement.[134] Whether in jest or to prove a larger point, the BPW club members performed the pageant without the help of male actors. Photographs show that women once again dressed up to take on the male parts. If a woman who assumes male dress in performance is playing with ideas about gender, whether or not she does so consciously,[135] then the many mentions in the BPW club records of women in male dress are not just a frivolous example of social activities: they represent more fundamental questions about gender for businesswomen.

Cross-dressing also has a different significance for women than for men. "Precisely because 'man' is the presumed universal ... drag changes meaning depending on who's wearing it."[136] Women do not gain power by portraying women, but they potentially access greater power by assuming a male identity. BPW club members were aware of this when they dressed as men – just as they were aware of the same issue when they entered the male world of business. Women in drag "can call into question the social conventions of gender roles, and ... as a result, the very category of gender."[137] Women in male-dominated business worlds were also calling into question the social conventions of gender. And while the BPW clubs on the whole tried to stress that businesswomen were appropriately conventional, cross-dressing pageants and games indicate an understanding that gender norms were upset by the entry of women into some categories of business and the professions.

All the photographs demonstrate the independence and freedom of their subjects: costumed affairs in which women cross-dressed show that, on some level, women wanted to assert that they were truly independent. They could vote, go out to work, and support themselves financially without men, and they could "marry" and hold weddings without men. Some fun was being had at the expense of men. But the symbolic power of the BPW clubwomen dressing as men – which they did in more than one context – is important. They were deliberately assessing their positions as independent women in society and in the labour force. Such rituals depicted businesswomen's "perceived life choices" and "reflected their view of the world."[138]

While some articles and discussions demonstrate a light-hearted mockery of what business and professional women knew to be real injustices in their work worlds and in their personal lives, the women also dealt with these injustices more seriously and more publicly. Despite their social conservatism and the biases inherent in their membership's position of relative privilege in society, the Vancouver and Victoria BPW clubs were headquarters of sorts for political action. Clubwomen fought the very real discrimination that they, along with all other working women, faced. In order to maintain a respectable public profile, they operated within an "inside-outside" approach. Outwardly, they maintained a fairly conservative profile even when pushing for equal treatment of all women in the workforce and for better treatment of businesswomen in the business community. Inwardly, however, they occasionally poked fun at (or critiqued in a more serious manner) the injustices that they faced as working women in a "man's world."

For self-employed women, the clubs were the only place in which these issues could be addressed. As Chapters 2 and 3 demonstrate, female entrepreneurs formed a relatively small proportion of all women in the labour force. Club membership was a corrective to the male-dominated business worlds in which self-employed women (and also many wage-earning professional women) worked. The BPW clubs were arguably all the more important for entrepreneurs, who were isolated within the business world and sought out a place to meet with like-minded women. The social and political activities of the clubs in British Columbia show that even when they seemed aimed at a particular group of respectable middle-class white women, they were an important marker of the ways in which gender shaped the work of *all* women. Club records reveal business and professional women's responses to the pressures of their society through social gatherings, through ritual parodying of normative traditions in their work and home lives, and through political action.

5
"You have to think like a man and act like a lady"

Gender, Class, and Businesswomen

en have long controlled, dominated, and defined the business world, and notions of masculinity have long been part of the definition of a businessman.[1] In stressing the connections between masculinity, independence, and self-employment, David Burley argues that self-employed women were an "anomaly in a man's world."[2] David Monod also addresses the patriarchal nature of certain types of entrepreneurship, pointing out that women were "barred from the brotherhood that underlay the professional ethos" of twentieth-century Canadian shopkeepers.[3] Other scholars have suggested that traits reserved for men in business included competition and aggression; moreover, men's business behaviour was shaped "according to an heroic, individualistic and nationalistic agenda"[4] that afforded no place for women. In the early twentieth century, it would have been difficult even to consider women as entrepreneurial because entrepreneurship suggested a realm marked by manhood, brotherhood, independence, competition, and aggression – traits not associated with women.

Yet, while entering a masculine realm of work, female entrepreneurs found a way to present themselves as both feminine and businesslike –

This chapter takes its title from "Think Like a Man, Act Like a Lady," *The Business and Professional Woman* (May-June 1967), Add Mss 799, 588-A-4, City of Vancouver Archives. A version of this chapter was previously published as "You Have to Think Like a Man and Act Like a Lady": Businesswomen in British Columbia, 1920-80, *BC Studies*, no. 151 (Autumn 2006): 69-95.

characteristics that would seem antithetical. If the business world was dominated by men and by manly characteristics such as aggression and competition, the way for women to assert their place in an entrepreneurial context was to stress that they could be businesslike in an appropriately feminine manner. Strategically, women attempted to "avoid the stigma that followed their entry into the male professional space" by stressing their femininity.[5] Entrepreneurial women in British Columbia, as well as outside observers, relied on conventional understandings of appropriate gendered behaviour to legitimize their place in the business world. To demonstrate that they were respectable, businesswomen emphasized their devotion to fashion and to their families. They found a way to enter a "school of manhood" without becoming manly. They spoke of their roles as mothers and wives and presented themselves as "womanly" women. The media also stressed businesswomen's ladylike behaviour and appearance, emphasizing qualities that their readership could recognize as markers of femininity. Businesswomen displayed a public image of respectable femininity; however, as I will show in this chapter, the media also did its part to represent self-employed women as overtly feminine.

These constructions of femininity were also classed. The self-employed women who were most prominent in their communities, women who joined business and professional women's (BPW) clubs, advertised in newspapers and city directories, and were featured in local newspaper articles, were those who fit an image of middle-class white womanhood in all aspects of their lives save their proprietorships. Those who seemed most eager to present themselves in particular ways were those who had the most to lose in terms of status, reputation, and relative privilege. Penny capitalists, largely working-class women who ran marginalized businesses and who were rarely profiled, were also somewhat protected from these issues, in part because they were not highly visible. They ran their businesses out of economic need and regardless of potential stigma. However, even in marginal home-based enterprises or service-oriented self-employment, issues of femininity are still evident. Working-class women were less likely to own cement factories or real estate offices, but their femininity was plain in the enterprises they did operate: hairdressing, sewing, and keeping a boarding house were, as Chapter 3 illustrates, options for self-employment, and these types of enterprises afforded some income but less censure because they were sex-typed as feminine work.

The definition of conventional, respectable, or ladylike behaviour was also race-specific. Those who were most likely to maintain a prominent profile in the community and who concerned themselves most with behavioural conventions were middle-class white women. Non-white entrepreneurs – and their opinions on issues of femininity and business – are harder to locate. They did exist: Sue Lee Ping Wong, a widow with eleven children, supported her family in Kelowna by making and selling tofu in the 1930s. Mrs. K. Ushijima operated a dry goods store and also worked as a dressmaker in Vancouver in 1918. And First Nations women, although they were not well enumerated by census takers, reported that they were self-employed as hunters and fishers and sold goods in an informal market economy within their own communities.[6] This is true of many non-white, and non-middle-class, women in the province, who used a variety of informal entrepreneurial strategies to support themselves and their families.

As American historian Wendy Gamber states, the business world of the early twentieth century was "rigidly sex-segregated. Hampered by limited capital and constrained by social convention, most female entrepreneurs clustered in occupations that mirrored traditional conceptions of women's work."[7] Gender conventions affected both the types of businesses that women chose to pursue and how others viewed and described businesswomen. Those who ran businesses that catered to women or used skill sets that had long been defined as women's work could rely on their field of work to demonstrate their femininity. Women who sold clothing, hats, and other products to women or who ran restaurants or girls' schools were operating in a public, entrepreneurial world marked as masculine. But their choice of business could be described as a female preserve. The work itself was an extension of women's traditional homemaking skills – cooking, sewing, cleaning – or their clientele was female. Thus, sex segregation made sense economically in that women who sold goods to women would be more successful. Sex-segregated enterprises were also more conventional; while entrepreneurship was typically defined as masculine behaviour, these types of enterprises and the businesswomen who ran them could be viewed as appropriately feminine.

It was even more important to represent women who operated businesses that traditionally had been run by men as feminine in behaviour and appearance. Such women were often described as exceptional in the period under study because both the act of self-employment and the type of self-employment chosen placed them in a particularly masculine public work world. The women themselves, and media representations of these women, stressed their ladylike attributes. People were more comfortable with women working in men's fields if it was clear that such women were still conventional in other ways.

Gender was therefore extremely important in determining how businesswomen were represented or represented themselves, while class and race were important in determining who was eliminated from the discussions about businesswomen and gender conventions. British Columbians needed reassurance that women who worked in the male-dominated business world were still feminine in manner and appearance, if not in choice of occupation. This version of femininity was marked by middle-class traits of respectable womanhood. Even more interestingly, depictions of respectable businesswomen changed very little in the first half of the twentieth century. While the types of work that drew women into the labour force changed, the gender codes to which businesswomen conformed remained constant. Certain markers of conventional middle-class femininity continued to be associated with businesswomen at mid-century and beyond, including emphasis on ladylike appearance and behaviour, overt references to motherhood, and even the sex-segregation of most businesswomen into feminine enterprises. As late as 1979, "work" was still being defined "as a masculine word."[8] This was particularly evident in the world of female entrepreneurship, where media representations of businesswomen, and the women themselves, continued to emphasize their femininity as though this would minimize the masculine nature of their work.

The records of the BPW clubs highlight the attitudes and actions of not only the mostly middle-class women in professional work but also the entrepreneurial women in the province.[9] The club records are an important source for understanding how businesswomen wanted to be represented and the kinds of businesses they associated with respectable middle-class femininity.

BPW club records demonstrate that businesswomen wanted to be both respectable and womanly. These women emphasized their middle-class femininity and actively participated in the construction of an appropriately feminine public identity, distinct from the masculine attributes associated with business ownership. The membership lists for the Victoria and Vancouver clubs indicate that they attracted a very specific type of proprietor, with hairdressers, café owners, milliners, and photographers prominent.[10]

The businesswomen who were not members of BPW clubs are perhaps more significant than those who were. Club membership lists did not include laundresses, cleaning women, or other self-employed women with small, home-based businesses who might have operated in an informal economy as penny capitalists. Very small enterprises cushioned the poor and provided disadvantaged working-class people – such as widowed or abandoned women – with a way to adapt and survive. But these businesses were working-class responses to economic crisis, not the kinds of businesses mentioned in BPW club records. Women who ran home-based businesses and whose work was feminized to the point of being almost invisible as a form of entrepreneurship did not typically join BPW clubs. Membership was not overtly restrictive: in Vancouver, as in other BPW clubs in the province, an active member could be any woman who was "gainfully employed in business, a profession or industry."[11] However, it appears that occupations like keeping a boarding house, doing laundry, or selling farm produce were not viewed as professions. Female penny capitalists were aware that the clubs were not meant for them. It is possible that they chose not to join the clubs or did not feel welcome. Practical considerations, such as membership fees, also prevented working-class women from joining. Many small business owners, struggling to make ends meet and supporting dependants, had little time to take part in club life and little extra income to pay club fees.

Even so, the issues of concern to more numerous and less vocal entrepreneurs in the province were sometimes mirrored in the characteristics and activities of the BPW clubwomen. All self-employed women tended to be older than their wage-earning counterparts and married, whereas wage-earners were single. Most struggled to manage their family's claims on their time, to choose a business type from which they could reap some profit but escape reproach, and to support themselves. They were also all affected by debates in the newspapers or by media profiles, even when those profiled were members of a privileged group. And all of them were potentially affected when members of the BPW clubs spoke out on social and political issues, such as the right to work and to vote (discussed in Chapter 4).

CONDUCT AND APPEARANCE IN A MAN-MADE WORLD

The BPW clubs embraced a particular construction of womanhood, which found expression in the way that club members represented themselves. For instance, at a luncheon held by the Vancouver club in 1923, Ethel Rease Burns "of the School of Expression, Alberta College, Edmonton," spoke on "Motherhood and Business." She asked her audience, "What's the matter with the business world that it would contaminate women who go out into it? It is a man-made world," where, too often, "a man leaves his ideals at home." After establishing that the business world was masculine, Burns suggested that a woman "must go into the business world and take her ideals with her, and her highest ideal is true motherhood."[12]

Burns's speech outlined a few common themes that many BPW club-women would continue to espouse. First, she acknowledged that the business world was masculine and that some people did not see a place for women in it. Second, she stressed that women could succeed in business: a general optimism regarding women's potential was a key part of the rapid formation of BPW clubs in the 1920s. But – and this is the third theme that threads through much of the literature on businesswomen – the woman who did so should take her ideals with her, ideals that were not the same as those of men. Burns specifically identified the "gift of motherhood" as a quality that only women could bring to the business world. While not all women were mothers, Burns highlighted motherhood as a marker of womanhood. BPW club members emphasized the woman-liness of female entrepreneurs to set them apart from (and perhaps to remove them from direct comparison to, or competition with) business-men. Burns stressed that businesswomen's success would come from emphasizing their uniquely female attributes rather than from behaving exactly like men.

The Vancouver BPW club began to publish *The Vancouver Business Woman* in 1923. The newsletter reported the activities of local business-women and announced club news, but it also served as a space for busi-nesswomen to network and consider issues they deemed important. In 1927, the newsletter reprinted an article by Emma Dot Partridge, then secretary of the National Federation of Business and Professional Women's Clubs in the United States. Partridge stated that women "take business as a challenge to make good in a man-made world and still struggle with a feeling of insecurity."[13] Her comments illustrate a belief that the world of business was masculine. Partridge argued that businesswomen were too serious and too courteous: "Busy men are gruff, why not busy women? ... The world is used to expecting the woman to act the hostess and, if she is anything less than gracious, comment is made." Women, she argued, have "not yet achieved the frankness and open-ness that the impersonality of business demands." In short, she suggested women should behave more like men if they wanted to succeed. In many respects, businesswomen acknowledged the gruff masculinity of the business world but strove to maintain their femininity in the work world. However, Partridge's com-ments did demonstrate that whether or not women ought to change, they were different from men – a common theme throughout the club records.

An unnamed author of a 1934 article in *The Vancouver Business Woman* stated chummily that although "we women are known as the chatty sex ... we find it harder to get acquainted with one another than our brothers of the sterner sex." The author suggested that women were not like men. Moreover, men had set the standards of conduct, and women needed to find new ways to accommodate themselves to the old order of things. "We find it difficult to 'whang' each other on the shoulder, or playfully knock each other's hats off, which ... seems an unfailing way of breaking up the ice with men."[14]

Business and professional women found many ways to ensure that they would not be viewed as manly, even if they worked in particularly masculine areas of business. An obvious point of departure was to emphasize a feminine appearance as a sign that women could be "in business" while remaining womanly. A 1925 advertisement for a beauty shop in *The Vancouver Business Woman* stated: "As a businesswoman, your personal appearance is an important thing."[15] Businesswomen were cognizant of the need to maintain a professional, neat, and even feminine appearance, in part to avoid being considered masculine in the business world. Thus, the advertisements stressed what women already knew.

At the 1932 convention of the Canadian Federation of Business and Professional Women's Clubs in Vancouver, Irene Green opened a round-table discussion on "The Psychology of Dress." The convention report noted that this was "a topic of eternal interest to women, no matter what their age, business or profession."[16] Green told the audience that it was not enough for a businesswoman to be efficient, "without any regard to her personal appearance. Because woman is established in the business world today she does not have to dress mannish to command respect, and the woman who becomes tailor-made clothes should avoid being masculine in her effect."[17]

Green's speech suggests that in earlier decades businesswomen needed to appear masculine in order to prove their worth. However, Green clearly believed that, by the 1930s, women could assert their femininity and still command respect in the business world.[18] She articulated the growing belief that middle-class businesswomen could appear conventional and maintain an aura of respectable femininity while working in what had once been an exclusively male business world.

It is also possible that businesswomen did not want to appear mannish for fear of being considered lesbians. A masculine appearance – as others have noted with respect to "independent women" in the United States in the nineteenth and early twentieth centuries – could signify that they were "somehow 'other' than women," that they were "Amazonians" who had "unsexed" themselves, that they were the third sex, or that they were sexually interested in women.[19] Businesswomen might not have wanted to be too masculine in appearance because it represented what they considered to be sexual deviance, ranging from being completely sexless to being dangerously oversexed, and included an implication of same-sex desire. Green, while not referring to sexuality directly, steered women away from masculine dress. She segregated women into three types – the ingénue, the athletic, and the dramatic – and claimed that while athletic types were easiest to dress, "it was best to avoid the over masculine modes." The dramatic was the "most dangerous type," presumably because a tendency toward flamboyance was not suitable in the business world. This suggests a certain class-based definition of dressing for success, one that encompassed tasteful conservatism: Green recommended that women conform to "the dictates of good taste and suitability of occasion."[20]

The importance of this seemingly inconsequential discussion cannot be overstated: it emphasizes that businesswomen in the 1930s wanted to be considered feminine and that their appearance was almost as important as the work they did. Green even argued that for a woman to "plan and build a wardrobe which resulted in her being well and suitable [sic] dressed on all occasions required *as much* brains and executive ability as organizing and running the business itself."[21] While there is no clear evidence that club members agreed with her assessment of the importance of appearing feminine, two references to the discussion exist in the Victoria BPW club notes. Furthermore, the *Victoria Daily Times* used the round-table discussion as its feature item in a story about the Canadian federation's convention, titling the article "Dressing Well Good Business."[22]

The importance that businesswomen attached to appearance continued. In 1937, Vancouver BPW club president Pearl Eaton stated that businesswomen "need no further reminder of the value of being well groomed."[23] In 1951, the Victoria club hosted an event called "The Business and Professional Woman as an Individual." The primary focus was appearance: the scheduled topics were hair care, use of cosmetics and accessories, and clothes to wear to work.[24] In 1961, the Victoria club presented a career preview for young women in which "Make-up and Clothes for a Working Day" formed one of the day's sessions. "Beauty Counsellor and Model" Mrs. Noel Morgan (whose own first name was not given) discussed hair, skin, personal hygiene, and clothes.[25]

Businesswomen who sold women's clothing advertised their goods based on the shared understanding that attire was a critical aspect of any enterprising woman's success. Mary Constance Dress Shop advertised "Fabulous Fashions For a Business Woman's Social Life," such as after-five cocktail and short formal dresses, while Raymar Fashions appealed to "Business Women of Victoria ... Look Smart in the Office! Choose from our complete selection of business-like dresses in the newest style trends and colors to please the most discriminating woman."[26]

Figure 4 shows three advertisements that were typical of the "Business Women's Week" special spread and of businesswomen's advertisements more generally. Victoria BPW Club member Minnie Beveridge's advertisements (here and elsewhere) stressed the femininity of her millinery business, which she opened in 1938, and the importance of hats as part of a businesswoman's fashionable attire. The Crown Dress and Hat Shop, in operation for more than twenty years, advertised the importance of elegance, suggesting a middle- to upper-class definition of what constituted fashionable women's wear. BPW club member Alice Mallek operated a women's clothing store on her own after her husband's death. Her advertisement catered to "career women in every field" but also stressed the importance of fashion.

BPW club members repeatedly reassured businessmen, other men, and other women that they were not going to become manly by entering into business. They stressed other characteristics besides appearance that demonstrated femininity. In 1952, the president of the International Federation of Business and Professional Women's Clubs, Dame Caroline Haslett, told the annual convention of the Canadian federation that women "don't need to copy men. They should keep courtesy alive as much as possible and should aim for an equality that does not eliminate graciousness."[27] Haslett emphasized that women were different from men: businesswomen sought equality, but they posed no threat to gender conventions already in place. This is also what a newspaper article about Haslett, titled "Business Women Have No Intention to Become 'Carbon Copy' of Men," suggested.[28] While Haslett probably did state that BPW club members could be gracious, feminine, and still businesswomen, the media highlighted these aspects of her talk to reassure readers that businesswomen were not threatening the normal order of the business world. The write-up of Haslett's visit in the Canadian federation's national newsletter stressed the same points: Haslett "proves conclusively that a woman may reach the top in a recognized man's field and still not lose her endearing qualities. One is immediately struck ... with her femininity, her charm of manner."[29]

The emphasis in the 1920s and 1930s on businesswomen's feminine qualities persisted after the Second World War, as Haslett's visit confirms.

Wardrobe Elegance
for Victoria's
Business Women

Our selection of good clothes at
reasonable prices are worth your
time and money. Come in and see
them. See how they fit in with
your busy life.

- ● SUITS
- ● DRESSES
- ● COATS

Millinery - Accessories

Crown Dress & Hat Shop

615 VIEW STREET   PHONE EV 3-7914

FIGURE 4 Advertisements
for Business Women's Week,
Victoria, British Columbia,
1962 | *Victoria Daily Times,*
13 October 1962, 22-23

A SALUTE TO THE
BUSINESS WOMEN
OF CANADA

Down through the years we have
been proud to serve career women
in every field with the latest in
quality and Fashion.

1696 Douglas   EV 2-8151

A
Minnie Beveridge
HAT
*Is Your Best
Fashion
Accessory*

Soft Velours, felts and many
other fabrics. Try the flattery
of a soft velvet cloche, semi-
Breton, high, wide and hand-
some stitched black velvet . . .
choose your hat from original
stylings.

9^{95} to 21^{95}

See Our Budget-Price

HAT BAR

That little extra hat costs so
little. So many styles in fall
colors.

6^{95} to 8^{95}

Expert Renovations and Alterations
Member Business and Professional Women's Club

MILLINERY

764 Fort Street   Open All Day
Wednesday   EV 3-3452

Businesswomen in the 1950s and beyond continued to represent themselves as different from men but equally capable. In 1963, Elsie Gregory MacGill, then president of the CFBPWC, spoke in Vancouver to British Columbia BPW clubs. MacGill spoke of what she called a "caste system" that held women back in the labour force and stated that social attitudes impeded women's progress. There were, she asserted, "two kinds of work – men's work and women's work – and they are not interchangeable."[30] *Vancouver Sun* reporter Kathy Hassard pointed out that MacGill had, however, "outfoxed the Canadian caste system" by working as an aeronautical engineer.

Elsie MacGill was not self-employed, although she was doing what she and Hassard felt had long been considered men's work. In fact, it *had* been men's work: MacGill was the world's first female aeronautical engineer.[31] But even in a piece written by one working woman about another working woman (head of a national organization and a success in her chosen profession), the need to stress MacGill's womanly attributes was evident: "Why did this slight, very feminine little woman embark on such a career?" Hassard asked. It is doubtful that Hassard would have described a male aeronautical engineer as large or masculine should the situation have been reversed.

As business and professional women made inroads into less orthodox professions, their achievements were celebrated and their femininity emphasized. Beginning in the early 1950s, BPW clubs across Canada annually celebrated Business Women's Week to "focus attention on the achievements of women in business, trades and the professions and on the part [that] many of these women are playing in the economic, cultural and public life of Canada."[32] Articles about the event published each year in the Victoria and Vancouver press focused on women's achievements, but the highlight of the news coverage was fashion shots of local businesswomen. In 1960, the *Victoria Daily Colonist* published a series of large photographs of Victoria BPW club members. One featured Margaret Harvey, who was "in the field of real estate," in a leopard-print hat with matching purse, fur-trimmed jacket, and white gloves.[33]

Newspaper articles pasted in the Vancouver club scrapbook, undated but appearing with a collection of clippings from the 1950s and 1960s, suggest that this interest in fashion continued. While the importance of Business Women's Week was stated, photographs pictured Vancouver club member Bertha Bell wearing "a charming and versatile jacketed dress in hazelnut brown antelope crepe" and "busy club woman Miss

FIGURE 5   BPW Club member Mrs. Margaret Harvey models
businesslike fashions during Business Women's Week, Victoria, British
Columbia, 1960 | *Victoria Daily Colonist*, 16 October 1960, 19

Barbara Macfarlane," featuring "one of the new flattering cuffed shallow
necklines."[34]

In 1961, British Columbia premier W.A.C. Bennett congratulated businesswomen and provided his "enthusiastic support to the nation-wide
recognition of Business Women's Week." Bennett implied that businesswomen were women, mothers, and wives first and businesswomen second:
"It is characteristic of our business and professional women that they regard
their careers not separately and selfishly but as adjuncts in support of the

family and the community, the foundation stone of our Western civilization."[35] Women might have entered the world of business, but Bennett, like many other observers, chose to emphasize women's familial commitments. The message was forceful: women could be businesswomen, and they could even be successful, but if they wished to maintain a position of feminine respectability and status, they had to appear ladylike, gracious, and feminine.

This helps to explain why businesswomen struggled throughout the first half of the twentieth century to downplay the ways in which they might, to their detriment, be considered masculine or manly, and why they accentuated their feminine attributes. For those women who did enter the masculine work world, one of their best tactics for survival might have been to exaggerate their feminine qualities.

MAINTAINING A FEMININE IMAGE: "NO CIGARETTES FOR HER!"

While an emphasis on femininity was most typical in descriptions of businesswomen, manliness was a titillating and irrefutable aspect of one businesswoman's life. Eleanor Johnson, profiled by P.W. Luce in the *Vancouver Sun* after her 1951 death, drove her own cab in Victoria before the First World War and later became a real estate and financial agent. She owned and operated a cement company and got the contract to build the first sewers in Burnaby. Johnson also worked as the marine and financial editor of the *Vancouver Sun* after the First World War.[36] Her manliness was notable and unusual. Luce proclaimed that Johnson was "born a woman but for more than seventy years she longed for the impossible: She yearned to be a man!" Known as Billy, she "invaded this strictly masculine field" of newspaper reporting, along with masculine fields of entrepreneurship such as driving a taxi and operating a cement company.[37]

Unlike most entrepreneurial women, Johnson did not attempt to be womanly: her appearance and her choice of businesses were distinctly masculine. While her manly appearance was the main topic of the profile, Luce attempted to stress that "Billy" was respectable: "A big, wholesome-looking woman, with a complexion that was the envy of her more feminine confreres, she was always immaculately groomed."[38] Later in the article he noted that she was a "massive woman" who "always wore mannish clothes." The final years of Johnson's life were a mystery. She left Vancouver in 1941 and did not resurface until September 1951, when her body was found in a hotel in Arizona. Luce tragically opined that Johnson "died as she had lived, a woman who trod a solitary path."

Johnson's story was unusual and certainly did not represent the majority. Even when women operated businesses most closely associated with men, reporters typically emphasized their femininity. This was the case in British Columbia and elsewhere. In 1962, the *Victoria Daily Times* printed a story about a Montreal businesswoman titled "'Boss' Holds Man's Job – And 'He' Is a Woman."[39] Laurette Grayel was the owner-director of a Montreal delivery company. Her work was identified as men work, but Grayel was portrayed (and likely portrayed herself) as womanly. The reporter described Grayel as an "attractive, 46-year-old blonde," pointedly demonstrating to readers that she was feminine in appearance if not in occupation. The accompanying photograph showed Grayel in heels and a dress, handing a package to one of her deliverymen. The incongruity of such a feminine woman in a masculine job must have been startling enough to warrant reprinting in a British Columbia newspaper. The piece was also placed in the Vancouver BPW club scrapbook.

Grayel stated that her work was "no business for a woman" and that there were "times when you must forget you are a woman." She implied that the kind of work she did was not meant to be done by women and, therefore, she took on manly characteristics to get the job done. Yet the article managed to stress her femininity and her success at the same time as it proclaimed that her business was a "man's job." According to the author, the only way that Grayel could successfully do a man's work was by occasionally forgetting that she was a woman, but also by maintaining an attractive appearance and making sure that her outward femininity was not in question. She recognized this, but so did the reporter who focused on her appearance and behaviour. A story about a woman who owned a scrap metal dealership stressed similar attributes: Mrs. Hyman Kessler "always wears skirts when she goes out on the job, and never smokes, although she is a heavy smoker at home." Much like Grayel, Kessler stated that in her business "you have to think like a man and act like a lady."[40]

These comments suggest a link between class, respectability, and ladylike behaviour. Acting like a lady, a word loaded with class implications, meant wearing skirts and not smoking in public. At the beginning of the twentieth century, to smoke and to be respectable was a contradiction for women.[41] Only less-respectable women – defined by social historian Matthew Hilton as prostitutes, actresses, and old women in rural communities! – smoked in public.[42] And a 1906 British newspaper article accused female smokers of being slack, casual, and neglectful of home and family.[43] Of course, people of all classes smoked, if not always in public. By 1949, smoking was no longer a luxury or a preserve of the rich, or of men.[44] Women's smoking rates rose during both world wars: as women entered more public spaces as workers, they also took up smoking in ever-increasing numbers.[45] Advertising also had an effect on women. North American advertisers saw the profitability of encouraging addiction among women, and they actively sought to do so between the 1920s and the 1940s.[46] However, I suggest that the links between a lack of respectability and cigarette smoking lingered, even if more women were happily smoking in public by the 1950s. For women like Kessler, projecting a respectable middle-class business image meant leaving the cigarettes at home. Wearing pants and smoking are arguably crucial cultural signposts of women's increasingly rapid entry into the workforce and, indeed, their freedom from the strictures of fashion and culture. Kessler's comments suggest that a certain conservatism remained in the business world at mid-century, where women's emancipation did not extend to clothing and cigarettes.

After her first husband's death in 1950, Wendy McDonald assumed ownership of BC Bearing Engineers, an industrial products and bearings company in Burnaby, British Columbia. McDonald was heralded as a woman who "juggled a career and raised 10 children in an era when women were barely cleaning boardrooms, much less presiding over them."[47] That she had worked as a model in her twenties was emphasized in two profiles published in 1999.[48] *Chatelaine* magazine described her as a "woman of her time and ahead of it" but also noted that she "peels off a chunky clip-on earring at the start of phone calls."[49] Here again we have an image of a powerful woman operating a business in a male-dominated work environment, a woman whose power is minimized by references to appearance and femininity. Comments about McDonald's fashion accessories and past modelling career seem intended to reinforce her femininity despite her type of business. While profiles written as her career was ending celebrated her successes, they presented her as exceptional for operating in a male domain and even for managing to run a company at all. The profile in *British Columbia's Business Leaders* notes that when McDonald's first husband went to war and left her with power of attorney, "she didn't even know what the term meant." And she "confessed" that, in the 1960s, it took years for her to really know what she was doing.[50] While these confessions may be true, the emphasis on her lack of knowledge, her marriages and many children, and her early modelling career all serve to reinforce her femininity: profiles of businessmen rarely focus on domestic issues or on a businessman's relative ignorance of his line of work.

Emphasizing womanliness prevented outright condemnation of entrepreneurial women. If businesswomen proved that they could be as successful as men while still behaving in a feminine manner and while still becoming wives or mothers, then their existence did not threaten the gender conventions that equated businesslike behaviour with masculine behaviour. The message they conveyed was that women operating businesses that had long been associated with men did not want to be men: women wanted to do men's work but remain womanly.[51] Businesswomen in "male" fields recognized the interaction that occurred between their gendered identities and their business identities.

The type of business that a self-employed woman chose to operate made a difference in how she might be portrayed or how she might portray herself. While some women ran businesses that were typically viewed as men's work – such as Johnson's cement company, Kessler's scrap metal business, or McDonald's bearings company – others ran businesses in fields deemed to be more appropriate for their sex. Yet women who operated businesses in trades that were clearly associated with domesticity were in some ways unbusinesslike to the point of being invisible in the business world. Factors such as the feminized niche in which women operated, the small size of their businesses, and the reality that businesses such as boarding houses operated out of the home meant that the women were rarely recognized as entrepreneurs in their own right. Women who owned small businesses in "typically feminized areas"[52] were rarely mentioned in the context of being in the business world, perhaps because the work they did was so closely related to unpaid domestic work. Boarding houses are one example of this: many women operated boarding houses in British Columbia, particularly in the early twentieth century, but an examination of the 1901 census indicates that many women who had boarders in their households were not enumerated as boarding-house keepers, nor were they listed as self-employed or as having income. Their husbands had wage-earning jobs or were absent. We can assume that the women looked after the boarders, who were paying for their lodgings and food, but the census does not always indicate this entrepreneurial relationship.

Moreover, very few boarding-house keepers joined the BPW clubs. In the 1920s, Victoria club member Miss A.J. Salter operated Devonshire House, advertised as "a Ladies' Hostel and Residential Club."[53] Salter did not represent the typical boarding-house keeper, however: a married woman heading her own household and taking in boarders to support her children was far more typical. When Emily Carr joined the Victoria BPW Club in 1926, her occupation was listed as artist, but Carr was also a boarding-house keeper in Victoria.[54] She did not consider boarding-house keeping her main occupation, however, and as a single woman of prominence and some status (despite her prolonged periods of penury) she was also an atypical boarding-house keeper.

Women who ran hotels in British Columbia were more likely than boarding-house keepers to be acknowledged as businesswomen. The Okanagan's Armstrong Hotel was notable for its "strong women proprietors." Florence Drage began an eleven-year tenure as owner in 1930. In 1950, James and Jean Phillips owned the hotel, and Jean managed it. She was "criticized in some quarters for running the establishment, especially as it contained a bar, and women were still expected to keep a low profile." Apparently, Phillips did take part in what the author of this article termed "more womanly things." She went to church and sang in the choir, and one acquaintance recalled that there was "no mistaking she was a lady, but she was a strong woman, too. People didn't really hold managing that business against her."[55] The reference to Phillips as a lady seems to connote middle-class respectability. Hotel keepers were running larger and more commercially profitable businesses than were boarding-house keepers, none of whom appeared on the Victoria or Vancouver BPW membership lists, despite their prevalence in both cities.[56] Hotel keeping had a place in the more public business arena, and hotels were usually separate from the home, making them a different kind of enterprise than boarding houses. That boarding-house keepers were more likely to be working-class women may also explain why they were not as likely as hotel keepers to be members of BPW clubs. The Victoria BPW club's 1948 membership list included two hotel proprietors, Erma Vautrin and Norma MacDonald. The latter, who owned the Oak Bay Beach Hotel, was still an active businessperson and a member of the Victoria Chamber of Commerce in 1957.[57]

Indeed, whether one was defined as a businesswoman was often a statement of class rather than a statement of type of work, particularly in the early twentieth century. This is reflected in the mostly middle-class membership of the BPW clubs. The working-class entrepreneurs who were invisible, working in their homes and fitting John Benson's definition of penny capitalists (see Chapter 1), were not members. While self-employment was a marker of a businesswoman, it was not the only marker, making it difficult to separate entrepreneurial from wage-earning business and professional women. In addition, being self-employed was no guarantee that a woman would be defined as a businessperson. Subsistence self-employment existed on the fringes of what it meant to be a man or woman of business.

Some entrepreneurial women worked outside the home but in feminized trades. Like the more domestic home-based businesswomen, they were rarely acknowledged as self-employed. In 1935, *Fortune* magazine published a series of articles on "Women in Business," one of which distinguished between "women engaged in the business exploitation of femininity" and those engaged in the "vital industries" dominated by men.[58] As Kathy Peiss elaborates, men's ventures were considered to be vital, a word that connotes indispensability, while women's ventures, being neither vital nor indispensable, were unbusinesslike.[59] The *Fortune* piece further stated that women's success with businesses that exploited femininity proved only that "women are by nature feminine." Being feminine was the antithesis of being businesslike, even for women operating businesses that were recognizably entrepreneurial.

Some women in British Columbia entered the beauty industry and made a niche for themselves. Beauty salon owners, corsetières, and milliners were well represented in the Vancouver and Victoria BPW club membership lists. The women stressed their middle-class femininity in comments about their businesses and in advertisements. Minnie Beveridge opened her millinery shop in Victoria in 1938. In 1954, in the *Daily Colonist,* Beveridge described her millinery work as a hobby that had developed into her living. Reporter Dee Lavoie wrote that Beveridge had taken into account a woman's personality and clothing when she created a hat for her; there was "a hat for every person."[60] The article focused on the designs, fabric, and shapes of Beveridge's hats rather than her business acumen. Lavoie portrayed her as a fashion expert, a recognized "authority on hats and how to wear them," but not as a business expert, despite her years of successful entrepreneurship.

Beveridge advertised directly to the community of businesswomen to which she belonged and noted her membership in the BPW club. She also appealed to her customers' sense of fashion: "The shape that flatters is yours this fall," her advertisements announced in 1960, with "Lovely, Lofty" hats from Minnie Beveridge Millinery.[61]

Observers' comments about businesswomen also focused on particular attributes when they described women and their enterprises. After she was widowed in the 1940s, Alice Mallek continued to operate the women's wear shop that she and her husband had opened in 1913. A profile of Mallek in the *Daily Colonist* in the mid-1950s stated: "Mrs. Mallek loves furs, like most women, and on her racks can be found some of the loveliest creations."[62] Articles highlighting businesswomen stressed either the femininity of the proprietors or the femininity of their goods: this profile stressed both. G.E. Mortimer described Mallek as a kindly woman of "lively ideas and mischievous good humor." Her carpeted salon was described as a "smart downtown dress shop," while she was described as respectable, womanly, and as dignified and elegant as her store. Mortimer described this "proprietress" as a "silver-haired widow."[63] Descriptions that focused on women's dignity or their femininity were a common feature of profiles such as this one. Certainly, class was one of the markers of Mallek's success, and her dignified appearance identified her as a respectable, middle-class businesswoman.

A retiring president of the Vancouver BPW club told the *Vancouver Daily Province* in the 1950s, "Though I'm known in business circles as Mrs. Theresa Galloway (she once owned a beauty parlor), I'm very happily married, and to a man who believes a wife should also be an individual."[64] Catering to a female clientele, Galloway's business had appealed to traditional understandings of gender divisions within Canadian society. Reporter Winifred Lee stressed that Galloway was respectable and womanly but also ambitious, hard-working, and community-minded, a "friendly hospitable person" who would tackle anything from sewing lace on lingerie to cooking a meal to leading a women's committee. Galloway had also "constantly agitated for better conditions and hours of work" for women. She embodied the ideal businesswoman: respectable, friendly, womanly, and businesslike, but in a feminine trade.

While Lee wrote of Galloway's work on behalf of other women and her extensive committee work, the article's subtitles included phrases such as "A Gay Person," "Happily Married," and "No Cigarettes For Her!" "I'm very sentimental," Galloway claimed. "I just can't bear to part with my daughter's baby things." Lee noted that "sloppy clothing for young people" aroused Galloway's disdain, and that she drew the line at smoking and drinking for women: "If women only knew how ugly they look with a cigarette dangling from their lips, I'm sure they'd stop." For Galloway, cigarettes seemed to represent an undignified image from which respectable entrepreneurs ought to distance themselves – as the scrap metal dealer, the widowed Mrs. Kessler, did by only smoking at home. Although she does not state it, Galloway may also have associated cigarettes with lower-class women, not with middle-class businesswomen, again illustrating a concern in business circles to maintain a relatively conservative image despite the wider societal appeal of cigarettes in the 1950s. Cigarette advertising often portrayed fun-loving, independent women and glamorous socialites. But "the seductive aspect of the cigarette was never too far removed," and a prejudice against women smoking in the streets also lingered.[65] The ability to light up was liberating for some women, just as owning a business was – but businesswomen still conformed to an image of respectable, conservative femininity, not one of fun-loving, liberated young workers.

Women also used "a discourse of community, domesticity, neighborliness and service" to gain a place in the world of residential real estate.[66] Traditional gendered ideas about women's roles, and the association of women with family and home, provided a way for women to enter the industry. An article in *The Business and Professional Woman* in 1963 titled "Women CAN Sell Real Estate" profiled the Vancouver all-woman real estate firm of Triangle Realty. "Can womanly qualities of charm, grace, enthusiasm and attention to detail form the basis of a successful business?" asked Virginia Beirnes.[67] Clearly, Beirnes believed that they could and that physical appearance and "womanly qualities" contributed to the women's success: "Mrs. Woodsworth is a charming silver blonde; Mrs. Linnell and Mrs. Ashdown, vivacious redheads, and all are mature women with families."[68] This physical description accentuated the fact that successful businesswomen could also be wives and mothers. Beirnes seems to have chosen her adjectives carefully, alerting her readership to the women's charm and maturity but also playfully noting the stereotype of the lively redhead. Beirnes concluded that "know-how, combined with charm, grace and enthusiasm, spell success in the real estate business for women."[69] The author and her readership undoubtedly made the link between these markers of ladylike behaviour and a middle-class feminine ideal.

Despite the success stories, it was difficult to be recognized as a woman *and* as an entrepreneur. Women who operated overtly domestic or feminine enterprises out of their home were rarely recognized as being in the business world. They were penny capitalists, frequently warding off poverty with businesses that required little capital and fell under the broad category of women's work. No profiles exist lauding home-based boardinghouse keepers or laundresses as successful businesswomen. Women who moved out of the house and into a capitalist marketplace to open businesses in fields deemed suitable to women were sometimes so successful at appearing feminine that they were hardly recognized as being in business either. They were heralded as community-minded mothers, wives, and dignified widows, with their careers as hat makers or beauty shop owners seeming almost incidental. For Billy Johnson, the taxi driver, cement company owner, and newspaper reporter, it was easier to be mannish. Unlike most female entrepreneurs, she seems to have made no effort to appear feminine. Her careers and appearance aptly demonstrate that business was actually a man's world, one that she embraced more forthrightly than most women. Johnson acted like a man, looked like a man, and entered a man's world of business, but she was also described as a woman who "trod a solitary path."

In 1923, Vancouver BPW Club president Mabel Ingram pointed out that "there are women in all branches of business and the professions today, we are shut out of nothing, and the men are recognizing more and more that we are in the business world to stay and to shoulder our share of the big things of the world."[70] Club members repeatedly asserted this conviction. A story published in *Vancouver Business Woman* in 1925 about a "plucky" female holly farmer is one such example: M.E. Dunn noted that it was "refreshing to see a woman strike out on a new line of work. 'Madam Farmer' ought to be congratulated." The profile emphasized that the aspiring farmer was entering a less predictable line of work for a woman and celebrated her "pioneer spirit" and "strength of mind."[71] However, the BPW clubs, dedicated to promoting the interests of business and professional women and stimulating "social intercourse,"[72] were not always optimistic. In 1932, the president of the Canadian federation stated that women had "only one foot on the threshold of business as the equal of man."[73]

The types of businesses that women operated represented a meeting point between societal pressures upon women and their need to make economic decisions. Despite the highlighted stories of plucky holly farmers or intrepid cab drivers, businesswomen in the province made gendered choices overlaid with capitalist choices. The interaction between gender and business is a critical part of the story because most women chose particular enterprises based on their expectations of business success – in essence, capitalist considerations – but also based on societal expectations of appropriate avenues for entrepreneurial women. It behooved women to pay attention to the latter expectations and open businesses in enterprises long associated with women in order to succeed economically.

That the kinds of work other members of society thought suitable for women affected women's economic choices was illustrated in a 1950 article in the *Veteran's Advocate*. The article reported on a meeting of the Toronto BPW club at which male guests took part in a panel discussion. Panelists advised businesswomen to become "more emotionally stable" and to follow professions in which women were successful.[74] Women's entrepreneurial choices were guided by gender expectations and by societal assumptions about their supposed emotional instability, which the panel clearly believed would hinder them in business.

Businesswomen in British Columbia stressed their femininity by emphasizing their roles as mothers or wives, by heeding their personal appearance, by acting "ladylike," and by consciously stressing the ways in which they were softer, more feminine than, and thus different from, their male counterparts in business. Women stressed these attributes themselves, but so did the commentators who reported on club events and who interviewed BPW clubwomen. What we see in the province is not an outright condemnation of women who operated businesses. Rather, we see a concerted effort by the women themselves, by outside observers, and by the media to assert the essential womanliness of female entrepreneurs. They were described and bounded by their feminine qualities, something that is clear in the advertisements for female-owned businesses and in newspaper articles or archival club records that mention female proprietors. This tendency was even more pronounced in profiles of women who operated businesses in masculine fields.

The womanliness of female entrepreneurs was stressed to such a degree that it seems calculated to negate the very fact of their self-employment. If they could be portrayed as good wives and mothers, as attractive or youthful, small or feminine, then their encroachment into the male-dominated business world was less threatening. If women were still different from men and still acted like ladies, they were not such a threat to an established order in which men – not women – were independent, self-reliant, and the owners of firms and businesses. As long as women resisted acting like men in the world of business (refraining from "whanging" each other on the shoulder, wearing masculine clothes, or smoking on the job) and continued to take care of their appearance and present themselves in a feminine manner, the fact that they happened to be business owners could be tolerated and even faintly celebrated.

"Darkened by Family Obligations"

Reflections on the Business of Women

In 1994, Robin Fisher argued that historical writing about British Columbia, like the province itself, "still has a sense of the frontier about it. The historian is expected to sally forth, stake out a new piece of ground, build fences and tame the wilderness."[1] In the course of laying out what he considered to be the limitations of the province's historiography, Fisher provided advice for emergent historians. He suggested we ought to move beyond piling up "new information about the past" and learn to "grapple vigorously with ideas."[2]

Fisher's comments were made fifteen years ago, and many of them are still germane, although scholarship in the province has changed in the years since his provocation was first uttered.[3] My study of female self-employment addresses his first challenge by contributing more than just another layer on the pile of information about British Columbia. Fisher also proposed that British Columbia historians should be thinking about getting into the twentieth century,[4] and this study is distinctively and quite literally "post-colonial." It is important to get beyond the province's formative years and address twentieth-century British Columbia, although the influence of colonial demographics on the province's evolution must not be discounted. Again, while Fisher's comments are not particularly recent, there continues to be much interest today, academic and popular, in nineteenth-century British Columbia. British Columbia historians are still discussing, and rightly so, a region awash with the conflicts of early encounters and with what Cole Harris called the "resettlement" of the region.[5] More recent social history is still relatively new terrain, although there are some excellent exceptions.[6] Still, as the 2007 edited collection *Myth and Memory: Stories of Indigenous-European Contact* notes, the province continues to be preoccupied with the contact zone.[7] My work takes us into the more recent past, although I do not discount the lingering effects of early encounters between original inhabitants and re-settlers.

Fisher also complained that we have avoided taking a broad view of the province by examining "tiny fragments of the past through a microscope. The narrower the focus, of course, the bigger the gaps that remain."[8] While he was not advocating more data collection, he suggested that more attention be paid to broader issues in the province's history.[9] My research demonstrates general trends by looking at patterns in women's self-employment over a large period of time: one cannot help examining a broad view of the province when looking at aspects of British Columbia's history across a half-century period. One of the more general issues considered in this work is how the province's frontier history has continued to influence female labour force participation. Vestiges of the province's early demographics, such as a high ratio of white men to white women (and, in turn, women's specific opportunities to commercialize traditional sex roles in early British Columbia), continued to affect the nature of female self-employment in the province long after the ratio evened out. Remnants of British Columbia's frontier-like beginnings have undoubtedly influenced other developments in the province. More studies that examine patterns over a broad period of time may help to fill other gaps in our perspective on British Columbia's history.

Finally, Fisher avers that British Columbia is "not simply a replica of other places: it is unique and special. And it is that uniqueness that British Columbia's historians should be concerned to define."[10] I grapple specifically and extensively with British Columbia's distinctiveness in one area: women's labour force and marital patterns, principally in the arena of self-employment. Proportionately more women were married, *and* more women were self-employed, in British Columbia than in the rest of Canada. The female population's involvement in self-employment was significant and deserves specific study because it uncovers another aspect of women's distinctive experiences in the province. In his appeal for more demographic histories of British Columbia, John Douglas Belshaw suggests that women's experiences "as entrepreneurs, as land-owners, and as political players was greater than non-demographically-minded histories have suggested."[11] My work demonstrates that the female population did exercise options that were not exercised in quite the same way in the rest of the country.

Historians of women and work have looked at waged and non-waged women's work, but entrepreneurs have rarely been singled out for attention. Scholars need to differentiate between types of work and ought to consider female self-employment more carefully. Self-employed women's participation in the labour force has been hidden historically because there were relatively few entrepreneurial women in the labour force. This does not make them less worthy of study. That there were real and perceived barriers to female employment in general and self-employment in particular makes the small number who became businesswomen all the more interesting. As Chad Gaffield has noted about the discipline of history, we can learn something about whole societies "by looking at an admittedly partial experience. Such work illustrates the value of examining in detail the unusual rather than dismissing it as marginal, as statistical noise."[12]

Self-employment is an important aspect of women's work experiences in the province, but self-employed women were different from wage-earning women. In this study, I make extensive use of census data to formulate important connections between women's marital patterns, ages, families, and the labour force options open to them as a result of these variables. Self-employed women in British Columbia and elsewhere in Canada were older, more likely to have children, and more likely to be married or once-married than were wage-earning women. Thus, family issues preoccupied them in specific ways, and their experiences were different than those of wage earners. Scholars in labour, business, or women's history have not adequately explored these differences. Labour historians have focused on wage earners; business historians have focused on male-dominated corporations or individual businessmen; and women's historians have focused on women's labour force experiences without differentiating between self-employed and wage-earning women.

This study illuminates differences between self-employed and wage-earning women. It also acknowledges that, much like women's wage-earning opportunities, women's self-employment in British Columbia and elsewhere was limited to a small number of occupational groups. Women in business have not been examined separately from female employees, in part because the types of work open to them were similar: they often found themselves in feminine-typed occupations such as cooking, cleaning, and sewing. Women operating boarding houses, hair salons, restaurants, and other retail operations involving laundry or women's and children's clothing were perceived to be doing "women's work." However, I argue that they ought to be considered entrepreneurs in their own right, their success measured by the ability of their businesses to aid their families and to stack up against the limited kinds of paid work available to women in the province. The size of business or level of income is a less useful measure of success in this context.

Simply by working for themselves, entrepreneurial women entered a world highly gendered as male: the language of success, capitalism, and business was masculine. Even women who were not remarkable or exceptional in terms of the type of business they operated followed a path that was not considered, suggested, or encouraged for women. They were unconventional in terms of their minority status, but that has also meant they have remained hidden. And when their work was home-based, feminine, and family-oriented, it was even harder to see them as businesspeople. That they operated their own businesses but were not often referred to as businesswomen or entrepreneurs indicates that our definitions of businesses and businesspeople, commonly expressed as male success stories, need widening.

Businesswomen were literally surrounded by men. If this was the case for self-employed women operating feminine businesses, it was even more pronounced for women who ran businesses in male-dominated fields. This is another distinctive aspect of female self-employment: despite a still-strong association with feminine industries, entrepreneurial women were more likely to work in male-dominated occupations than were wage-earning women. Therefore, some businesswomen challenged woman's place doubly, by being in business at all *and* by running businesses that were normally run by men.

Even these women were often hidden from view. Rarely were they overtly described as self-made women and captains of industry. The ways in which businesswomen were defined by others, and defined themselves, provide some explanation of how female-owned businesses were catalogued and understood in what were male-dominated work worlds. While census data helps to pull businesswomen into view and can highlight similarities and differences between self-employed women and other working men and women, it cannot illustrate how they made sense of their status as entrepreneurs. The records of the business and professional women's (BPW) clubs of British Columbia demonstrate more directly how businesswomen described their entrepreneurship and how they compared themselves to other women and men in the labour force. Women relied on feminine imagery and ideas about what constituted feminine work to explain their presence in the world of business. They did this in five ways: by working in "feminine" industries; by emphasizing the trappings of femininity, such as appearance and respectability, particularly when they were not operating feminine enterprises; by invoking the language of family responsibility to justify their endeavours; by working out of the home; and by continuing the businesses of their fathers or husbands. These elements of female self-employment are not expressed in census data, but they are better understood through an examination of clubwomen's experiences in British Columbia.

In 1997, Katherine Gay noted that women's aspirations in the labour force generally "are still constrained by a limited range of job opportunities," that their "obligation to family frequently interrupts and compromises careers," and that many women "can't or won't" separate their business lives from their personal lives.[13] Rather than see these constraints as limitations to entrepreneurial success, Gay proclaimed that

> in entrepreneurialism, they [women] have found a place in the world where, baby, it just doesn't get better than this. After all, their alternative is to work in a hierarchy determined by men and supported by women, with less freedom and authority and a smaller chance of reward. An entrepreneurial career is a harbour from many of the external storms of being female. It offers the purest form of pay-for-performance possible, without the filters of bureaucracy and bias.[14]

This, of course, was not the whole story for women at the end of the twentieth century, nor was self-employment this liberating in 1901. Gay also argues that female self-employment is a "new and unfamiliar road, darkened by family obligations, absent business networks, a society reluctant to give its full endorsement, good old fashioned fear, and few visible examples to follow."[15]

Some of the possibilities *and* limitations inherent in female self-employment in 1901 were still present at the end of the century, as Gay's commentary indicates. Yet, like other more contemporary observers, she mistakenly assumes that female self-employment is a relatively recent phenomenon, a "new and unfamiliar" road for women. Canadian statistics do indicate that female entrepreneurship increased rapidly in the last twenty-five years of the twentieth century. Between 1975 and 1986, the number of self-employed women in Canada rose three times as fast as the number of self-employed men.[16] However, female entrepreneurship was just as prominent at the beginning of the century. While 10 percent of all employed women were self-employed in 1993,[17] more were self-employed in earlier decades – 19.5 percent in 1901, and a still high 11 percent in 1931.[18]

"Self-employment for Canadian women is far from being simply a late twentieth-century phenomenon."[19]

Moreover, while self-employment may be viewed in some respects as a "harbour" from the male-dominated pressures of the rest of the labour force, many women have only taken refuge there because they had no other choice at the time. And the harbour was still a male-dominated place. The constraints on women's labour force aspirations in the 1990s were also present in 1901, for self-employed *and* wage-earning women.

While self-employment did not always provide a safe harbour for women in the first half of the twentieth century, female entrepreneurs coped with a limited range of employment possibilities by opening businesses in areas that capitalized on their feminine attributes. If they operated more masculine businesses, which some women also did, they stressed their feminine qualities to escape censure. In addition, economic need often dictated women's entrepreneurial decisions. Rather than actively choosing self-employment because they sought personal and financial success, many women entered self-employment because they needed to feed their families but could not find wage-earning work because of their location, age, or marital status. Sometimes continuing to operate a family farm or taking in boarders was the best choice out of a not-very-promising set of options. "My husband left and it's what I know how to do," a British Columbia cattle rancher explained in a 1991 survey, a comment that could as easily have been made in 1901. But she added, "As well, I love it."[20] Economic need did not mean that women had no other reasons for running businesses, and this was the case at the beginning of the century as well as at the end of it. Importantly though, in the first half of the nineteenth century, whether they worked in female- or male-dominated occupations, self-employed women stressed their femininity and the need to support family, particularly if they had lost a spouse through death or desertion.

Contemporary discussions of women's participation in the labour force suggest that entrepreneurship is a choice made by women who have surveyed their work possibilities and recognized, as did women in the early to mid-1900s, that it is difficult to combine wage-earning work and family. In 1999, the Canadian magazine *Chatelaine* published what became an annual showcase of Canada's top women entrepreneurs. The first series noted that the number of self-employed women in Canada had grown 42 percent between 1992 and 1997 – although in the late 1990s the rates of self-employment were still lower than they had been at the beginning of the century. "More women in the work force were self-employed in 1901 than in 1996," as Peter Baskerville notes.[21] The feature stressed women's emancipation through entrepreneurship, claiming that women in business were loving their work, breaking into new enterprises, and "shattering stereotypes."[22]

The *Globe and Mail* has also stressed choice, specifically highlighting the lives of "mompreneurs," women with children who operate their own businesses in order to accommodate their lives as wives and mothers.[23] There is even a Canadian magazine, *The Mompreneur,* "for women who are balancing the role of motherhood with being an entrepreneur."[24] Kathryn Bechthold, the creator of the magazine and of Mompreneur Networking Group Inc. (and an associated website), states that her network "provides information, inspiration and education to Mompreneurs looking for success with running their own businesses and balancing their family lives."[25]

The trend goes beyond this networking group. *Today's Parent,* a popular Canadian parenting magazine that covers a wide range of topics, featured mompreneurs in a 2006 article. "Many a mom has been tempted to leave a not-so-fulfilling job to head down the entrepreneurial road. What's not to love? You could set your own hours (no ducking from the boss when you come in late!), spend more time with your children, and put your heart and soul into work you feel passionate about – all perks your current job can't offer."[26] And in January 2009, *Today's Parent* asked its readers, "Could you be a mom entrepreneur?" Author Kim Shiffman suggests that many self-employed women in Canada "are mothers who opted to drop out of the career rat race," and she notes the perks: "what mom wouldn't want to choose her own work hours and spend more time with her kids?" However, she warns that business ownership involves long hours, and "fewer than half of small businesses live to celebrate their third anniversary."[27]

While demanding, self-employment promises more flexibility than wage-earning occupations in which hours of work are rigid. Some of the reasons that women have historically turned to self-employment are mirrored in the experiences of today's mompreneurs. And, clearly, the discussion of entrepreneurs and mompreneurs is salient and increasingly relevant to women in the twenty-first century. However, modern commentators who celebrate the rise of women's home-based businesses would do well to remember that businesswomen of the past faced issues similar to those of women today: how to financially provide for their families, look after their children, and – sometimes – survive the loss of a spouse or financial partner. They would also do well to remember that the choice is sometimes a result of other doors closing. Women of child-bearing age sometimes find it difficult to fit family needs around their careers. Limitations in the labour force sometimes compel women to consider options – like self-employment – that allow them to set their own hours.

Family considerations and limited access to a wider range of employment possibilities help to explain why women turned to self-employment between 1901 and 1951, just as they help to explain women's business decisions in the 1990s and beyond. But the interconnected factors of marital status, age, and the family claim also clarify the nature of female self-employment. The study of these variables in one province demonstrates the importance of comparative studies and the need to differentiate between groups of women in the labour force.

This story of entrepreneurial women in British Columbia covers women in different towns, operating a variety of different types of businesses in the first half of the twentieth century. The ways in which they were defined, and defined themselves, provide some understanding of businesswomen who operated in male-dominated work worlds. Entrepreneurial women constituted a small proportion of the total female labour force, but they exhibited differences from the rest of the labour force that deserve attention. My aim in this book has been to explore women's employment options in early-twentieth-century British Columbia and explain their decisions to open businesses. In examining the lives of businesswomen and BPW club members in the province, what comes to light are their struggles to succeed in what was quite evidently a man's world, but also the degree to which family and marital status played a part in business choice. Thus, we begin to see the links between gender, labour, and business history.

My work also indicates that region matters: British Columbia's gender imbalance in the first half of the twentieth century meant that women had high rates of marriage, but they also worked in relatively high numbers and were more likely to be self-employed in the province than in the rest of Canada. Frontier characteristics help explain their willingness to open businesses. The economic and social development of the province continued to be affected by its frontier years long after the features we might consider to be most characteristic of frontiers had dissipated, and this also shaped women's decisions to open their own businesses. Thus, businesswomen's identities as mothers, wives, and widows affected their entrepreneurial decisions in meaningful ways, as did their location in British Columbia. For a small but significant number of women in British Columbia, issues of employment options, class, and their own (and others') understanding of their femininity affected their working lives in distinct ways.

Further study is required to tease out how much difference regionalism makes to female entrepreneurship in other parts of Canada, just as further study of individual entrepreneurial women in British Columbia – including the very important, although often obscured, stories of non-white businesswomen in the province – is a logical next step. The ways in which British Columbia differs from the rest of the country can only be understood if researchers situate the province within a broader context, just as entrepreneurial women's distinctive qualities can only be illuminated through comparison with other working men and women. I urge other scholars to use this study as a beginning point from which to consider how women's paid work encompasses more than wage-earning work, and how business and entrepreneurship can be more broadly defined to include many types of female-run enterprises. I hope others will expand this research to flesh out the histories of individual enterprising women, to address the ways that ethnicity and race can complicate the stories of female entrepreneurship, and to better understand female self-employment in other regions of the country. Clearly, examining how self-employed women understood their roles within the gendered world of business provides further insight into many other aspects of women's work and into the study of female *and* male entrepreneurship in twentieth-century Canadian history.

Self-Employed Women in the Victoria and Vancouver Business and Professional Women's Clubs, 1921-63

Last name	First name	Marital status	Years mentioned	Occupation	City
Adams	Lydia	S	1924	Chiropractor	Victoria
Arsens	Helen	M	1961	Store owner	Victoria
Badgley	Elizabeth	S	1923	Arts teacher	Vancouver
Baker	R.	M	1927	Book store owner	Vancouver
Ballantyne	M.	M	1952	Florist	Victoria
Bartholomew	Phyllis		1930s?	Antiques dealer	Victoria
Barton	Winnifred	S	1923	Dressmaker	Vancouver
Beckwith	Heather	M	1927, 1931	Milliner	Victoria
Bell	Margaret	M	1921	Violin teacher	Victoria
Bell	Viva	S	1948	Corsetière	Victoria
Bengston	Minnie	S	1955	Guest house prop. (& nurse)	Victoria
Beveridge	Norah	S	1941, 1948	Milliner	Victoria
Bidwell	Muriel	S	1946	Glass engraver	Victoria
Blythe	Mima	M	1931	Milliner	Victoria
Brown	Emily	S	1921	Florist	Vancouver
Carr	Irene	M	1926	Artist	Victoria
Carroll	Isabella	S	1942, 1948	Corsetière	Victoria
Conacher			1927, 1931	Photographer	Victoria

Surname	First name		Years	Occupation	City
Cooper	Rozella	M	1947, 1948	Restaurant owner	Victoria
Costar	Winnifred	M	1946, 1948	Dressmaker	Victoria
Darling	Dollie	M	1931, 1948, 1949	Beauty shop owner	Victoria
Dodds	Pamela	M	1948	Music teacher	Victoria
Donagh	Dora	S	1922, 1931	Artist	Victoria
Drake		M	1935	Bakery owner	Victoria
Foxall	Nettie	S	1925, 1931, 1935	Photographer	Victoria
Fraser		M	1930s?	Hairdresser	Victoria
Gibbon	Marjorie	S	1948	Designer	Victoria
Gibson	Marjorie	S	1948	Photographer	Victoria
Goy	Julie	S	1925	Clothing/Dressmaker	Vancouver
Greaves		M	1931	Photographer	Victoria
Griffin	Beatrice	S	1926, 1931	Music teacher/Musician	Victoria
Hall	Jane	S	1948	Dressmaker	Victoria
Harradine	Norah		1924	Owner, commercial school	Vancouver
Hastings	Alice		1932	Star Steam Laundry	Vancouver
Heath	Winnifred	M	1961	Green Lantern Gift Shop	Victoria
Heeney	Dorothy	M	1948	Milliner	Victoria
Henderson	Olive	M	1962	Beauty salon owner	Victoria
Herd	Minnie	S	1931	Milliner	Victoria
Kitto		S	1921	Artist	Victoria
Langworthy		M	1927	Florist	Vancouver
Le Lacheur	Ruth	S	1961	Partner, Green Lantern	Victoria
Livingstone		S	1941	Crown Millinery	Victoria
Lund		M	1922	Dance teacher	Victoria
Lythgoe	Dr. Leyda	M	1955	Psychiatrist	Victoria

Last name	First name	Marital status	Years mentioned	Occupation	City
Macdonald	Norma	M	1948, 1957	Hotel prop.	Victoria
Macdonald		M	1927	Owner, oriental store	Vancouver
Mallek	Alice	M	1941, 1948	Furrier/Clothes	Victoria
Maynard	Ethel	M	1926, 1931, 1941	Jeweller	Victoria
Maynard	Ida	M	1932	Shoe store	Victoria
McCrea		M	1924, 1931	Photographer	Victoria
McGregor	Kate	S	1924	Music teacher	Victoria
McLenaghen		S	1932	Blue Bird Hat Shop	Vancouver
McMartin		M	1931, 1941	Leather goods store	Victoria
Moggey	Vivian	S	1927	Music teacher	Victoria
Monk	Phyllis		1926	Merchant, lingerie	Vancouver
Moody			1923	Tea room	Vancouver
More	Bessie	M	1948	Milliner	Victoria
Morgan		M	1924	Authoress	Victoria
Morgan	Mary Cecilia	M	1946	Dressmaker	Victoria
Morrison	Cecilia	M	1948	Dressmaker	Victoria
Neiman	Adele	M	1946	Army supply store owner	Victoria
Pearce	Winnifred	M	1948	Café owner	Victoria
Pearson		M	1923	Owner, tea room	Vancouver
Raine	Olive	S	1931	Milliner	Victoria
Rose	Sonia	M	1948	Jeweller	Victoria
Salter		S	1926	Owner, hostel	Victoria
Schramli		M	1931	Merchant	Victoria
Shanks	Loretta	M	1947	Lingerie shop owner	Victoria
Sherratt	Hazel	M	1951	Masseur	Victoria

Surname	First name	Status	Year(s)	Occupation	City
Sparks	Edith		1948	Milliner	Victoria
Sprott	Anna	M	1927	Owner, business college	Vancouver
Steel	Dr. Anne		1957	Doctor?	Victoria
Stewart	Margaret	M	1931	Musician	Victoria
Strathern	Ada	S	1931	Music teacher	Victoria
Sweeney		M	1921	Artist	Victoria
Talbot	Mabel	M	1959	Milliner	Victoria
Taylor	Juanetta	M	1951	Restaurant owner	Victoria
Van Beeker	E.	S	1931	Masseuse	Victoria
Vautrin	Erma	M	1948	Hotel prop.	Victoria
Wade	Vera	M	1961, 1963	Dress shop owner	Victoria
Westall		M	1951	Wigs (hairdresser)	Vancouver
Westcott	May	S		Owner, Academy of Useful Arts	Vancouver
Wilkes		M	1931	Furrier	Victoria
Willis		M	1923	Artist	Victoria
Wilson	Nellie		1932	Hosiery, lingerie shop	Vancouver
Wingate	Brownie	S	1939	Commercial artist	Victoria.
Woodward	Barbara	M	1946, 1948	Artist/Author	Victoria
Woollatt		M	1924	Antiques dealer	Victoria
Wright	Jean	M	1951	Masseur	Victoria
York	Elizabeth	S	1941, 1948	Holley's Café	Victoria

NOTES: This list does not include all BPW club members who were self-employed between 1921 and 1963, only those specifically noted in club records. In addition, club records did not usually indicate employment status; I have listed women who were very likely self-employed based on their occupational title and women who were specifically referred to in the Vancouver or Victoria BPW club minutes and records as entrepreneurs. The point here is that in occupations that were or were likely to be entrepreneurial, the rate of marriage was high. Marriage was a far more likely state among self-employed than among wage-earning women between 1901 and 1951.

SOURCE: Victoria BPW Club Records (BC Archives) and Vancouver BPW Club Records (City of Vancouver Archives).

Membership List of the Victoria Business and Professional Women's Club, 1931, by Occupational Category

Last name	First name	Marital status	Occupation
Clerical – Wage Earners			
Blythe	Muriel	S	Stenographer
Bradshaw	E.	S	Secretary
Brown	Kate	S	Stenographer
Cameron	Mabel	S	Secretary
Cruickshanks	Gladys	S	Secretary
Fraser	Jessie	S	Stenographer
Gray	Clarice	S	Stenographer
Hafer	F.	S	Stenographer
Howell	Edith	S	Stenographer
Johnson	May	M	Stenographer
Macrae	E.M.	S	Bank clerk
Monteith	M.	M	Secretary
Morris	Hilda	S	Bank clerk
Murie	F.	M	Secretary
McLaren	Kate	S	Stenographer
McLeod	Gene	S	YWCA secretary
Nickerson	H.	S	Stenographer
Paul	A.J.	S	Law office
Pogson	E.	S	Insurance
Reynolds	Elsie	S	Stenographer
Richards	Bessie	S	Bank clerk
Richards	Elsie	S	Insurance
Richardson	Elsie	S	Bank clerk
Roberts	Mary	S	Secretary
Taylor	Tephi	S	Secretary
Thomas	B.G.	S	Secretary
Unwin	Mabel	S	Stenographer
Wigley	M.A. (Bay)	S	Accountant
Wills	Elizabeth	M	Stenographer
Woodcock	Margaret	S	Stenographer

▶

Last name	First name	Marital status	Occupation
Professional – Wage Earners			
Austin		M	Librarian
Clay	Margaret	S	Librarian
Craig	Sadie	S	Manageress
Donough	Kate	S	Customs inspector
Forbes	Agnes	S	Nurse
Girling		M	Nurse
Hall	Margaret	M	Librarian
Hodge	Meta	S	Nurse
Hodges	Nancy	M	Society editor, newspaper
Kelly	Helen	S	Nurse
Macrae	Kate	S	Nurse
McBride	A.	S	Social service
Ormiston	May	S	Nurse
Shaw	Geraldine	S	Librarian
Snyder	Olive	S	Social service
Sylvester	Louise	S	Teacher
Taylor		M	Nurses' home
Thornley	Ethel	S	Nurse
Whitehead		S	Governess
Retail Workers – Wage Earners			
Abbott	Ida	M	Saleslady
Burwood	Ivy	S	Saleslady
Lacey	Ada	S	Saleslady
Lamport	M.	M	Saleslady
Rose		M	Saleslady
Self-Employed			
Beckwith	Winnifred	S	Milliner
Conacher	Isabella	S	Photographer
Darling	Dollie	M	Beauty shop owner
Donough	Dora	S	Artist
Foxall	Nettie	S	Photographer
Greaves		M	Photographer
Griffin	Beatrice	S	Musician
Grute	Margaret	M	Art pottery
Herd	Minnie	S	Milliner
Maynard	E.G.	M	Jeweller
Maynard	Ida	M	Fashion bootery (shop)
McCrea		M	Photographer
McMartin		M	Leather goods (shop)
Raine	Olive	S	Milliner

Last name	First name	Marital status	Occupation
Schramli		M	Merchant
Stewart	Margaret	M	Musician
Turley	Eva	S	Academy of Useful Arts
Wilkes		M	Furrier
Willis	W.A.	M	Art pottery

Other (occupation status unknown)

Herbert	E.J.	S	Unknown
Holland	Francis	M	Architect
Kenworthy		S	Unknown
Matheson		M	Unknown
Morton	E.M.	S	Unknown
Roberts	Emily	S	Girls' private school
Shaw	Jennie	S	Unknown
Strathern	Ada	S	Music teacher
Sweeney	Lillian	M	Unknown
Van Beeker	E.	S	Masseuse
Wallace	May	S	Law student
White	E.H.	M	Unknown
White	J.L.	M	Unknown

SOURCE: "Membership List, Victoria Business and Professional Women's Club, 1931," Attendance and Registration Book, BPW Club Records, 89-1386-3, British Columbia Archives.

Membership List of the Victoria Business and Professional Women's Club, 1948, by Occupational Category

Last name	First name	Marital status	Occupation	Member in 1931?
Clerical – Wage Earners				
Beek	Verna	S	Secretary	
Bidwell	Margaret	S	Stenographer	
Buckingham	Daisy		Clerk	
Cameron	Mabel	S	Secretary (retired)	Y (Secretary)
Campbell	Meryl		Clerk	
Cliff	Mary	S	Payroll clerk	
Cumming	Mary	M	Office clerk	
Downing	K.	S	Secretary	
Drake	Alice	M	Office clerk	
Dykes	Dorothy	S	Traffic clerk	
Edney	Dorothy	S	Stenographer	
Farquharson	Kate	M	Secretary	
Fraser	Jessie	S	Secretary	Y (Stenographer)
Gray	Ethel	S	Insurance	
Hall	Jane	S	Secretary	
Hall	Madge	M	Insurance	Y (Librarian)
Hebden	Marjorie	M	Clerk	
Henderson	Constance	M	Bank clerk	
Henderson	Lily	S	Bookkeeper	
Laughlin	Marguerite	M	Secretary	
Lord		M	Secretary	
Masters	Ruby	M	Steno-bookkeeper	
McClement	Mae	M	Bookkeeper	
Mitchell	Marion	M	Wholesale clerk	
Moore	Helen	S	Secretary	
Palmason	Avis	M	Advertising (newspaper)	
Paterson	Kate	M	Secretary (retired)	
Pembridge	Lottie	M	Insurance	
Phipps	Agnes	M	Secretary	

▶

Last name	First name	Marital status	Occupation	Member in 1931?
Rainforth	Margaret	M	Bookkeeper	
Rich	Nona	S	Chief clerk	
Richardson	Elsie	S	Bank clerk (retired)	Y (Bank clerk)
Ross	Harriet	M	Secretary	
Smith	Bessie	M	Sec. bookkeeper	
Smith	Lillian	M	Secretary	
Stevenson	Winifred	M	Secretary	
Stewart	Eleanor	S	Stenographer	
Woodcock	Margaret	S	Secretary	Y (Stenographer)

Professional – Wage Earners

Last name	First name	Marital status	Occupation	Member in 1931?
Baird	Marjorie	S	Supt. Victorian Order of Nurses	
Barton	Lillian	S	Teacher	
Burwash	Ella	M	Librarian	
Carey	Gladys	M	Practical nurse	
Clay	Margaret	S	Librarian	Y (Librarian)
Crighton	Dorothy	S	Librarian	
Cruickshank	Helen	S	Nurse	
Forbes	Elizabeth	S	Social editor (newspaper)	
Guild	Mary	M	Teacher	
Herson	Alice		Nurse	
Hodges	Nancy	M	Newspaper	Y (Newspaper)
Lovel	Irene	S	Teacher	
Lucas	Eva	S	Nurse	
Maunsell	Eleanor	M	Commercial teacher	
Roberts	Jane	S	Hospital matron	
Simpson	Jean		Teacher	
Sylvester	Louise	S	Teacher (retired)	Y (Teacher)
Tuck	Isla	S	Teacher (retired)	
Webster	Dorothy	S	Nurse	
Woods	Gertrude	M	Civil service	
Worthington	Iola	S	Commercial teacher	

Retail Workers – Wage Earners

Last name	First name	Marital status	Occupation	Member in 1931?
Ambrose	Dorothy	M	Saleslady	
Carslake	Ida	M	Saleslady	
Devine	Olive	M	Saleslady	
Ellis	Winnifred	S	Cashier	
Higgins	Jessie	S	Cashier	
Lamport	Mary	M	Saleslady	Y (Saleslady)
Mackley	Mary		Saleslady	

Last name	First name	Marital status	Occupation	Member in 1931?
Maxwell	Violet	M	Cashier	
Norrie	Doris	M	Saleslady	
Parsell	Edith	S	Cashier	
Webb	Mary	M	Saleslady	

Self-Employed

Bell	Margaret	M	Corsetière	
Beveridge	Minnie	S	Milliner	
Carroll	E.I.	M	Lingerie shop	
Connacher	Isabella	S	Photographer	Y (Photographer)
Cooper	Rozella	M	Café owner	
Costar	Winnifred	M	Dressmaker	
Curry	Mabel	M	Milliner (retired)	
Darling	Dollie	M	Hairdresser (owns shop)	Y (Store owner)
Gibson	Marjorie	S	Photographer	
Harvey	Bernice	S	Dressmaker	
Heeney	Dorothy	M	Milliner	
Macdonald	Norma	M	Hotel prop.	
Mallek	Alice	M	Ladies' wear (owns shop)	
McMartin		M	Leather goods (shop)	Y (Leather goods)
More	Bessie	M	Milliner	
Morrison	Cecilia	M	Dressmaker	
Nichols	Kily	M	Caterer	
Pearce	Winifred	M	Café owner	
Rose	Sonia	M	Jewellery store	Y (Saleslady)
Sparks	Edith		Milliner	
Vautrin	Erma	M	Hotel prop.	
Woodward	Barbara	M	Artist and author	
York	Elizabeth	S	Café owner (retired)	

Other (occupational status unkown)

Abbott	I.M.	M	Post office	Y (Saleslady)
Brown	Mae		YWCA	
Dodds	Pamela	M	Music teacher	
Fitz	Eileen	M	Hairdresser	
Germaine	Jessie	S	Dietician (retired)	
Gibbon	Marjorie	S	Designer	
Kitts	Ethel	S	Pharmacist	
McLean	M.V.	M	Real estate	
McNaughton	Florence	M	Doctor's directory	
Press	Marjorie	S	Employment	
Rayfuse	Winifred	M	Rentals	

Last name	First name	Marital status	Occupation	Member in 1931?
Richards	Elsie	S	Real estate	Y (Insurance)
Walls	Doris	M	Retired	
Wilson	Violet	S	Radio	

SOURCE: "Membership List, Victoria Business and Professional Women's Club, 1948," BPW Club Records, 89-1386-2, British Columbia Archives.

Notes

Chapter 1: Businesswomen in British Columbia

1 Joy Parr, "The Skilled Emigrant and Her Kin: Gender, Culture, and Labour Recruitment," *Canadian Historical Review* 68, 4 (December 1987): 530.
2 Wendy Gamber, "A Gendered Enterprise: Placing Nineteenth-Century Businesswomen in History," *Business History Review* 72, 2 (Summer 1998): 190.
3 See David Burley, *A Particular Condition in Life: Self-Employment and Social Mobility in Mid-Victorian Brantford, Ontario* (Montreal/Kingston: McGill-Queen's University Press, 1994), 236. While Burley makes the connection here between manliness and self-employment, he is certainly not the first or only scholar to do so. Mary A. Yeager states in her introduction to the three-volume collection *Women in Business* that the business world has been made and recorded largely by men. See Yeager, "Introduction," in *Women in Business,* vol. 1, ed. Mary A. Yeager (Northampton, MA: Elgar, 1999), ix-x.
4 Marjory Lang and Linda Hale, "Women of the *World* and Other Dailies: The Lives and Times of Vancouver Newspaperwomen in the First Quarter of the Twentieth Century," *BC Studies,* no. 85 (Spring 1990): 4-5.
5 Gay Page, cited in Lang and Hale, "Women of the *World* and Other Dailies," 5.
6 The small population of white women in colonial British Columbia prior to 1901 is dealt with by Adele Perry, *On the Edge of Empire: Gender, Race, and the Making of British Columbia, 1849-1871* (Toronto: University of Toronto Press, 2001). Her book provides an excellent analysis of gender and of women's "place" in colonial British Columbia.
7 Ibid., 193. My study focuses primarily on white women in British Columbia. While First Nations women often worked in jobs that can be described as entrepreneurial, they were not conceptualized as entrepreneurs and they were also poorly recorded in the census. Later in this chapter, I address the issue of race and entrepreneurship in more detail.
8 Bride ships contained young single women, "living freight ... destined for the colonial and matrimonial market," as the *British Colonist* described them upon their arrival in Victoria,

British Columbia, in September 1862. The arrival is also described in N. de Bertrand Lugrin, *The Pioneer Women of Vancouver Island, 1843-1866* (Victoria: Women's Canadian Club, 1928), 146-49. For more on the story of the women's arrival on the first so-called bride ship, the *Tynemouth,* see also Jackie Lay, "To Columbia on the Tynemouth: The Emigration of Single Women and Girls in 1862," in *In Her Own Right: Selected Essays on Women's History in BC,* ed. Barbara Latham and Cathy Kess (Victoria: Camosun College, 1980), 19-41.

9   The Canadian Families Project database, based on a 5 percent sample of the 1901 census, allowed for a very thorough examination of census data: it is now available for public use at http://web.uvic.ca/hrd/cfp/what/index.html.

10 Chris Clarkson, *Domestic Reforms: Political Visions and Family Regulation in British Columbia, 1862-1940* (Vancouver: UBC Press, 2007), 7.

11 Ibid.

12 Ibid., 45.

13 Ibid., 100-1. Here, Clarkson cites Peter Baskerville, "Women and Investment in Late-Nineteenth-Century Urban Canada: Victoria and Hamilton, 1880-1901," *Canadian Historical Review* 80, 2 (June 1999): 191-218.

14 Clarkson, *Domestic Reforms,* 111.

15 My PhD dissertation, which covers the years from 1901 to 1971, reveals some of the changes occurring in the second half of the century. See Melanie Buddle, "The Business of Women: Gender, Family, and Entrepreneurship in British Columbia, 1901-1971" (PhD diss., University of Victoria, 2003).

16 See Barbara Latham and Cathy Kess, eds., *In Her Own Right: Selected Essays on Women's History in BC* (Victoria: Camosun College, 1980); Barbara Latham and Roberta Pazdro, eds., *Not Just Pin Money: Selected Essays on the History of Women's Work in British Columbia* (Victoria: Camosun College, 1984); and Gillian Creese and Veronica Strong-Boag, eds., *British Columbia Reconsidered: Essays on Women* (Vancouver: Press Gang Publishers, 1992).

17 Lindsey McMaster, *Working Girls in the West: Representations of Wage-Earning Women* (Vancouver: UBC Press, 2007).

18 See Creese and Strong-Boag, *British Columbia Reconsidered,* and their article "Taking Gender into Account in British Columbia: More Than Just Women's Studies," *BC Studies,* nos. 105-6 (Spring/Summer 1995).

19 Sylvia Van Kirk, "A Vital Presence: Women in the Cariboo Gold Rush, 1862-1875," in *British Columbia Reconsidered,* ed. Creese and Strong-Boag, 22.

20 Peter Baskerville, "'She Has Already Hinted at Board': Enterprising Urban Women in British Columbia, 1863-1896," *Histoire sociale/Social History* 26, 52 (November 1993): 208. Baskerville has also examined women and credit, and women and investment, and he has noted the prominence of female entrepreneurs in British Columbia in this research. See Baskerville, "Women and Investment in Late-Nineteenth-Century Urban Canada," 191-218. See also Baskerville, "Familiar Strangers: Urban Families with Boarders, Canada, 1901," *Social Science History* 25 (2001): 321-46.

21 Baskerville, "'She Has Already Hinted at Board'," 205.

22 Ibid., 226. See also Baskerville, "Women and Investment in Late-Nineteenth-Century Urban Canada," 191.

23 For a good examination of one kind of self-employment, in just one city, see Jean Barman, "Vancouver's Forgotten Entrepreneurs: Women Who Ran Their Own Schools," *British Columbia Historical News* 31, 4 (Fall 1998): 21-29. Small mentions of businesswomen and

short biographies of female entrepreneurs can be found in other sources, but these are not thorough treatments of gender and self-employment. See Alexander Freund and Laura Quilici, "Exploring Myths in Women's Narratives: Italian and German Immigrant Women in Vancouver, 1947-1961," *BC Studies*, nos. 105-6 (Spring/Summer 1995): 159-82; Cathy Converse, *Mainstays: Women Who Shaped BC* (Victoria: Horsdal and Schubart, 1998); Lang and Hale, "Women of the *World* and Other Dailies," 3-23; Rosemary Neering, *Wild West Women: Travellers, Adventurers and Rebels* (Vancouver: Whitecap Books, 2000). For a good study of gender imbalance and women's social position, see Perry, *On the Edge of Empire*.

24 Robin Fisher, "Matters for Reflection: *BC Studies* and British Columbia History," *BC Studies*, no. 100 (Winter 1993-94): 64.

25 John Douglas Belshaw, "The West We Have Lost: British Columbia's Demographic Past and an Agenda for Population History," *Western Historical Quarterly* 29, 1 (Spring 1998): 42. It should be noted that Belshaw is one of a limited number of historians who have not dismissed the roles of female entrepreneurs in British Columbia's history. In his book about the coalfields and miners of Vancouver Island, he includes examples of women running businesses in coal-mining towns and credits them as entrepreneurs in their own right. See Belshaw, *Colonization and Community: The Vancouver Island Coalfield and the Making of the British Columbian Working Class* (Montreal/Kingston: McGill-Queen's University Press, 2002).

26 Yeager, "Introduction," xxii. Yeager also wrote the first chapter (titled "Will There Ever Be a Feminist Business History?") of her collection *Women in Business*. It is a useful survey of some of the main challenges to incorporating the "experiences of women in business" into "the history of business." See Yeager, "Will There Ever Be a Feminist Business History?" in *Women in Business*, 31.

27 Gamber, "A Gendered Enterprise," 192.

28 Ibid.

29 Joan Wallach Scott, *Gender and the Politics of History* (New York: Columbia University Press, 1988), 41. The chapter cited here is titled "Gender: A Useful Category of Historical Analysis" and was first published as an article in the *American Historical Review* 91, 5 (December 1986).

30 Joan Wallach Scott, "Comment: Conceptualizing Gender in American Business History," *Business History Review* 72, 2 (Summer 1998): 242.

31 Ibid.

32 Yeager, "Introduction," xiii.

33 Ibid.

34 Wendy Gamber, *The Female Economy: The Millinery and Dressmaking Trades, 1860-1930* (Urbana: University of Illinois Press, 1997). Her articles are also extremely useful for anyone interested in gender and entrepreneurship. See "A Gendered Enterprise," mentioned above, as well as Gamber, "A Precarious Independence: Milliners and Dressmakers in Boston, 1860-1890," *Journal of Women's History* 4, 1 (Spring 1992): 60-88; and Gamber, "Gendered Concerns: Thoughts on the History of Business and the History of Women," *Business and Economic History* 23, 1 (Fall 1994): 129-140.

35 See Angel Kwolek-Folland, *Engendering Business: Men and Women in the Corporate Office, 1870-1930* (Baltimore: Johns Hopkins University Press, 1994); and Kwolek-Folland, *Incorporating Women: A History of Women and Business in the United States* (New York: Twayne, 1998), 11.

36 Kwolek-Folland, *Incorporating Women*, 11.

37   As Gamber articulates, Stimson, the author of the phrase "school of manhood," and many
     other men of his day linked the characteristics of business success – ambition, assertiveness,
     competitiveness – to masculinity. But she also notes that scholars have followed in Stimson's
     footsteps, using the phrase unwittingly. Gamber, "A Gendered Enterprise," 191.
38   Ibid.
39   Michael Bliss, *Northern Enterprise: Five Centuries of Canadian Business* (Toronto: Mc-
     Clelland and Stewart, 1987). See back jacket of 1990 paperback edition.
40   Ibid., 351. Bliss is here referring to family dynasties of the early 1900s. However, he also
     dismisses the existence of businesswomen in the 1960s: see Bliss, *Northern Enterprise*,
     502.
41   Ibid., 352.
42   Graham Taylor and Peter Baskerville, *A Concise History of Business in Canada* (Toronto:
     Oxford University Press, 1994).
43   Peter Baskerville, *A Silent Revolution? Gender and Wealth in English Canada, 1860-1930*
     (Montreal/Kingston: McGill-Queen's University Press, 2008).
44   John Benson, *The Penny Capitalists: A Study of Nineteenth-Century Working-Class Entre-
     preneurs* (New Brunswick, NJ: Rutgers University Press, 1983), 6.
45   John Benson, *Entrepreneurism in Canada: A History of "Penny Capitalists"* (Lewiston, NY:
     E. Mellen Press, 1990), 77, 86.
46   Bettina Bradbury, "Pigs, Cows, and Boarders: Non-Wage Forms of Survival among
     Montreal Families, 1861-91," in *The Challenge of Modernity: A Reader on Post-Confederation
     Canada*, ed. Ian McKay (Toronto: McGraw-Hill Ryerson, 1992), 68. For a more detailed
     treatment of non-wage survival in Montreal, see Bettina Bradbury, *Working Families:
     Age, Gender, and Daily Survival in Industrializing Montreal* (Toronto: McClelland and
     Stewart, 1993).
47   Scott, "Comment," 242.
48   Ibid., 243.
49   Franca Iacovetta and Mariana Valverde, eds., "Introduction," in *Gender Conflicts: New
     Essays in Women's History*, ed. Iacovetta and Valverde (Toronto: University of Toronto Press,
     1992), xix.
50   Ibid., xviii.
51   Gisela Bock, "Women's History and Gender History: Aspects of an International Debate,"
     Gender and History 1, 1 (Spring 1989): 16.
52   Iacovetta and Valverde, *Gender Conflicts*, xvi. Note: the Introduction is written collect-
     ively by all of the authors whose essays are included in the book.
53   Gamber, "A Gendered Enterprise," 193.
54   Yeager, "Introduction," xxi.
55   Gamber, "A Gendered Enterprise," 196.
56   Anthony Giddens and David Held, *Classes, Power, and Conflict: Classical and Contempor-
     ary Debates* (Berkeley: University of California Press, 1982), 20-25.
57   Bertell Ollman, "Marx's Use of 'Class,'" *Dialectical Marxism: The Writings of Bertell Ollman*,
     http://www.nyu.edu/projects/ollman/docs/class.php. See also, of course, Karl Marx, *Cap-
     ital* (Moscow: Foreign Languages Publishing House, 1957); and Karl Marx and Friedrich
     Engels, *The Communist Manifesto*, trans. Samuel Moore (Chicago: Charles H. Kerr, 1945).
58   Scott, "Comment," 247.
59   Gamber, "A Gendered Enterprise," 195.

60　Gamber uses this term, and it is appropriate since women's businesses were much smaller than men's businesses: see "A Gendered Enterprise," 195. John Benson's definition of penny capitalists would also suffice: see *The Penny Capitalists,* 6.

61　Gamber, "A Gendered Enterprise," 193.

62　Catherine A. Cavanaugh and Randi R. Warne, "Introduction," in *Telling Tales: Essays in Western Women's History,* ed. Catherine A. Cavanaugh and Randi R. Warne (Vancouver: UBC Press, 2000), 13.

63　See the Canadian Families Project database, based on a 5 percent sample of the 1901 census (http://web.uvic.ca/hrd/cfp/data/index.html). Note: one of the difficulties with using the information on First Nations women who declared that they were self-employed is that they were poorly enumerated. Census takers in 1901 did not reliably record their age, marital status, or even their names, making it harder to rely on the census to glean information about these self-employed women.

64　Canada, Dominion Bureau of Statistics, *Census of Canada 1931,* vol. 11, tables 1a and 1b.

65　*Wrigley's British Columbia Directory, 1918* (Vancouver: Wrigley Directories, 1918). Other sources, such as the Okanagan Historical Society's Reports, provide stories of Asian businesswomen such as Sue Lee Ping Wong. Mrs. Wong moved to Kelowna in the 1930s. Her second husband died in 1960, leaving her with eleven children. She supported her family by making and selling tofu. See Tun Wong, "Sue Lee Ping Wong," *Okanagan History: The Sixty-Third Report of the Okanagan Historical Society* 63 (1999): 156-159.

66　Tomoko Makabe, *Picture Brides: Japanese Women in Canada,* trans. Kathleen Chisato Merken (Toronto: Multicultural History Society of Ontario, 1995), 80.

67　Ibid., 85.

68　In 1942, Mrs. Murata was forced to leave Vancouver for the "ghost town" of Slocan as part of the Japanese Canadian relocation or internment during the war. It was this uprooting that led to the closure of her business.

69　Makabe, *Picture Brides,* 83.

70　See Freund and Quilici, "Exploring Myths in Women's Narratives," 159-82. This article is not solely about entrepreneurial women, but it does recount the stories of Italian women who worked as boarding-house keepers.

71　The Canadian Families Project's database for the 1901 census would allow for a more detailed analysis of race and racial categories of people of different employment statuses, for instance. But the sample size of 5 percent is too small for such subdivisions to be useful for a study of self-employed women.

72　*Henderson's British Columbia Gazetteer and Directory and Mining Companies with which is Consolidated the Williams' British Columbia Directory for 1900-1901* (Victoria and Vancouver: Henderson Publishing, 1901). One difficulty with comparing directories to census data is that the directories do not definitively indicate whether a woman was self-employed. On the other hand, women listed as proprietors in city directories were not always enumerated by census takers as self-employed. The 1900-1 directory shows many women operating hotels and selling dry goods, fruits, and tobacco. Some may have been running stores that were owned by someone else. In Vancouver alone I found a widowed restaurant owner, at least five music and vocal teachers, four women running dry goods and grocery stores, and a number of hotel owners. In Victoria, there were close to ten hotels with female "proprietresses." Again, that they ran the hotels is not proof that they owned them, which may help explain why so few female-run hotels appear in the 5 percent sample of the 1901 census.

Chapter 2: The Marriage of Business and Women

1   Chris Clarkson, *Domestic Reforms: Political Visions and Family Regulation in British Columbia, 1862-1940* (Vancouver: UBC Press, 2007), 115-16. Clarkson questions the efficacy of the law, suggesting it was rarely applied effectively, which corroborates my findings that high numbers of self-employed women were married but to men who no longer lived with or supported them or their children. If these men had been paying support, these single mothers might not have opened businesses.

2   Carolyn Strange, *Toronto's Girl Problem: The Perils and Pleasures of the City, 1880-1930* (Toronto: University of Toronto Press, 1995), 3. Strange uses the phrase "working girl" extensively to describe the archetypal working girl of urban centres, the young single wage-earning woman. The term has also been used as a euphemism for prostitutes, but Strange, and also Christine Stansell, differentiate between prostitutes and working girls, although Stansell notes that some women were both. See Christine Stansell, *City of Women: Sex and Class in New York, 1789-1860* (New York: Alfred A. Knopf, 1986), 97 and 181. In a British Columbia context, Lindsey McMaster also addresses the growing number of young working girls in the labour force and how they became the focus of intense public debate in the early twentieth century. Lindsey McMaster, *Working Girls in the West: Representations of Wage-Earning Women* (Vancouver: UBC Press, 2007).

3   Wendy Gamber, "Gendered Concerns: Thoughts on the History of Business and the History of Women," *Business and Economic History* 23, 1 (Fall 1994): 129.

4   Mary A. Yeager, "Introduction," in *Women in Business,* vol. 1, ed. Mary A. Yeager (Northampton, MA: Elgar, 1999), xvii.

5   John Douglas Belshaw calls this the thorny issue of First Nations' demographic history and suggests that our sense of the pre-contact population and its subsequent decline is still based on what he calls "impressionistic guesstimates." This, he argues, means that much of the meaning of the province's history suffers from an "inadequate contextual setting." See John Douglas Belshaw, "The West We Have Lost: British Columbia's Demographic Past and an Agenda for Population History," *Western Historical Quarterly* 29, 1 (Spring 1998): 40. Cole Harris and Robin Fisher have also speculated on – and differed in their conclusions about – First Nations population decline and recovery rates. See Cole Harris, *The Resettlement of British Columbia: Essays on Colonialism and Geographical Change* (Vancouver: UBC Press, 1997); and Robin Fisher, *Contact and Conflict: Indian-European Relations in British Columbia, 1774-1890,* 2nd ed. (Vancouver: UBC Press, 1992).

6   Canada, Census Office, *Census of Canada 1901.*

7   In 1901, 12.2 percent of all adult women in British Columbia worked for pay, compared to 14.5 percent in the rest of Canada. In ongoing years, the percentages were as follows: 1911, 15 percent (BC) and 13.9 percent (Canada); 1921, 14.2 percent (BC) and 15.3 percent (Canada); 1931, 17.2 percent (BC) and 17 percent (Canada); 1941, 18.2 percent (BC) and 20.3 percent (Canada); 1951, 23 percent (BC) and 23.7 percent (Canada). Note that I have removed British Columbia data from the Canadian data in order to present British Columbia compared to the rest of Canada. Here, as in all other data presented in my research, data for 1901 is from the Canadian Families Project database, based on a 5 percent sample of the 1901 census (http://web.uvic.ca/hrd/cfp/data/index.html). For labour force characteristics, 1911 to 1951, see Canada, Dominion Bureau of Statistics, *Census of Canada 1931,* vol. 1, table 82, and vol. 7, tables 1 and 40; *Census of Canada 1941,* vol. 1, table 58, and vol. 3, table 1; and *Census of Canada 1951,* vol. 4, table 1.

8 The archetypal elements of frontiers in general, and the British Columbia frontier in particular, are dealt with more extensively elsewhere. See Melanie Buddle, "'All the Elements of a Permanent Community': A History of Society, Culture and Entertainment in the Cariboo" (master's thesis, University of Northern British Columbia, 1997). See also Barry M. Gough, "The Character of the British Columbia Frontier," *BC Studies*, no. 32 (Winter 1976-77): 28-40; and S.D. Clark, *The Developing Canadian Community*, 2nd ed. (Toronto: University of Toronto Press, 1968), 82.

9 Jean Barman, *Constance Lindsay Skinner: Writing on the Frontier* (Toronto: University of Toronto Press, 2002), 10.

10 Harris, *The Resettlement of British Columbia*, 102, 142-45, and 159. For more on early British Columbia's resource-based economy and immigration, particularly of men seeking work, see Hugh J.M. Johnston, "Native People, Settlers and Sojourners, 1871-1916," and Allen Seager, "The Resource Economy, 1871-1921," in *The Pacific Province: A History of British Columbia*, ed. Hugh J.M. Johnston (Vancouver: Douglas and McIntyre, 1996).

11 Harris, *The Resettlement of British Columbia*, 172.

12 Ibid., 179.

13 Ibid., 192.

14 Ibid. Chapter 6 is entitled "The Struggle with Distance."

15 For data on total adult population, gainfully employed adult population, and marital status of adult population, see Canada, Dominion Bureau of Statistics, *Census of Canada 1921*, vol. 2, table 24; *Census of Canada 1931*, vol. 1, table 17B; vol. 7, tables 25-29; *Census of Canada 1941*, vol. 1, tables 20 and 63; vol. 3, table 7; vol. 7, table 5; *Census of Canada 1951*, vol. 2, tables 1 and 2; vol. 4, table 11. Data for 1901 is from the Canadian Families Project database. For my figures, I have taken British Columbia data out of Canadian totals in order to compare the province to the rest of the country. Limited data is available for 1911; it is found in comparative historical statistics in 1941 and 1951 census volumes and tables listed here.

16 Data on Canadian figures is taken from the same census tables listed in endnote 15.

17 Elizabeth Herr, "Women, Marital Status, and Work Opportunities in 1880 Colorado," *Journal of Economic History* 55, 2 (June 1995): 340-41.

18 Adele Perry, "Oh I'm Just Sick of the Faces of Men: Gender Imbalance, Race, Sexuality, and Sociability in Nineteenth-Century British Columbia," *BC Studies*, nos. 105-6 (Spring/ Summer 1995): 28. See also Adele Perry, *On the Edge of Empire: Gender, Race, and the Making of British Columbia, 1849-1871* (Toronto: University of Toronto Press, 2001), especially Chapters 6 and 7.

19 R. Byron Johnson, cited in Perry, "Gender Imbalance," 38.

20 That is, a higher proportion of adult women were married in the province than in the rest of the country in every census year between 1901 and 1951 for which data is available. Data for 1911 is not available, but in 1921, 65.9 percent of all adult women were married in British Columbia, compared to 58.7 percent in the rest of Canada; by 1951, 69.1 percent of all adult women in British Columbia were married, compared to 64.1 percent in the rest of Canada. Data for 1901 is from the Canadian Families Project database; all other data is from the published census of Canada, 1921-71. See endnote 15 for specific census volume and table numbers. Note that I have removed BC numbers from Canadian totals in the figures presented here.

21 Percentage of all adult women who were single: 1901, 33.9 percent (BC) and 47.1 percent (Canada). Data for 1911 is not available. 1921: 25.5 percent (BC) and 32.4 percent (Canada).

1931: 28.7 percent (BC) and 34.4 percent (Canada). 1941: 26.5 percent (BC) and 33 percent (Canada). 1951: 19.2 percent (BC) and 26.3 percent (Canada). I have removed BC numbers from Canadian totals in the figures presented here. See endnote 15 for specific census volumes and table numbers.

22 Perry, *On the Edge of Empire*, 145. Perry's book provides a more nuanced analysis of the role of white women in the settlement of British Columbia. Despite their scarcity and, therefore, their "value," the women who immigrated in the 1860s and 1870s did not always benefit from their position. Perry notes that it is hard to reconcile some women's sad marital histories "with boosterism about white women's choice spot in the marriage market." See Perry, *On the Edge of Empire*, 139, 167, 172.

23 Peter Baskerville, "Women and Investment in Late-Nineteenth-Century Urban Canada: Victoria and Hamilton, 1880-1901," *Canadian Historical Review* 80, 2 (June 1999): 205.

24 On this phenomenon in nineteenth-century British Columbia, see Perry, "Oh I'm Just Sick of the Faces of Men." Charlene Porsild points to the same frontier characteristics, including low numbers of women and their high rates of marriage, in the case of the Yukon between 1896 and 1905. See Charlene Porsild, *Gamblers and Dreamers: Women, Men, and Community in the Klondike* (Vancouver: UBC Press, 1998), 14-20.

25 See endnote 7 for references and for data on adult women's labour force participation in each census year, 1901 to 1951.

26 For example, for adult men, rates of self-employment in British Columbia were 26.9 percent in 1901, 22.4 percent in 1931, and 17.8 percent in 1951. The rates in the rest of the country were consistently higher: 40.8 percent in 1901, 29.3 percent in 1931, and 24.2 percent in 1951. Sources for male self-employment figures are the same as those listed in the previous note for female self-employment.

27 Seager, "The Resource Economy, 1871-1921," 238-39.

28 Canada, Dominion Bureau of Statistics, *Census of Canada 1921*, vol. 4, table 4; and *Census of Canada 1951*, vol. 4, table 11.

29 Johnston, "Native People, Settlers and Sojourners, 1871-1916," 182. Chinese men who worked as domestics often lived together in boarding houses; an informal census of Victoria in 1871, taken by a police constable, revealed that over one-third of households in Victoria housed only men and also noted a high number of Chinese, all-male households. See Perry, *On the Edge of Empire*, 22. Using the Canadian Families Project database, I also found examples in the 1901 census of boarding houses operated by Chinese men.

30 Johnston, "Native People, Settlers and Sojourners, 1871-1916," 182-83.

31 See, for example, Joy Parr, *The Gender of Breadwinners: Women, Men, and Change in Two Industrial Towns, 1880-1950* (Toronto: University of Toronto Press, 1990); Bettina Bradbury, *Working Families: Age, Gender, and Daily Survival in Industrializing Montreal* (Toronto: McClelland and Stewart, 1993); and, in an American context, Joanne Meyerowitz, *Women Adrift: Independent Wage Earners in Chicago, 1880-1930* (Chicago: University of Chicago Press, 1988); and Stansell, *City of Women*. All of them mention the age and marital status of working women, and the latter two also deal with prescriptive literature on the "girl problem," produced by middle-class social reformers who noted the increase in the number of young single girls working in urban centres in the late nineteenth century.

32 Selected occupations were those that had higher than average rates of self-employment and that employed 15 or more women: over 20 jobs were included. I then looked at the marital status of all these workers, comparing it to the marital status for all gainfully

employed women in the province in 1931. The list of selected occupations and the numbers used to calculate these percentages can be found in Melanie Buddle, "The Business of Women: Gender, Family, and Entrepreneurship in British Columbia, 1901-1971" (PhD diss., University of Victoria, 2003), Appendix 2.3, 367.

33 Canada, Dominion Bureau of Statistics, *Census of Canada 1931*, vol. 7, tables 50 and 54; *Census of Canada 1941*, vol. 7, table 5; and *Census of Canada 1951*, vol. 4, table 11. For lists of the selected occupations and for data on employment status and marital status of women workers in British Columbia and the rest of Canada for these years, see Buddle, "The Business of Women," Appendix 2.1-2.4, 360-78.

34 *Wrigley's British Columbia Directory, 1918* (Vancouver: Wrigley Directories, 1918).

35 See Clarkson, *Domestic Reforms,* and see also my discussion in Chapter 1 of the effect of married women's property laws on business ownership.

36 In 1901, 4.9 percent of all married women in British Columbia worked for pay, compared to 2.9 percent in the rest of Canada. In 1931, 4.3 percent of married women in the province worked for pay, compared to 3.4 percent in the rest of Canada, and in 1951, 13.3 percent of married women in British Columbia worked, compared to 11.0 percent in Canada. This data is calculated from the 5 percent sample of the 1901 census and from published census data on marital status of adults and gainfully employed adults: see endnote 15 for references.

37 Herr, "Women, Marital Status, and Work Opportunities in 1880 Colorado," 341.

38 Ibid., 347.

39 Sylvia Van Kirk, "A Vital Presence: Women in the Cariboo Gold Rush, 1862-1875," in *British Columbia Reconsidered,* ed. Gillian Creese and Veronica Strong-Boag (Vancouver: Press Gang Publishers, 1992), 21-22.

40 Ibid., 22.

41 Ibid., 24. Again, given that married women could not own property until 1873, entrepreneurship was a statement and a reality, but perhaps not a legal reality. It would be interesting to examine legal or business records for women in British Columbia who claimed they owned their own businesses before 1873: what did claiming self-employment mean, legally, if married women could not own property in the Cariboo gold rush period, for example?

42 Herr, "Women, Marital Status, and Work Opportunities in 1880 Colorado," 359-60.

43 Porsild, *Gamblers and Dreamers,* 63-64.

44 Ibid., 68-69.

45 *Henderson's British Columbia Gazetteer and Directory, 1905* (Victoria and Vancouver: Henderson Publishing, 1905).

46 Ibid.

47 Canada, Dominion Bureau of Statistics, *Census of Canada 1901,* vol. 1, xviii.

48 Data for 1901 is taken from the Canadian Families Project database. Other data on household heads comes from the published census. See Canada, Dominion Bureau of Statistics, *Census of Canada 1921,* vol. 3, table 25; *Census of Canada 1931,* vol. 1, tables 4 and 98, and vol. 5, table 92; *Census of Canada 1941,* vol. 5, table 19; and *Census of Canada 1961,* Series 2.1, Catalogue 93-512, tables 27 and 31.

49 Information about these women, and other 1901 examples mentioned in this chapter, was taken from the Canadian Families Project's sample of the 1901 census.

50 Rosemary Neering, *Wild West Women: Travellers, Adventurers and Rebels* (Vancouver: Whitecap Books, 2000), 228.

51 This is speculative. It is also possible that George Seel was listed as household head, since he did reside there normally, and they were not separated.

52 Olive Fredrickson, with Ben East, *Silence of the North* (Toronto: General Publishing, 1972), 10. Fredrickson's story is also told in Neering, *Wild West Women,* 145-52.

53 Neering, *Wild West Women,* 149.

54 Claudia Goldin, *Understanding the Gender Gap: An Economic History of American Women* (Oxford: Oxford University Press, 1990), 133.

55 Susan Householder Van Horn, *Women, Work, and Fertility, 1900-1986* (New York: New York University Press, 1988), 64.

56 Van Kirk, "A Vital Presence," 25.

57 That is, when all married women are compared to all widowed or divorced women, a higher proportion of the widowed or divorced women worked, compared to the married group: 18 to 26 percent of all widowed or divorced women were in the labour force between 1901 and 1951 – the numbers were similar in each decade, although slightly higher in the province than in the rest of the country. Between 2 and 5 percent of all married women worked between 1901 and 1941, again in both British Columbia and the rest of Canada, although the percentage was always higher in British Columbia. Many more married women were in the labour force in 1951 – 13.3 percent in British Columbia and 11 percent in Canada – but this rate of participation was still less than that of widowed or divorced women in 1951. All of this data is calculated from the census tables referred to in endnote 15, this chapter.

58 Bettina Bradbury, "Surviving as a Widow in 19th-Century Montreal," *Urban History Review* 17, 3 (February 1989): 150.

59 Ibid.

60 Lorna R. McLean, "Single Again: Widow's Work in the Urban Family Economy, Ottawa, 1871," *Ontario History* 83, 2 (June 1991): 131.

61 On this point, McLean cites Diane Farmer, "Widowhood in the Parish of Notre Dame: An Examination of Death and Remarriage in Mid-Nineteenth-Century Lower Town" (master's research essay, Carleton University, 1981).

62 Jean Barman, "Vancouver's Forgotten Entrepreneurs: Women Who Ran Their Own Schools," *British Columbia Historical News* 31, 4 (Fall 1998): 27.

63 Jean Barman, *Sojourning Sisters: The Lives and Letters of Jessie and Annie McQueen* (Toronto: University of Toronto Press, 2003), 214-15.

64 Most studies of widowhood do not, for obvious reasons, focus on remarriage, because widowed women were no longer widows if they remarried. McLean notes that widowed women had "few choices," and she implies that remarriage was rarely one of them. Her article illustrates the economic measures that widows turned to in order to survive, including home-based enterprises such as taking in sewing or boarders. See McLean, "Single Again," 140.

65 Ibid., 133.

66 *Henderson's British Columbia Gazetteer and Directory and Mining Companies with Which Is Consolidated the Williams' British Columbia Directory for 1900-1901* (Victoria and Vancouver: Henderson Publishing, 1901). Mayo was the given name of Whitney's deceased husband.

67 Bradbury, *Working Families,* 199.

68 Lisa Wilson Waciega, "A 'Man of Business': The Widow of Means in Southeastern Pennsylvania, 1750-1850," *William and Mary Quarterly* 44 (1987): 60.

69 Bradbury, *Working Families,* 197-98.

70 Baskerville, "Women and Investment," 195.

71 Wendy Gamber, "A Precarious Independence: Milliners and Dressmakers in Boston, 1860-1890," *Journal of Women's History* 4, 1 (Spring 1992): 74.

72 Margaret Hobbs, "Gendering Work and Welfare: Women's Relationship to Wage-Work and Social Policy in Canada during the Great Depression" (PhD diss., University of Toronto, 1995), 41.

73 Ibid., 48.

74 Cited in Margaret Hobbs, "Equality and Difference: Feminism and the Defence of Women Workers during the Great Depression," in *Canadian Women: A Reader,* ed. Wendy Mitchinson et al. (Toronto: Harcourt Brace, 1996), 226.

75 *Prince Rupert Daily News,* 31 January 1946.

76 Joan Sangster, *Earning Respect: The Lives of Working Women in Small-Town Ontario, 1920-1960* (Toronto: University of Toronto Press, 1995), 79.

77 Ibid., 78.

78 Hobbs, "Gendering Work and Welfare," 49.

79 See Barman, "Vancouver's Forgotten Entrepreneurs," 24. Three of the six women who founded the school had husbands.

80 Beatrix Potter, *The Tale of Benjamin Bunny* (London: Frederick Warne, 1993), n.p. First published in 1904 by Frederick Warne.

81 Young women with children could also become entrepreneurs, but census data demonstrates that young women were a minority among the self-employed.

82 Lisa Wilson, *Life after Death: Widows in Pennsylvania, 1750-1850* (Philadelphia: Temple University Press, 1992), 1.

83 Jane Addams, *Democracy and Social Ethics* (New York: Macmillan, 1916). First published in 1902.

84 Angel Kwolek-Folland, *Incorporating Women: A History of Women and Business in the United States* (New York: Twayne, 1998), 45. Kwolek-Folland is in this case referring to early-nineteenth-century women, but the point remains valid into the twentieth century.

85 Julie A. Matthaei, *An Economic History of Women in America: Women's Work, the Sexual Division of Labor, and the Development of Capitalism* (New York: Schocken Books, 1982), 224.

86 Lucy Eldersveld Murphy, "Business Ladies: Midwestern Women and Enterprise, 1850-1880," *Journal of Women's History* 3, 1 (Spring 1991): 71.

87 Van Horn, *Women, Work, and Fertility,* 8.

88 Matthaei, *An Economic History of Women,* 214.

89 Kwolek-Folland, *Incorporating Women,* 8.

90 And will be said: see Chapter 3.

91 Van Horn, *Women, Work, and Fertility,* 29.

92 Matthaei, *An Economic History of Women,* 65.

93 Murphy, "Business Ladies," 70-71.

94 See Chuck Davis, ed., *The Greater Vancouver Book: An Urban Encyclopaedia* (Surrey, BC: Linkman Press, 1997), 240, 811; and E.O.J. Scholefield and F. W. Howay, *British Columbia from Earliest Times to the Present,* vol. 4 (Vancouver: S.J. Clarke, 1914), 928-32.

95 Bettina Bradbury deals with family economies, poverty, and the financial vulnerability of widows, in particular, in nineteenth-century Montreal in *Working Families.*

96 Goldin, *Understanding the Gender Gap,* 181.

97 Ibid., 184.
98 That is, the rates of self-employment in these five occupations are higher than the rates of self-employment in all occupations. In 1921, 70 percent of dressmakers and sewers were self-employed, while the overall self-employment rate for all women in the labour force in that year was 10.5 percent. See Canada, Dominion Bureau of Statistics, *Census of Canada 1921*, vol. 4, table 4; and *Census of Canada 1931*, vol. 13, table 29.
99 Canada, Dominion Bureau of Statistics, *Census of Canada 1921*, vol. 4, xli.
100 Canada, Dominion Bureau of Statistics, *Census of Canada 1931*, vol. 7, table 40. Note that the age groups used in the aggregate data were not uniform. The 20- to 24-years age group, a four-year age group, was followed by nine-year age groups: 25-34, 35-44, and so on, up to age 65, when another four-year age group was used for ages 65 to 69. The last age group used was for 70 years of age and over.
101 Canada, Dominion Bureau of Statistics, *Census of Canada 1931*, vol. 7, table 40.
102 Matthaei, *An Economic History of Women*, 51-53.
103 Debra Michals, "Toward a New History of the Postwar Economy: Prosperity, Preparedness, and Women's Small Business Ownership," *Business and Economic History* 26, 1 (Fall 1997): 50-51.
104 Ibid., 48.
105 Justine Mansfield, "Can the 'Two-Job Woman' Succeed at Home and in Business?" *The Business Woman*, 3, 1 (January 1928), p. 30, Add Mss 799, 588-A-4, City of Vancouver Archives.
106 Ibid., 9.
107 Neering, *Wild West Women*, 26-30. See also Jan Gould, *Women of British Columbia* (Saanichton, BC: Hancock House Publishers, 1975). Gould provides similar biographical information about Jowett.
108 See Chapter 4 for a more thorough discussion of the significance of certain groups of women cross-dressing in the context of social events, or for visual effect, as in this photograph.
109 Neering, *Wild West Women*, 15.
110 Harriet Rochlin, "The Amazing Adventures of a Good Woman," *Journal of the West* 12 (April 1973): 281-95.
111 Neering, *Wild West Women*, 19-26. Neering does not mention Cashman's nieces and nephews at all. I suspect they were either nearly grown and did not need her presence or were not living with her long enough to affect her travels and enterprises.
112 Ibid., 166-69.
113 Ibid., 107-10.
114 Ibid., 12-13.
115 Susan Ingalls Lewis, "Beyond Horatia Alger: Breaking through Gendered Assumptions about Business 'Success' in Mid-Nineteenth-Century America," *Business and Economic History* 24, 1 (Fall 1995): 98.
116 Ibid., 99.

CHAPTER 3: CAREERS FOR WOMEN

1 Many historians have written about women's work cultures. In a Canadian context, see, for example, Joy Parr, *The Gender of Breadwinners: Women, Men, and Change in Two Industrial Towns, 1880-1950* (Toronto: University of Toronto Press, 1990); and Joan Sangster,

Earning Respect: The Lives of Working Women in Small-Town Ontario, 1920-1960 (Toronto: University of Toronto Press, 1995). For a good treatment of women's work culture in an American context, see Patricia Cooper, *Once a Cigar Maker: Men, Women, and Work Culture in American Cigar Factories, 1900-1919* (Urbana: University of Illinois Press, 1987). Historians of women have also explored the idea of women's separate spheres (both at home and at work). For early and seminal discussions of "women's spheres," see Nancy F. Cott, *The Bonds of Womanhood: Women's Sphere in New England, 1780-1835* (New Haven, CT: Yale University Press, 1977); and Carroll Smith-Rosenberg, "The Female World of Love and Ritual," *Signs* 1 (Autumn 1975): 1-29. On the extent to which businesswomen operated in separate female cultures, see Lucy Eldersveld Murphy, "Business Ladies: Midwestern Women and Enterprise, 1850-1880," *Journal of Women's History* 3, 1 (Spring 1991): 65-89; and Wendy Gamber, *The Female Economy: The Millinery and Dressmaking Trades, 1860-1930* (Urbana: University of Illinois Press, 1997).

2 Canada, Dominion Bureau of Statistics, *Census of Canada 1941,* vol. 1, 328.

3 Ibid.

4 The 1921 census listed office employees, clerks, and messengers within their relevant occupational groups but did not list stenographers or typists as specific occupations in any occupational groups. While the 1931 census listed 5,559 female stenographers/typists in British Columbia. See Canada, Dominion Bureau of Statistics, *Census of Canada 1931,* vol. 7, table 50; and *Census of Canada 1921,* vol. 4, table 4.

5 Jeff O'Neill, "Changing Occupational Structure," *Canadian Social Trends* 23 (Winter 1991): 9.

6 For data on occupational groups and the distribution of the female labour force between 1901 and 1951, see Canada, Dominion Bureau of Statistics, *Census of Canada 1951,* vol. 4, table 2. This table provides historical statistics for the first half of the twentieth century. The 1901 data presented here on the female labour force and occupational groups is from the published census and not from the Canadian Families Project sample. In order to compare the provincial situation to that of the rest of the country, data for British Columbia has been removed from Canadian totals in the numbers presented here.

7 In 1901, just 7 percent of the female labour force in British Columbia, and 5 percent in the rest of the country, worked in clerical occupations, but I included this group because from 1911 to 1951 it included high percentages of women workers. The trade/finance category would, like the clerical category, become prominent for women after 1901, but there were few women in that category in 1901. Agriculture was a relatively important category for women – in 1911 in particular, 4.5 percent of the female labour force worked in agriculture – but other than this year, the category included less than 4 percent of all employed women in either British Columbia or the rest of the country.

8 The percentage was almost exactly the same fifty years later, but it was also almost exactly the same in British Columbia as in the rest of Canada. In 1901 and in 1951, 92 percent of the female labour force in British Columbia worked in the same four occupational groups. In the rest of the country, the percentage was 93 percent in 1901 and 92 percent in 1951.

9 Canada, Dominion Bureau of Statistics, *Census of Canada 1951,* vol. 4, table 2. In the trade/finance and clerical occupational groups, the differences were not as big. In 1931 in British Columbia, 11.5 percent of the female labour force worked in trade/finance and 19.9 percent in clerical. In the same year in the rest of Canada, the figures were 8.3 percent and 17.5 percent, respectively. In 1951, 14.6 percent of employed women in the province worked in trade/finance and 30.7 percent in clerical. In the rest of Canada, the numbers

were 10.7 percent and 27.1 percent, respectively. For the service occupations, the difference was also small but steady in that more women worked in service in the province than in the rest of the country: in 1931, 53.3 percent of employed women in British Columbia, and 52 percent in the rest of Canada, worked in service, while in 1951 the numbers were 39 percent in British Columbia and 36 percent in the rest of Canada.

10 For a detailed look at specific jobs done by women at the beginning of the century, see the Canadian Families Project's database, based on a 5 percent sample of the 1901 census of Canada (http://web.uvic.ca/hrd/cfp/data/index.html).

11 Lindsey McMaster, *Working Girls in the West: Representations of Wage-Earning Women* (Vancouver: UBC Press, 2008), 11.

12 Robert A.J. McDonald, *Making Vancouver: Class, Status, and Social Boundaries, 1863-1913* (Vancouver: UBC Press, 1996), 124.

13 Ibid.

14 R.E. Caves and R.H. Holton, "An Outline of the Economic History of British Columbia, 1881-1951," in *Historical Essays on British Columbia*, ed. J. Friesen and H.K. Ralston (Toronto: McClelland and Stewart, 1976), 159. Caves and Holton note that manufacturing grew enormously between 1911 and 1951, and that it became more diverse. The workforce of the province more than doubled between 1911 and 1951, while the service and trade sectors more than tripled in size and the manufacturing sector nearly tripled. Despite this, the growth was still related to fish and fish processing and to pulp, paper, and lumber processing; the growth was not in the processing of new staples but "rather a growth of the processing of the old staples" (159). Caves and Holton also note that from 1939 to 1955 the population of the province rose by a very high 70 percent, a response to employment opportunities in manufacturing sectors. People were employed in logging but also in related wood products industries: in sawmills, plywood and pulp and paper factories, and furniture plants, for example. Thus, even as the population got bigger and employment opportunities diversified, the manufacturing sector remained tied to resource extraction and the processing and exporting of these resources. See Caves and Holton, 159-163.

15 Sylvia Ostry, *The Occupational Composition of the Canadian Labour Force* (Ottawa: Dominion Bureau of Statistics, 1967), 14.

16 Graham Lowe, *Women in the Administrative Revolution: The Feminization of Clerical Work* (Cambridge, UK: Polity Press, 1987), 4.

17 Marsha Courchane and Angela Redish, "Women in the Labour Force, 1911-1986: A Historical Perspective," in *False Promises: The Failure of Conservative Economics*, ed. Robert C. Allen and Gideon Rosenbluth (Vancouver: New Star Books, 1992), 151-53.

18 Canada, Dominion Bureau of Statistics, *Census of Canada 1921*, vol. 4, xiii.

19 Lowe, *Women in the Administrative Revolution*, 11. See also Shirley Tillotson, "'We May All Soon Be First-Class Men': Gender and Skill in Canada's Early Twentieth-Century Urban Telegraph Industry," *Labour/Le Travail* 27 (Spring 1991): 97-125; and Sangster, *Earning Respect*.

20 Lowe, *Women in the Administrative Revolution*, 16.

21 Sangster, *Earning Respect*, 36.

22 Pat Armstrong and Hugh Armstrong, *The Double Ghetto: Canadian Women and Their Segregated Work* (Toronto: McClelland and Stewart, 1978), 39.

23 Ibid., 40.

24 Courchane and Redish, "Women in the Labour Force," 151-52.

25 Wendy Gamber, "A Gendered Enterprise: Placing Nineteenth-Century Businesswomen in History," *Business History Review* 72, 2 (Summer 1998): 204.
26 Ibid., 203-4.
27 Gamber, *The Female Economy*, 2.
28 Kathy Peiss, "'Vital Industry' and Women's Ventures: Conceptualizing Gender in Twentieth-Century Business History," *Business History Review* 72, 2 (Summer 1998): 224.
29 Kathy Peiss, "On Beauty ... and the History of Business," in *Beauty and Business: Commerce, Gender, and Culture in Modern America*, ed. Philip Scranton (New York: Routledge, 2001), 12. Like Gamber, Peiss is discussing American examples, but I suggest that these patterns are also clear in the Canadian context.
30 Gabrielle Carrière, *Careers for Women in Canada: A Practical Guide* (Toronto: J.M. Dent and Sons, 1946), 134.
31 Ibid.
32 Gamber, "A Gendered Enterprise," 209. See also Gamber, *The Female Economy*, for a lengthier examination of sex-typing in the sewing trades.
33 Gamber, "A Gendered Enterprise," 204.
34 *Wrigley's British Columbia Directory, 1918* (Vancouver: Wrigley Directories, 1918).
35 See membership information for the Victoria and Vancouver business and professional women's clubs in Chapter 4: these women were all members.
36 On Denny and Geoghegan, see *Who's Who in British Columbia, 1937-1939* (Vancouver: S.M. Carter, 1939), 25-26. See also Carolyn Gossage, *A Question of Privilege: Canada's Independent Schools* (Toronto: Peter Martin Associates, 1977), 251-53. On Jessie Gordon, see Gossage, *A Question of Privilege*, 263-64; and Jean Barman, "Vancouver's Forgotten Entrepreneurs: Women Who Ran Their Own Schools," *British Columbia Historical News* 31, 4 (Fall 1998): 22.
37 See Gossage, *A Question of Privilege;* and Jean Barman, *Growing Up British in British Columbia: Boys in Private School* (Vancouver: UBC Press, 1984).
38 Barman, "Vancouver's Forgotten Entrepreneurs," 21-22.
39 See Veronica Strong-Boag and Kathryn McPherson, "The Confinement of Women: Childbirth and Hospitalization in Vancouver, 1919-1939," *BC Studies*, nos. 69-70 (Spring-Summer 1986): 156-58.
40 David Burley, *A Particular Condition in Life: Self-Employment and Social Mobility in Mid-Victorian Brantford, Ontario* (Montreal/Kingston: McGill-Queen's University Press, 1994), 236. See also his Introduction, which elaborates on the connection between entrepreneurship and masculinity.
41 Gamber, *The Female Economy*, 6.
42 Ibid., 20.
43 David Mitchell and Shari Graydon, eds., *British Columbia's Business Leaders of the Century* (Vancouver: BIV Special Publications, Quebecor Printing, 1999), 96-97.
44 Chuck Davis, ed., *The Greater Vancouver Book: An Urban Encyclopaedia* (Surrey, BC: Linkman Press, 1997), 844.
45 The only exception: in 1901 in Canada these occupations accounted for slightly less than 60 percent of all female self-employment; milliners made up much of the balance. However, they formed a small and rapidly declining proportion of all female self-employment after 1921. The occupations in Table 5 were selected for their consistently high rates of female self-employment over the period 1901 to 1951. These occupations had relatively

high numbers of businesswomen compared to other jobs *and* high rates of female self-employment.

46 In 1921, 100 percent of all dressmakers and sewers in Canada were female, and from 1931 on dressmaking and sewing were only categories for the female labour force. With this difference, in 1931 there were 854 female dressmakers and sewers in British Columbia and 680 male tailors and sewers in the province. By 1951, there were 48 male "sewers" and 448 tailors in British Columbia, compared to 1,133 female dressmakers and seamstresses and 222 "tailoresses." In 1921, of all lodging-house keepers in British Columbia, 41.5 percent were men; for the rest of Canada, 16.9 percent were men. In 1931, 19 percent of all lodging-house keepers in British Columbia were men; in the rest of Canada, just 7.5 percent were men. In 1951, 32 percent of all lodging-house keepers in British Columbia were men. See Canada, Dominion Bureau of Statistics, *Census of Canada 1921,* vol. 4, table 4; *Census of Canada 1931,* vol. 7, tables 50, 53 and 54; and *Census of Canada 1951,* vol. 4, table 11.

47 See endnote 46 for references to specific census tables that list employment data for men and women.

48 Canada, Dominion Bureau of Statistics, *Census of Canada 1961,* vol. 7, part 1, Catalogue 99-522, 12.21.

49 For data on share of total employment, see the Canadian Families Project database; Canada, Dominion Bureau of Statistics, *Census of Canada 1931,* vol. 7, tables 50, 53, and 54; and *Census of Canada 1951,* vol. 4, table 11.

50 See, for instance, Nancy Grey Osterud, *Bonds of Community: The Lives of Farm Women in Nineteenth-Century New York* (Ithaca, NY: Cornell University Press, 1991); and Mary Neth, *Preserving the Family Farm: Women, Community, and the Foundations of Agribusiness in the Midwest, 1900-1940* (Baltimore: Johns Hopkins University Press, 1995). In a Canadian context, see Marjorie Griffin Cohen, *Women's Work, Markets, and Economic Development in Nineteenth-Century Ontario* (Toronto: University of Toronto Press, 1988); Mary Kinnear, "'Do You Want Your Daughter to Marry a Farmer?' Women's Work on the Farm, 1922," in *Canadian Papers in Rural History,* vol. 6, ed. D.H. Akenson (Gananoque, ON: Langdale, 1988), 137-153; Veronica Strong-Boag, "Pulling in Double Harness or Hauling a Double Load: Women, Work and Feminism on the Canadian Prairie," *Journal of Canadian Studies* 21, 3 (1986): 32-52.

51 Osterud argues that farm tasks were gender-specific, but that men and women switched roles when necessary. A sense of partnership pervades her discussion of rural family economies: see Osterud, *Bonds of Community.* See also Virginia E. McCormick, "Butter and Egg Business: Implications from the Records of a Nineteenth-Century Farm Wife," *Ohio History* 100 (Winter/Spring 1991): 57-67.

52 McCormick, "Butter and Egg Business," 58.

53 These examples are taken from the Canadian Families Project database.

54 H. Glynn-Ward, *The Glamour of British Columbia* (New York: Century, 1926; repr., Toronto: Doubleday, Doran and Gundy, 1932.), 88. H. Glynn-Ward was Hilda Howard's pseudonym; her married name was Hilda Glynn Howard. See Anne Innis Dagg, *The Feminine Gaze* (Waterloo: Wilfrid Laurier University Press, 2001), 111.

55 O'Keefe Family Records, MS 1890, m/f A01254, A01255, BC Archives.

56 Ibid.

57 In 1901, 75 percent of female farmers in British Columbia were widowed/divorced. In 1931, 59 percent were widowed/divorced, compared to 5.2 percent of male farmers. By 1951,

slightly fewer female farmers – 38.5 percent – were widowed/divorced, compared to 3.6 percent of male farmers in the province. Data for the rest of Canada was similar but was marked by even higher rates of widowhood/divorce for female farmers, and rates of 3 to 5 percent for male farmers. Data for the marital status of female and male farmers in 1901 is taken from the Canadian Families Project database. The 1911 census data is incomplete. From 1921 on, data on employment status and marital status is taken from the following volumes of the published census: Canada, Dominion Bureau of Statistics, *Census of Canada 1921*, vol. 4, table 4; *Census of Canada 1931*, vol. 7, tables 50, 53, and 54, and vol. 13, table 29; *Census of Canada 1941*, vol. 7, table 5; and *Census of Canada 1951*, vol. 4, table 11.

58 They would not have been able to call themselves farmers had their husbands been present: that title would have been given to the male head of household in cases where both husband and wife were present. Even if the woman owned the land, if she was married, she was a farmer's wife, not a farmer. I did not find any cases where women listed in the census as farmers had spouses living with them.

59 Joan Lang, *Lost Orchards: Vanishing Fruit Farms of the West Kootenay* (Nelson, BC: Ward Creek Press, 2003), 46. It is unknown, in this case, whether the census also acknowledged her as a farmer: her incapacitated husband was likely still the "farmer" on paper and in name, if not in practice.

60 Rosemary Neering, *Wild West Women: Travellers, Adventurers and Rebels* (Vancouver: Whitecap Books, 2000), 164-65.

61 *Victoria Colonist*, 8 May 1913.

62 See *Henderson's British Columbia Gazetteer and Directory*, 1900 to 1907 (Victoria and Vancouver: Henderson Publishing, 1900-7); *Wrigley's British Columbia Directory*, 1918, 1922 (Vancouver: Wrigley Directories, 1918, 1922); Lang, *Lost Orchards*, 46. See also Jean Barman, *Sojourning Sisters: The Lives and Letters of Jessie and Annie McQueen* (Toronto: University of Toronto Press, 2003), 154.

63 Lang, *Lost Orchards*, 35, 46.

64 Irene Howard, *The Struggle for Social Justice in British Columbia: Helena Gutteridge, the Unknown Reformer* (Vancouver: UBC Press, 1992), 141; and Rosemarie Parent, "The Story of Estella Hartt," *British Columbia Historical News* 32, 2 (Spring 1999): 30. As Howard points out, Gutteridge would become much better known in her post-poultry years as a union organizer, member of the CCF, and, in 1937, the first woman elected to Vancouver City Council.

65 I have not included female milliners in this discussion of women in the sewing trades because even though milliners had high rates of self-employment, the number of women working as milliners, compared to those working as seamstresses or dressmakers, was very low.

66 For a more detailed gender analysis of work in the sewing trades in particular, see Parr, *The Gender of Breadwinners;* Gamber, *The Female Economy;* and Sangster, *Earning Respect.*

67 David Monod, *Store Wars: Shopkeepers and the Culture of Mass Marketing, 1890-1939* (Toronto: University of Toronto Press, 1996), 46.

68 Ibid.

69 *Henderson's British Columbia Gazetteer and Directory, 1901* (Victoria and Vancouver: Henderson Publishing, 1901).

70 Canada, Dominion Bureau of Statistics, *Census of Canada 1921*, vol. 4, table 4.

71 Canada, Dominion Bureau of Statistics, *Census of Canada 1931*, vol. 10, table 2A.

72 Canada, Dominion Bureau of Statistics, *Census of Canada 1941*, vol. 10, table 5.

73 See Monod, *Store Wars*, 46; and Gamber, *The Female Economy*, 4.

74 It should be stressed that many women running boarding houses may not have owned their own properties; while married women could own property in twentieth-century British Columbia, it is likely that many marginal businesses were operated out of buildings owned by men. Women were in some cases renting their homes; in other cases, their husbands owned the properties, even if they had deserted their wives. The point, however, is not whether they owned the buildings. If they declared themselves to be self-employed and took in boarders for money, they owned their enterprises (in that they worked for themselves and profits went into their pockets), if not the buildings. And my argument is that, regardless of their profitability, even boarding houses should be considered as businesses: they allowed women a measure of self-sufficiency, and they represent something very different from a wage-earning occupation.

75 Canada, Dominion Bureau of Statistics, *Census of Canada 1931*, vol. 13, 79.

76 Ibid., 85.

77 Ibid., 79.

78 The 1951 numbers of self-employed lodging-house keepers seem quite low compared to those of the 1930s, but I could not find any specific references to changes in how the occupation was classified between 1931 and 1951 that explain this drop. One possibility might be the postwar construction of suburban housing developments and apartment buildings; as more people married and moved into their own homes in postwar Canada, the need for boarding houses declined. See Gilbert A. Stelter and Alan F.J. Artibise, eds., *The Canadian City: Essays in Urban and Social History* (Ottawa: Carleton University Press, 1991). Essays in this collection also note that "city beautiful" and urban reform movements after the First World War prompted housing reform and inspired new types of housing.

79 Of all female boarding-house keepers in the province, 44 percent were married in 1901, 66 percent were married in 1931, and 57 percent were married in 1951. In the rest of Canada, only 24 percent were married in 1901 (but the Canadian Families Project's 5 percent sample only caught 103 female boarding-house keepers in Canada, excluding the 12 caught by the sample in British Columbia). In later published census data, the rates of married boarding-house keepers in the rest of the country were very similar to the proportions in the province. Data for 1901 is taken from the Canadian Families Project database. The 1911 data is incomplete. From 1921 on, data on employment status and marital status is taken from the following volumes of the published census: Canada, Dominion Bureau of Statistics, *Census of Canada 1921*, vol. 4, table 4; *Census of Canada 1931*, vol. 7, tables 50, 53, and 54, and vol. 13, table 29; *Census of Canada 1941*, vol. 7, table 5; and *Census of Canada 1951*, vol. 4, table 11.

80 Canada, Dominion Bureau of Statistics, *Census of Canada 1921*, vol. 4, xl-xli.

81 Canada, Dominion Bureau of Statistics, *Census of Canada 1941*, vol. 1, 330.

82 *Vancouver Sun*, 21 May 1912, 15.

83 Ibid., 3 March 1920, 13.

84 *Victoria Daily Colonist*, 20 April 1945, 12.

85 Tomoko Makabe, *Picture Brides: Japanese Women in Canada*, trans. Kathleen Chisato Merken (Toronto: Multicultural History Society of Ontario, 1995), 83.

86 Other explanations for the high number of male-run boarding houses and the high number of men employed in domestic service work are discussed in Chapter 2.

87 Data for 1901 is taken from the Canadian Families Project database. The 1911 data is incomplete. From 1921 on, data on employment status and male/female share of total

employment is taken from the following volumes of the published census: Canada, Dominion Bureau of Statistics, *Census of Canada 1921,* vol. 4, table 4; *Census of Canada 1931,* vol. 7, tables 50, 53, and 54, and vol. 13, table 29; *Census of Canada 1941,* vol. 7, table 5; and *Census of Canada 1951,* vol. 4, table 11.

88 Hairdressing was the one job listed here that was becoming more feminine; by mid-century, women made up half of all employed barbers/hairdressers, and they made up more than half of all barbers/hairdressers by 1961.

89 Virginia Beirnes, "Women CAN Sell Real Estate," *The Business and Professional Woman* 28 (March-April 1963): 5, Add Mss 799, 588-A-4, City of Vancouver Archives.

90 McDonald, *Making Vancouver,* 128.

91 Data on real estate agents is found in tables on employment status provided in the published census: see endnote 87 for specific references. There were so few female real estate agents in 1901 that only one appeared in the Canadian Families Project's database, and that one was not in British Columbia.

92 See endnote 87 for specific references to census tables that provide data on men and women in specific occupations such as hotelkeeping, on employment status, and on male and female share of total employment.

93 Robert A. Campbell, *Sit Down and Drink Your Beer: Regulating Vancouver's Beer Parlours, 1925-1954* (Toronto: University of Toronto Press, 2001), 33.

94 Alexander Freund and Laura Quilici, "Exploring Myths in Women's Narratives: Italian and German Immigrant Women in Vancouver, 1947-1961," *BC Studies,* nos. 105-6 (Spring/Summer 1995): 172-73.

95 *Henderson's British Columbia Gazetteer and Directory, 1901,* does list many women as proprietors of hotels, particularly in urban areas, and the business and professional women's club membership lists also record some female hotel keepers. See Chapters 4 and 5 for BPW clubwomen who were also hotel keepers.

96 Marjorie Leffler, "The Island Hall Hotel History," *British Columbia Historical News* 27, 2 (Spring 1994): 21-22.

97 Allen Seager, "The Resource Economy, 1871-1921," in *The Pacific Province: A History of British Columbia,* ed. Hugh J.M. Johnston (Vancouver: Douglas and McIntyre, 1996), 238-39.

98 In totalling numbers of self-employed women in the 1901 database, I included only women whose self-employment was listed by census takers or, in a very few cases, those whose entrepreneurship was clear despite incomplete or seemingly incorrect data. I included, for example, women who were enumerated as both employees and as self-employed but whose occupation was entrepreneurial, and I included two women who stated they were farmers and household heads, but who were not listed as either employees or as self-employed. After 1901, such examples would probably have been omitted from published totals. Even if a woman appeared to be working for herself and seemed self-employed, I was cautious about making a decision where none had been made in 1901. This was to preserve consistency with later published data.

99 Ostry, *The Occupational Composition of the Canadian Labour Force,* 3.

100 Ibid., 41.

101 Armstrong and Armstrong, *The Double Ghetto,* 20, 22.

102 Ibid., 20.

103 Ibid., 31.

104 Canada, Dominion Bureau of Statistics, *Census of Canada 1941,* vol. 1, 329.

105 Gamber, *The Female Economy,* 3.
106 Ibid., 216.
107 Davis, *The Greater Vancouver Book,* 827.

CHAPTER 4: "THEY ARE QUICK, ALERT, CLEAR-EYED BUSINESS GIRLS"

1 Club records are a valuable source, but it must be noted that relatively few employed women, of all women in the labour force, belonged to BPW clubs. The number of women who joined and the ways that class and profession affected membership are discussed later in this chapter.
2 Candace Kanes, "American Business Women, 1890-1930: Creating an Identity" (PhD diss., University of New Hampshire, 1997), 332.
3 Ibid., 8.
4 Ibid.
5 Ibid., 9.
6 Deidre Brocklehurst, "A Visible Presence: The Victoria Business and Professional Women's Club, 1921-1960" (master's thesis, University of Victoria, 2001), 3.
7 "Women Invading All Walks of Life," *Vancouver Business Woman* 5, 6 (November 1927), Add Mss 799, 588-A-3, City of Vancouver Archives (hereafter CVA).
8 Angel Kwolek-Folland, *Incorporating Women: A History of Women and Business in the United States* (New York: Twayne, 1998), 57.
9 Mary A. Yeager, "Will There Ever Be a Feminist Business History?" in *Women in Business,* vol. 1, ed. Mary A. Yeager (Northampton, MA: Elgar, 1999), 19.
10 Angel Kwolek-Folland, *Engendering Business: Men and Women in the Corporate Office, 1870-1930* (Baltimore: Johns Hopkins University Press, 1994), 178.
11 *Saturday Evening Post* (1915), cited in Kwolek-Folland, *Engendering Business,* 178.
12 Ibid.
13 Ibid., 169.
14 Kanes, "American Business Women," 178.
15 Entry for 19 January 1925, Kumtuks Club Minute Book, p. 9, 89-1386-3, British Columbia Archives (hereafter BCA).
16 "Constitution and By-Laws of the Canadian Federation of Business and Professional Women's Clubs," 89-1387-1, BCA.
17 See Chapter 2 for rates of female self-employment in the province and in the rest of the country between 1901 and 1951.
18 Chuck Davis, ed., *The Greater Vancouver Book: An Urban Encyclopaedia* (Surrey, BC: Linkman Press, 1997), 415-16.
19 Ibid.
20 Kwolek-Folland, *Incorporating Women,* 91.
21 Kanes, "American Business Women," 127, 129.
22 Ibid., 30-31.
23 Ibid., 125.
24 Frances Paterson, "The Saga of Kumtuks," *The Business and Professional Woman* 21, 11 (March-April 1951), Add Mss 799, 588-A-4, CVA.
25 "History of the Victoria Business and Professional Women's Club," 89-1387-3, file 5, BCA.
26 Brocklehurst, "A Visible Presence," 43.
27 "History of the Victoria Business and Professional Women's Club," 89-1387-3, file 5, BCA.

28 Davis, *The Greater Vancouver Book,* 817. Dauphinee also served as president of the Canadian federation from 1932 to 1935. She is probably better known for her support of eugenics. She was the first teacher in British Columbia to teach children labelled as "feeble-minded" in a segregated classroom and promoted this segregation as well as the sexual sterilization of the feeble-minded. See Gerald Thomson, "'Through No Fault of Their Own': Josephine Dauphinee and the 'Subnormal' Pupils of the Vancouver School System, 1911-1941," *Historical Studies in Education* 18 (Spring 2006): 51-73.

29 Kumtuks/Victoria Club Record Book, 1923-29, 89-1386-3, BCA.

30 Excerpt from a club publication by Elizabeth Forbes, "With Enthusiasm and Faith: History of the Canadian Federation of B. and P.W. Clubs, 1930-1972," Add Mss 799, 588-A-3, CVA. The booklet was published by the Canadian Federation of Business and Professional Women in 1974.

31 Vancouver BPW Club Records, Add Mss 799, 608-A-1, file 4, CVA.

32 Brocklehurst, "A Visible Presence," 43.

33 Kumtuks/Victoria Club Minute Book, 1930-37, 89-1386-3, BCA.

34 BPW Club Records, 89-1387-3, file 3, BCA.

35 Elizabeth Forbes, author of the historical booklet "With Enthusiasm and Faith," was a Victoria BPW club member and newspaper editor.

36 J. Donald Wilson, "I Am Ready to Be of Assistance When I Can': Lottie Bowron and Rural Women Teachers in British Columbia," in *Women Who Taught: Perspectives on the History of Women and Teaching,* ed. Alison Prentice and Marjorie R. Theobald (Toronto: University of Toronto Press, 1991), 205-6, 221. Bowron did return to government work in 1928, when a Conservative government was elected. She was appointed rural teachers' welfare officer but was dismissed again in 1934 by Duff Pattullo's Liberal government. Unwillingly retired in 1934 at age fifty-four, Bowron lived at the Strathcona Hotel in Victoria until her death in 1964.

37 Lottie Bowron, "Club History, 1921-28," 89-1386-3, BCA.

38 Ibid.

39 "History of the Victoria Business and Professional Women's Club," 89-1387-3, file 5, BCA.

40 "Kumtuks Club History, 1921-28," 89-1386-3, BCA. Women who were widowed would also have appeared as married in the records of attendance and membership.

41 "History of the Victoria Business and Professional Women's Club," 89-1387-3, file 5, BCA.

42 "Canadian Federation News" (1946), 89-1387-3, file 5, BCA.

43 Entry for 20 February 1923, Vancouver BPW Club Minute Book, Add Mss 799, 608-A-1, CVA.

44 *Vancouver Business Woman* 2, 2 (1 July 1924): cover page, Add Mss 799, 588-A-3, CVA.

45 Lottie Bowron commented, as quoted earlier in this chapter, that women needed a club "like the Rotarians." Brocklehurst argues that Bowron envisioned a club whose primary aim was to provide service to the community and that Bowron used the Rotarians as the model for this element of the Kumtuks Club. See Brocklehurst, "A Visible Presence," 23.

46 Kanes, "American Business Women," 32.

47 Entry for February 1923, Kumtuks Club Minute Book, 89-1386-3, BCA.

48 Brocklehurst, "A Visible Presence," 14-15.

49 "Canadian Federation News" (March 1931), 89-1387-3, file 5, BCA.

50 Victoria BPW Club Minute Book, 89-1387-3, file 3, BCA.

51 Kumtuks/Victoria Club Minute Book, 1930-37, 89-1386-3, BCA.

52 Ibid.

53 "A Momentous Time," *The Business and Professional Woman* (June 1935): 4, 89-1387-1, file 2, BCA.

54 *The Business and Professional Woman* (May 1941), 89-1387-1, file 2, BCA.

55 "All Clubs Put Emphasis on War Work," *The Business and Professional Woman* (November 1940): 9, 89-1387-1, file 2, BCA.

56 Scrapbook (clippings), Victoria BPW Club Records, 74-A-436, BCA.

57 Kumtuks/Victoria Club Minute Book, 1930-37, 89-1386-3, BCA.

58 Brocklehurst, "A Visible Presence," 58.

59 Membership records listed women as Miss or Mrs. but did not highlight whether women were widowed or divorced. However, at the very least, we can determine whether they were single or not-single, i.e., married/widowed/divorced. See the membership lists in Appendixes 2 and 3, which indicate marital status of all members in 1931 and 1948. Note that more members were married in 1948 than in 1931.

60 Appendix 1 lists all the self-employed women that I was able to locate in the club records between 1921 and 1963, their stated occupation, name, and marital status. From this list of eighty-six women, fifty-one were recorded as "Mrs." See also Appendixes 2 and 3, containing membership lists of the Victoria BPW club from 1931 and 1948, respectively, which indicate marital status. Data is compiled from "Membership List, Victoria Business and Professional Women's Club, 1931," Attendance and Registration Book, BPW Club Records, 89-1386-3, BCA; and "Membership List, Victoria Business and Professional Women's Club, 1948," BPW Club Records, 89-1386-2, BCA.

61 Not all women responded to the propaganda encouraging them to leave the labour force, however; see Chapter 2 for a discussion of women's labour force participation rates during and after the war and the limited effect of postwar propaganda urging women to leave their jobs.

62 Victoria BPW Club Records, 89-1386-2, BCA.

63 See Appendixes 2 and 3.

64 See Table 6 and Appendixes 2 and 3. Despite my interest in entrepreneurs, professional and clerical wage-earning women made up more than half of the membership of the Victoria club. I have highlighted them here because as wage earners, their marriage rates changed quite significantly when marriage bars were lifted. Wage earners were the members whose marital rates changed most from 1931 to 1948.

65 Minute Book, BPW Clubs of BC and the Yukon, vol. 1, 1948-64, 91-3433-516, BCA.

66 Scrapbook (clippings), Victoria BPW Club, 89-1386-1, BCA. This scrapbook contained articles from three provincial newspapers, dated 8 August 1949, about the issue.

67 *Victoria Daily Times,* 8 August 1949, 3.

68 Minute Book, BPW Clubs of BC and the Yukon, vol. 1, 1948-64, 91-3433-516, BCA. The telegram was also reprinted in *The Business and Professional Woman* 20, 3 (November-December 1949): 9, 89-1387-1, file 2, BCA.

69 Victoria BPW Club Records, 89-1386-2, BCA.

70 Scrapbook (clippings), Victoria BPW Club Records, 74-A-436, BCA.

71 Marion Harland, "The Incapacity of Business Women," *North American Review* 149 (July 1889): 707-12.

72 Kwolek-Folland, *Incorporating Women,* ix.

73 Pearl Steen, Speech to the National Council of Women, Pearl Steen Fonds, Add Mss 272, 517-C-5, file 3, CVA. The speech is not dated, but it appears with clippings and files from the 1950s.

74 Program from one-day regional BPW club conference, February 1944. Victoria BPW Club Scrapbook (1930s and 1940s), 74-A-436, BCA. The members did not list specific laws in this declaration, although they specifically stated their support for nursery schools and recreational centres.

75 BPW Clubs of British Columbia and the Yukon, Minute Book, vol. 1, 1948-64, 91-3433-516, BCA.

76 Scott's original column and Fry's response are not listed in the BC Newspaper Index, and the letter by Fry, clipped out of the newspaper and entered into a BPW scrapbook, was not dated. I was unable to find the original article and letter in the *Sun*. However, the subject matter and tone of Scott's column are clear from Fry's response.

77 Vancouver BPW Club, Scrapbook and Miscellany, 1920s-80s, Add Mss 799, 588-A-5, CVA. This letter, clipped from the *Vancouver Sun*, is not dated but it appears with a series of clippings from the mid-1950s.

78 British Columbia, Ministry of Labour, Women's Programs, "Survey of Women Business Owners in British Columbia: Major Findings and Policy Implications" (Victoria: Author, 1986), "Appendix C: Reasons Why Women Become Business Owners." The study was undertaken in 1985.

79 Ibid., "Appendix D: Barriers Unique to Women as Business Owners."

80 British Columbia, Ministry of Economic Development, Small Business, and Trade, Businesswomen's Advocate, "Women in Business: Profile of Women Business Owners in British Columbia" (Victoria: Author, 1991), 6.

81 Paul Phillips and Erin Phillips, *Women and Work: Inequality in the Canadian Labour Market* (Toronto: Lorimer, 1993), 42.

82 Victoria BPW Club Records, 89-1386-2, BCA.

83 Victoria BPW Club Records, 89-1387-3, file 5, BCA. These programs did not begin until 1961, but they speak to the ongoing interests of the club.

84 Victoria BPW Club – conference programs, loose pamphlets, 89-1387-3, BCA.

85 Brocklehurst, "A Visible Presence," 44.

86 For a more detailed examination of the many issues that the Victoria BPW club, in particular, tackled, and the issues it advanced, see Brocklehurst, "A Visible Presence." Her study outlines in detail the various bills and legislation pertaining to women that the club supported between 1920 and 1961, as well as other issues related to work and women that the club addressed.

87 Kumtuks Club Record Book, 1920s, 89-1386-3, BCA.

88 Brocklehurst, "A Visible Presence," 31-32.

89 Entry for 19 September 1930, Kumtuks/Victoria Club Minute Book, 1930-37, 89-1386-3, BCA.

90 Entry for 3 November 1930, ibid..

91 Minute Book, BPW Clubs of BC and the Yukon, vol. 1, 1948-64, 91-3433-516, BCA.

92 Brocklehurst suggests that the club's racial biases had "disappeared" by the late 1940s, but she also notes there is no evidence that the club membership was more integrated. Even if examples of overt racism from club members were rare by 1950, most of the members were still white. See Brocklehurst, "A Visible Presence," 88-89.

93 Pearl Steen Fonds, Add Mss 272, 517-C-4, CVA. Steen's surname was Eaton when she was president of the club.

94 Entry for 21 August 1930, Kumtuks/Victoria Club Minute Book, 1930-37, 89-1386-3, BCA.

95 "History of the Victoria Business and Professional Women's Club," 89-1387-3, file 5, BCA.

96 Vancouver BPW Club Minutes, Add Mss 799, 608-A-1, CVA.

97 CFBPWC Convention Minutes, 1932, 89-1387-3, file 3, BCA. This box includes a variety of loose pamphlets and convention programs, including provincial and federal pamphlets, probably included in the records by Victoria's conference delegates.

98 Ibid.

99 Ibid.

100 Kumtuks/Victoria Club Minute Book, 1930-37, 89-1386-3, BCA.

101 "Report of the Provincial President," BPWC of BC and the Yukon, 1974, 89-1387-1, BCA.

102 "Women's Clubs Hold Convention," *Vancouver Weekly,* 18 July 1974, in BPW Scrapbook, Add Mss 799, 588-A-5, CVA.

103 Brocklehurst, "A Visible Presence," 1.

104 Vancouver BPW Club Records, Add Mss 799, 608-A-1, file 3, CVA.

105 Jean Barman, "Vancouver's Forgotten Entrepreneurs: Women Who Ran Their Own Schools," *British Columbia Historical News* 31, 4 (Fall 1998): 27; and Davis, *The Greater Vancouver Book,* 838.

106 Hilda Hesson, " T.B.W.," *The Business and Professional Woman* 22, 2 (September-October 1951), Add Mss 799, 588-A-5 CVA.

107 "Women's Club Debates, Is Man Really a Person?" *Globe and Mail,* 29 July 1954, 10.

108 Ibid.

109 Valerie J. Korinek, "'Mrs. Chatelaine' vs. 'Mrs. Slob': Contestants, Correspondents and the *Chatelaine* Community in Action, 1961-1969," *Journal of the Canadian Historical Association* 7 (1996): 274. See also Valerie J. Korinek, *Roughing It in the Suburbs: Reading Chatelaine Magazine in the Fifties and Sixties* (Toronto: University of Toronto Press, 2000).

110 Korinek, "'Mrs. Chatelaine' vs. 'Mrs. Slob,'" 275.

111 Ibid., 253.

112 "Women's Club Debates." An undated newspaper article, titled "Shoe Is on the Other Foot When Tables Turned on Men," covers the same debate: see Scrapbook (clippings), Victoria BPW Club Records, 74-A-436, BCA.

113 Kumtuks Club scrapbook, 89-1386-1, BCA. The photographs were loosely placed inside the cover of one of many scrapbooks in this box, and the only information listed was the date, September 1925, and the title, "Fete Galante, Gonzales."

114 Pearl Steen Fonds, Add Mss 272, 517-C-4, file 3, CVA.

115 The height difference is evident in a number of the photographs but not in the one shown in Figure 3.

116 Lisa M. Fine, "Between Two Worlds: Business Women in a Chicago Boarding House, 1900-1930," *Journal of Social History* 19 (Spring 1986): 511. For a broader look at working women in Chicago, see also Lisa M. Fine, *The Souls of the Skyscraper: Female Clerical Workers in Chicago, 1870-1930* (Philadelphia: Temple University Press, 1990).

117 Fine, "Between Two Worlds," 513.

118 Ibid., 511.

119 Ibid., 514.

120 Ibid., 515.

121 Ibid., 516.

122 Ibid., 517.

123 Joy Parr, *The Gender of Breadwinners: Women, Men, and Change in Two Industrial Towns, 1880-1950* (Toronto: University of Toronto Press, 1990), 30.

124 Ibid.

125 Ibid., 32.

126 See, for instance, Anne Herrmann, "Imitations of Marriage: Crossdressed Couples in Contemporary Lesbian Fiction," in *Lesbian Subjects: A Feminist Studies Reader,* ed. Martha Vicinus (Bloomington: Indiana University Press, 1996), 102-15. The Introduction by Vicinus also points out that the "not-said" and the "not-seen" are important analytical tools in lesbian studies. She argues that lesbians can be everywhere and yet unmentioned.

127 Martha Vicinus, *Independent Women: Work and Community for Single Women, 1850-1920* (Chicago: University of Chicago Press, 1985), 158-59.

128 Lillian Faderman, *Surpassing the Love of Men: Romantic Friendships and Love between Women from the Renaissance to the Present* (New York: William Morrow, 1981), 190.

129 Ibid. Faderman also notes that they were often New Women, feminists and pioneers in a profession – as were many of the clubwomen discussed in my work.

130 Sheila Jeffreys, "Does It Matter If They Did It?" in *Not a Passing Phase: Reclaiming Lesbians in History, 1840-1985,* ed. Lesbian History Group (London: Women's Press, 1989), 23.

131 Scrapbook, Victoria BPW Club Records, 89-1386-1, BCA. The scrapbook contains clippings, photographs, and miscellaneous notes about the Kumtuks Club's activity in the 1920s, and Bowron's name is listed on the cover as the owner of the book.

132 Entry for 17 July 1931, Kumtuks/Victoria Club Minute Book, 1930-37, 89-1386-3, BCA. This was one of many references to the two women in the records of the Victoria club but the only reference suggesting that they vacationed together.

133 The pageant is mentioned in the Victoria BPW Club Minutes, 1951-52, 89-1386-2, BCA. Photographs of the pageant appeared in a separate box of Victoria BPW Club records, in an album of photographs of various club activities from the 1930s to the 1960s (89-1386-1, BCA).

134 Fine mentioned a similar party that took place in 1916 in a Chicago women's residence: the women staged a suffrage meeting, and all the participants dressed as different "types" of suffragettes. Fine, "Between Two Worlds," 513.

135 Sara Maitland, cited in Lesley Ferris, *Acting Women: Images of Women in Theatre* (New York: New York University Press, 1989), 147.

136 Alisa Solomon, "It's Never Too Late to Switch," in *Crossing the Stage: Controversies on Cross-Dressing,* ed. Lesley Ferris (London: Routledge, 1993), 145.

137 Ibid., 146.

138 Fine, "Between Two Worlds," 517.

CHAPTER 5: "YOU HAVE TO THINK LIKE A MAN AND ACT LIKE A LADY"

1 David Burley, *A Particular Condition in Life: Self-Employment and Social Mobility in Mid-Victorian Brantford, Ontario* (Montreal/Kingston: McGill-Queen's University Press, 1994), 236. Burley is not the only scholar to make the connection between manliness and self-employment: in her Introduction to the three-volume collection *Women in Business,* Mary Yeager states that the business world has been made and recorded largely by men. See Mary A. Yeager, "Introduction," in *Women in Business,* vol. 1, ed. Mary A. Yeager (Northampton, MA: Elgar, 1999), ix-x. On the gendering of the business world as masculine, see also Angel Kwolek-Folland, *Engendering Business: Men and Women in the Corporate Office, 1870-1930* (Baltimore: Johns Hopkins University Press, 1994), and *Incorporating Women: A History of Women and Business in the United States* (New York: Twayne, 1998).

2   Burley, *A Particular Condition in Life,* 102.
3   David Monod, *Store Wars: Shopkeepers and the Culture of Mass Marketing, 1890-1939* (Toronto: University of Toronto Press, 1996), 88.
4   Stana Nenadic, "The Social Shaping of Business Behaviour in the Nineteenth-Century Women's Garment Trades," *Journal of Social History* 31, 3 (Spring 1998): 639.
5   Monod, *Store Wars,* 88.
6   Robert McDonald notes that immigrant women contributed to the family economy in Vancouver, running boarding houses, for instance, and I found scattered evidence of non-white women providing services as restaurant and shop owners. See Robert A.J. McDonald, *Making Vancouver: Class Status, and Social Boundaries, 1863-1913* (Vancouver: UBC Press, 1996); *Wrigley's British Columbia Directory, 1918* (Vancouver: Wrigley Directories, 1918); Tun Wong, "Sue Lee Ping Wong," *Okanagan History: The Sixty-Third Report of the Okanagan Historical Society* 63 (1999): 156-59. See also the Canadian Families Project's database, based on a 5 percent sample of the 1901 census (http://web.uvic.ca/hrd/cfp/data/index.html) for examples of First Nations women who declared they were self-employed.
7   Wendy Gamber, *The Female Economy: The Millinery and Dressmaking Trades, 1860-1930* (Urbana: University of Illinois Press, 1997), 27.
8   Margaret Hewett Robertson, "Work Is a Masculine Word," *The Business and Professional Woman* (October-November 1979): 6-8, Add Mss 799, 588-A-4, City of Vancouver Archives (hereafter CVA).
9   BPW clubwomen were not all self-employed. My research focuses on the self-employed members, but wage-earning and self-employed club members alike encountered gendered tensions and wrestled with their professional images.
10 For a list of self-employed clubwomen and their occupations, see Appendix 1. The list includes such occupations as "authoress," guest house proprietor, and many types of store owners, ranging from women's clothing to shoes, flowers, and jewellery. See also Appendixes 2 and 3, which provide membership lists for the Victoria club in 1931 and 1948.
11 Vancouver BPW Club Records, Minutes and Correspondence, Add Mss 799, 608-A-1, file 6, CVA.
12 Vancouver BPW Club Minute Book, Add Mss 799, 608-A-1, CVA.
13 Emma Dot Partridge, "On Taking One's Work Too Seriously," *The Vancouver Business Woman* 4, 8 (January 1927): 7-8, Add Mss 799, 588-A-3, CVA.
14 *The Vancouver Business Woman* 9, 51 (September 1934): 2, Add Mss 799, 588-A-3, CVA.
15 *The Vancouver Business Woman* 3, 7 (December 1925): 8, Add Mss 799, 588-A-3, CVA.
16 "Report of the 3rd Convention of Canadian Federation of Business and Professional Women's Clubs, Held in Vancouver, B.C., July 13th to 16th 1932 at Hotel Vancouver," Kumtuks/Victoria Club Minute Book, 1930-37, 89-1386-3, BC Archives (hereafter BCA). Green was a member of the Vancouver School Board.
17 "Minutes of a Preliminary Session of the Third Annual Convention, CFBPWC," 89-1387-3, file 3, BCA.
18 Note that Green was almost certainly talking about wage-earning professional women as well as self-employed women in this context.
19 See Lee Virginia Chambers-Schiller, *Liberty, A Better Husband: Single Women in America – The Generations of 1780-1840* (New Haven, CT: Yale University Press, 1984), 176-77, 198-99. See also Martha Vicinus, *Independent Women: Work and Community for Single Women, 1850-1920* (Chicago: University of Chicago Press, 1985), 15, 32.
20 "Report of the 3rd Convention."

21 Ibid. (emphasis added).

22 *Victoria Daily Times,* 14 July 1932, 8.

23 Pearl Eaton, "Secretarial Work" (speech given at 1937 CFBPWC convention), Pearl Steen Fonds, Add Mss 272, 517-C-5, CVA. Steen's surname was Eaton at the time she gave the speech.

24 Victoria BPW Club Records, 89-1386-2, BCA.

25 1961 Programme, BPW Club Career Preview, 89-1387-3, BCA.

26 *Victoria Daily Times,* 13 October 1962, 23.

27 Newspaper clipping (paper unknown), 1952, Vancouver BPW Club Scrapbooks and Miscellany, 1920s-80s, Add Mss 799, 588-A-5, CVA.

28 Ibid.

29 "Convention Chatter," *The Business and Professional Woman* 23, 1 (July-August 1952): 7, Add Mss 799, 588-A-4, CVA.

30 *Vancouver Sun,* 22 May 1963.

31 See Chuck Davis, ed., *The Greater Vancouver Book: An Urban Encyclopaedia* (Surrey, BC: Linkman Press, 1997), 827-28. Biographical information on MacGill's famous mother, Helen Gregory MacGill, who also achieved a number of "firsts" for women, is included here. And if being an engineer wasn't enough, Elsie MacGill also wrote a biography of her mother titled *My Mother, the Judge: A Biography of Judge Helen Gregory MacGill* (Toronto: Ryerson Press, 1955).

32 *Victoria Daily Times,* 14 October 1961, 21.

33 *Daily Colonist,* 16 October 1960, 19.

34 Vancouver BPW Club Records, Scrapbooks and Miscellany, 1920s-80s, Add Mss 799, 588-A-5, CVA. This newspaper clipping is not dated, and the newspaper is unknown, but it is with a collection of clippings from the 1960s.

35 *Victoria Daily Times,* 14 October 1961, 21.

36 P.W. Luce, *Vancouver Sun,* 3 November 1951, Magazine Section, 6. See also Marjory Lang and Linda Hale, "Women of the *World* and Other Dailies: The Lives and Times of Vancouver Newspaperwomen in the First Quarter of the Twentieth Century," *BC Studies,* no. 85 (Spring 1990): 17-18.

37 Taxi drivers were typically self-employed in the period, as were realtors, unlike contemporary real estate agents or taxi drivers, who often work for someone else. Interestingly, as Chapter 3 indicates, both of these jobs were more prominent amongst women in British Columbia than in the rest of the country. Thus, while "Billy" was unusually masculine, these were two jobs that highlighted a difference between the province and the rest of Canada. Owning a cab company or real estate firm was less unusual for women in British Columbia than for women elsewhere in Canada.

38 Luce, *Vancouver Sun,* 3 November 1951, 6.

39 "'Boss' Holds Man's Job – And 'He' Is a Woman," *Victoria Daily Times,* 13 October 1962, 23.

40 Kessler, a widow in Hamilton, Ontario, had inherited her husband's scrap metal business. In the 1960s she was profiled in the national federation's newsletter. While not from British Columbia, her reflections on business and gender are appropriate given the context, and they are applicable to other BPW club members and entrepreneurs. Most surprising, although her interview took place in the supposedly more liberated late 1960s, the tone of the piece and the attitude of Kessler herself seem old-fashioned, and the piece reads much like the business profiles from the pre-war era. "Think Like a Man, Act Like a Lady," *The Business and Professional Woman,* May-June 1967, Add Mss 799, 588-A-4, CVA.

41 Matthew Hilton, *Smoking in British Popular Culture, 1800-2000* (Manchester: Manchester University Press, 2000), 141.

42 Ibid., 143.

43 Ibid., 141.

44 Ibid., 124-25.

45 Ibid., 145-46. See also Penny Tinkler, *Smoke Signals: Women, Smoking and Visual Culture in Britain* (Oxford, UK: Berg Publishers, 2006). Tinkler argues that the "prevalence of women smoking grew dramatically" between 1920 and 1950 and that particularly during the Second World War it became more acceptable for women to smoke at all and to smoke in public. Tinkler, *Smoke Signals*, 11.

46 See Cheryl Krasnick Warsh, "Smoke and Mirrors: Gender Representation in North American Tobacco and Alcohol Advertisements before 1950," *Histoire sociale/Social History* 31, 62 (1998): 183-222.

47 "100 Top Women Entrepreneurs," *Chatelaine*, November 1999, 77. See also David Mitchell and Shari Graydon, eds., *British Columbia's Business Leaders of the Century* (Vancouver: BIV Special Publications, Quebecor Printing, 1999), 96-97.

48 See Mitchell and Graydon, *British Columbia's Business Leaders*, 96-97; see also "100 Top Women Entrepreneurs," 77.

49 "100 Top Women Entrepreneurs," 77.

50 Mitchell and Graydon, *British Columbia's Business Leaders*, 96-97.

51 See Candace Kanes, "American Business Women, 1890-1930: Creating an Identity" (PhD diss., University of New Hampshire, 1997), 68. She makes a similar point in an American context.

52 Kwolek-Folland, *Incorporating Women*, 125.

53 *Vancouver Business Woman* 4 (1 August 1926): 3, Add Mss 700, 588-A-3, CVA. I did not find Salter on any surviving BPW club membership lists, but her advertisement in this Vancouver publication highlighted that she was a Victoria BPW club member.

54 Kumtuks Club Book, 1921-29, 89-1386-3, BCA. "Miss Emily Carr, Artist" is noted as a new member in 1926 in the club minutes. Carr began her career as a landlady in 1913, operating an apartment building, but by 1916 she had converted the upstairs apartments into rooms for boarders. She ended her career as a landlady, which she "loathed," in 1935. See Maria Tippett, *Emily Carr: A Biography* (Toronto: Oxford University Press, 1979), 115-20, 233.

55 Devon L. Muhlert, "Armstrong Hotel Fits a Dowager's Role," *Okanagan History: The Sixty-First Report of the Okanagan Historical Society* 61 (1997): 84-89.

56 The only boarding-house keepers I located in the club records, Salter and Carr, were mentioned in other contexts but were not found on any of the surviving full membership lists.

57 Victoria Chamber of Commerce, *Annual Report and Business Directory (1957)*, 33 G 1, file 2, CVA.

58 "Women in Business: III," *Fortune* 12 (July-December 1935): 81, cited in Kathy Peiss, "'Vital Industry' and Women's Ventures: Conceptualizing Gender in Twentieth-Century Business History," *Business History Review* 72, 2 (Summer 1998): 219.

59 Ibid.

60 Dee Lavoie, *Daily Colonist*, 14 February 1954, 18.

61 *Daily Colonist*, 16 October 1960, 6.

62 G.E. Mortimer, *Daily Colonist*, 13 January 1957, 3.

63 Ibid.

64 Winifred Lee, *Vancouver Daily Province*. The article, clipped for the BPW club scrapbook, is undated but appears with clippings from the mid-1950s. Vancouver BPW Club Scrapbook, 1950-58, Add Mss 799, 588-A-5, CVA.

65 Hilton, *Smoking in British Popular Culture*, 151, 155. Hilton notes that advertising in the 1920s and 1930s in England was gender specific but also that men and women picked their brands based on other factors, such as cost. He also suggests that, after the Second World War, the idea that cigarette smoking was not respectable or inappropriate for women was disappearing. Penny Tinkle argues that in mid-century Britain, women smokers were portrayed as middle- or upper-class women of refinement: they had become respectable smokers, while less-respectable working-class women did not smoke in public. She suggests that this was a modern femininity that transgressed older Victorian notions and challenged the "long-standing association of women's smoking with sexual laxity" (Tinkler, *Smoke Signals*, 134). This new modern image did not appear in Britain until the interwar years, and it does not seem to have arrived in 1950s British Columbia, where smoking was still not respectable and middle-class mothers kept their smoking more private. The changes Tinkler noted were not yet evident in Galloway's world. Respectability and class position were still factors for women who smoked at mid-century in the circles that women like Galloway moved in.

66 Peiss, "'Vital Industry,'" 239.

67 Virginia Beirnes, "Women CAN Sell Real Estate," *The Business and Professional Woman* 28, 5 (March-April 1963): 5, Add Mss 799, 588-A-4, CVA.

68 Interestingly, the women's first names were not given in the article: the conservative formality of introducing women by their marital status persisted into the 1960s.

69 Beirnes, "Women CAN Sell Real Estate," 5.

70 Club luncheon, February 1923, Vancouver BPW Club Minute Book, 1922-26, 608-A-1, file 2, CVA.

71 M.E. Dunn, *Vancouver Business Woman* 3, 7 (December 1925), Add Mss 799, 588-A-3, CVA.

72 Article 3 of the club constitution states all of these aims and objectives. See *Vancouver Business Woman* 2, 2 (1 July 1924), Add Mss 799, 588-A-3, CVA.

73 "Presidential Address," August 1932, Pearl Steen Fonds, Add Mss 272, 517-C-5, CVA.

74 Article in *Veteran's Advocate*, 1 February 1950, Vancouver BPW Club Scrapbook (1950-58), Add Mss 799, 588-A-5, CVA.

CONCLUSION

1 Robin Fisher, "Matters for Reflection: *BC Studies* and British Columbia History," *BC Studies*, no. 100 (Winter 1993-94): 64.

2 Ibid.

3 A few interesting recent examples from UBC Press indicate that scholars are moving into the history of representation and "ideas" in the province. See, for example, Michael Dawson, *Selling British Columbia: Tourism and Consumer Culture, 1890-1970* (Vancouver: UBC Press, 2004). See also Lindsey McMaster, *Working Girls in the West: Representations of Wage-Earning Women* (Vancouver: UBC Press, 2007).

4 Fisher, "Matters for Reflection," 63.

5 See Cole Harris, *The Resettlement of British Columbia: Essays on Colonialism and Geographical Change* (Vancouver: UBC Press, 1997). This book and his most recent book indicate

our ongoing fascination with the province's early years. See Cole Harris, *The Reluctant Land: Society, Space, and Environment in Canada before Confederation* (Vancouver: UBC Press, 2008).

6 See the books mentioned above by Dawson and McMaster. In addition, Chris Clarkson's recent work addresses more "recent" themes. See Clarkson, *Domestic Reforms: Political Visions and Family Regulation in British Columbia, 1862-1940* (Vancouver: UBC Press, 2007). Clarkson also addresses, as many of us do, the province's early colonial years, but he moves into the legal and familial context of British Columbia in the twentieth century.

7 See John Lutz, ed., *Myth and Memory: Stories of Indigenous-European Contact* (Vancouver: UBC Press, 2007).

8 Fisher, "Matters for Reflection," 76.

9 Rather, he stated that we need to "devote less energy to dry details and empirical compilation." Fisher, "Matters for Reflection," 77.

10 Ibid., 76.

11 John Douglas Belshaw, "The West We Have Lost: British Columbia's Demographic Past and an Agenda for Population History," *Western Historical Quarterly* 29, 1 (Spring 1998): 41.

12 Chad Gaffield, "Historical Thinking, C.P. Snow's Two Cultures, and a Hope for the Twenty-First Century," *Journal of the Canadian Historical Association,* new series, 12 (2001): 20-21.

13 Katherine Gay, *In the Company of Women: Canadian Women Talk about What It Takes to Start and Manage a Successful Business* (Toronto: HarperCollins, 1997), 14.

14 Ibid., 15.

15 Ibid.

16 Gary Cohen, *Enterprising Canadians: The Self-Employed in Canada* (Ottawa: Statistics Canada, 1988), 9.

17 Pamela Best, "Women, Men and Work," *Canadian Social Trends* 36 (Spring 1995): 33.

18 See Chapter 2, Table 1.

19 Peter Baskerville, "Gender and Self-Employment in Urban Canada, 1901" (paper presented to the American Historical Association, Chicago, January 2003, quoted with permission of the author), 10.

20 British Columbia, Ministry of Economic Development, Small Business, and Trade, Businesswomen's Advocate, "Women in Business: Profile of Women Business Owners in British Columbia" (Victoria: Author, 1991), 10.

21 Baskerville, "Gender and Self-Employment in Urban Canada, 1901," 8.

22 "100 Top Women Entrepreneurs," *Chatelaine,* November 1999, 72-118.

23 Tralee Pearce, "Mompreneurs," *Globe and Mail,* 7 August 2004, L1.

24 The website for *The Mompreneur,* "Canada's Business Magazine for Women," is http://www.themompreneur.com.

25 Mompreneur, "About Us," http://www.themompreneur.com/about_us.htm.

26 Astrid Van Den Broek, "The Mother Corp.: Meet Five Mompreneurs," *Today's Parent,* March 2006, http://www.todaysparent.com.

27 Kim Shiffman, "Are You Entrepreneur Material?" *Today's Parent,* January 2009, 69.

Bibliography

ARCHIVAL COLLECTIONS

British Columbia Archives
British Columbia Directories, 1860-1929, m/f, call number D-9.
O'Keefe Family Records, MS 1890, m/f A01254, A01255.
Victoria Business and Professional Women's Club Records and the Kumtuks Club Records.

City of Vancouver Archives
Pearl Steen Fonds.
Vancouver Business and Professional Women's Club Records.

City of Victoria Archives
Victoria Chamber of Commerce Records, 33 G 1.

PUBLISHED PRIMARY SOURCES

Addams, Jane. *Democracy and Social Ethics.* New York: Macmillan, 1916. First published in 1902.
"All Clubs Put Emphasis on War Work." *The Business and Professional Woman* (November 1940): 9.
Beirnes, Virginia. "Women CAN Sell Real Estate." *The Business and Professional Woman* 28 (March-April 1963): 5.
Canadian Families Project. Database and user guide for the national sample of the 1901 Census of Canada. http://web.uvic.ca/hrd/cfp/data/index.html.
Carrière, Gabrielle. *Careers for Women in Canada: A Practical Guide.* Toronto: J.M. Dent and Sons, 1946.

"Club Songs." *Vancouver Business Woman* 5, 6 (November 1927).

"Convention Chatter." *The Business and Professional Woman* 23, 1 (July-August 1952): 7.

Fredrickson, Olive, with Ben East. *Silence of the North.* Toronto: General Publishing, 1972.

Glynn-Ward, H. *The Glamour of British Columbia.* New York: Century, 1926. Reprint, Toronto: Doubleday, Doran and Gundy, 1932.

Harland, Marion. "The Incapacity of Business Women." *North American Review* 149 (July 1889): 707-12.

Henderson's British Columbia Gazetteer and Directory. Victoria: Henderson Directory Co., 1890, 1900-07, 1918.

Henderson's British Columbia Gazetteer and Directory and Mining Companies with Which Is Consolidated the Williams' British Columbia Directory for 1900-1901. Victoria: L.G. Henderson, 1901.

Hesson, Hilda. "T.B.W." *The Business and Professional Woman* 22 (September-October 1951): 2.

Lugrin, N. de Bertrand. *The Pioneer Women of Vancouver Island, 1843-1866.* Victoria: Women's Canadian Club, 1928.

Mansfield, Justine. "Can the 'Two-Job Woman' Succeed at Home and in Business?" *The Business Woman* 3 (January 1928): 1.

"A Momentous Time." *The Business and Professional Woman* (June 1935): 4.

Partridge, Emma Dot. "On Taking One's Work Too Seriously." *Vancouver Business Woman* 4, 8 (January 1927): 7-8.

Paterson, Frances. "The Saga of Kumtuks." *The Business and Professional Woman* 21 (March-April 1951): 11.

Potter, Beatrix. *The Tale of Benjamin Bunny.* London: Frederick Warne, 1993. First published in 1904 by Frederick Warne.

Robertson, Margaret Hewett. "Work Is a Masculine Word." *The Business and Professional Woman* (October-November 1979): 6-8.

Scholefield, E.O.J., and F. W. Howay. *British Columbia from Earliest Times to the Present.* Vol. 4. Vancouver: S.J. Clarke, 1914.

"Think Like a Man, Act Like a Lady." *The Business and Professional Woman* (May-June 1967).

Who's Who in British Columbia, 1937-1939. Vancouver: S.M. Carter, 1939.

Wrigley's British Columbia Directory. Vancouver: Wrigley Directories Limited, 1918, 1922, 1926-32.

"Women Invading All Walks of Life." *Vancouver Business Woman* 5 (November 1927): 6.

NEWSPAPERS

British Colonist (Victoria); also the *Daily Colonist*
Globe and Mail
Prince Rupert Daily News
Vancouver Province; also the *Vancouver Daily Province*
Vancouver Sun
Victoria Daily Times

GOVERNMENT DOCUMENTS

British Columbia, Ministry of Economic Development, Small Business, and Trade. Businesswomen's Advocate. "Women in Business: Profile of Women Business Owners in British Columbia." Victoria: Author, 1991.

–. "Survey of Women Business Owners in British Columbia: Major Findings and Policy Implications." Victoria: Author, 1986.

Canada. Department of Labour. *Women at Work in Canada: A Fact Book on the Female Labour Force, 1964.* Ottawa: Queen's Printer, 1965.

Canada, Dominion Bureau of Statistics. Published Reports of the Census of Canada. Ottawa.

1901, Volumes 1-3
1911, Volumes 1-4
1921, Volumes 1-5
1931, Volumes 1-3, 5, 7, 10-12
1941, Volumes 1, 6-11
1951, Volumes 1-8, 10
1961, Volume 7, Part 1, Catalogue Numbers 99-511, 99-514, 99-515, 99-522, 99-524; Volume 7, Part 2, Catalogue Numbers 99-528, 99-534, 99-535, 99-536; Series 2.1, Catalogue Number 93-512; Series 2.2, Catalogue Number 93-530; Series 3.1, Catalogue Numbers 94-501 – 94-517; Series 3.2, Catalogue Numbers 94-518 – 94-532; Series SL, Catalogue Numbers 94-551, 94-552
1971, Volume 1, Part 4, Catalogue Number 92-730; Volume 3, Part 1, Catalogue Number 94-702; Volume 3, Part 2, Catalogue Numbers 94-716, 94-723, 94-726, 94-727; Volume 3, Part 3, Catalogue Numbers 94-733, 94-783; Volume 3, Part 5, Catalogue Numbers 94-749, 94-752; Volume 3, Part 7, Catalogue Numbers 94-771, 94-783

Statistics Canada. Summary tables: Time spent on various activities, by sex. www.statcan. ca/english/Pgdb/famil36a.htm (20 February 2003).

SECONDARY SOURCES

Armstrong, Pat, and Hugh Armstrong. *The Double Ghetto: Canadian Women and Their Segregated Work.* Toronto: McClelland and Stewart, 1978.

Barman, Jean. *Constance Lindsay Skinner: Writing on the Frontier.* Toronto: University of Toronto Press, 2002.

–. *Growing Up British in British Columbia: Boys in Private School.* Vancouver: UBC Press, 1984.

–. *Sojourning Sisters: The Lives and Letters of Jessie and Annie McQueen.* Toronto: University of Toronto Press, 2003.

–. "Vancouver's Forgotten Entrepreneurs: Women Who Ran Their Own Schools." *British Columbia Historical News* 31, 4 (Fall 1998): 21-29.

Baskerville, Peter. "Familiar Strangers: Urban Families with Boarders, Canada, 1901." *Social Science History* 25 (2001): 321-46.

–. "Gender and Self-Employment in Urban Canada, 1901." Paper presented to the American Historical Association, Chicago, January 2003.

–. "'She Has Already Hinted at Board': Enterprising Urban Women in British Columbia, 1863-1896." *Histoire sociale/Social History* 26, 52 (November 1993): 205-28.

–. *A Silent Revolution? Gender and Wealth in English Canada, 1860 to 1930.* Montreal/ Kingston: McGill-Queen's University Press, 2008.

–. "Women and Investment in Late-Nineteenth-Century Urban Canada: Victoria and Hamilton, 1880-1901." *Canadian Historical Review* 80, 2 (June 1999): 191-218.

Belshaw, John Douglas. *Colonization and Community: The Vancouver Island Coalfield and the Making of the British Columbian Working Class.* Montreal/Kingston: McGill-Queen's University Press, 2002.

–. "The West We Have Lost: British Columbia's Demographic Past and an Agenda for Population History." *Western Historical Quarterly* 29, 1 (Spring 1998): 25-47.

Benson, John. *Entrepreneurism in Canada: A History of "Penny Capitalists."* Lewiston, NY: E. Mellen Press, 1990.

–. *The Penny Capitalists: A Study of Nineteenth-Century Working-Class Entrepreneurs.* New Brunswick, NJ: Rutgers University Press, 1983.

Best, Pamela. "Women, Men and Work." *Canadian Social Trends* 36 (Spring 1995): 30-33.

Bliss, Michael. *Northern Enterprise: Five Centuries of Canadian Business.* Toronto: Mc-Clelland and Stewart, 1987.

Bock, Gisela. "Women's History and Gender History: Aspects of an International Debate." *Gender and History* 1, 1 (Spring 1989): 7-30.

Bradbury, Bettina. "Pigs, Cows, and Boarders: Non-Wage Forms of Survival among Montreal Families, 1861-91." In *The Challenge of Modernity: A Reader on Post-Confederation Canada,* ed. Ian McKay, 65-91. Toronto: McGraw-Hill Ryerson, 1992.

–. "Surviving as a Widow in 19th-Century Montreal." *Urban History Review* 17, 3 (February 1989): 148-60.

–. *Working Families: Age, Gender, and Daily Survival in Industrializing Montreal.* Toronto: McClelland and Stewart, 1993.

Brocklehurst, Deidre. "A Visible Presence: The Victoria Business and Professional Women's Club, 1921-1960." Master's thesis, University of Victoria, 2001.

Buddle, Melanie. "'All the Elements of a Permanent Community': A History of Society, Culture and Entertainment in the Cariboo." Master's thesis, University of Northern British Columbia, 1997.

–. "The Business of Women: Gender, Family, and Entrepreneurship in British Columbia, 1901-1971." PhD dissertation, University of Victoria, 2003.

Burley, David. *A Particular Condition in Life: Self-Employment and Social Mobility in Mid-Victorian Brantford, Ontario.* Montreal/Kingston: McGill-Queen's University Press, 1994.

Campbell, Robert A. *Sit Down and Drink Your Beer: Regulating Vancouver's Beer Parlours, 1925-1954.* Toronto: University of Toronto Press, 2001.

Cavanaugh, Catherine A., and Randi R. Warne. "Introduction." In *Telling Tales: Essays in Western Women's History,* ed. Catherine A. Cavanaugh and Randi R. Warne, 3-31. Vancouver: UBC Press, 2000.

Caves, R.E., and R.H. Holton. "An Outline of the Economic History of British Columbia, 1881-1951." In *Historical Essays on British Columbia,* ed. J. Friesen and H.K. Ralston, 152-66. Toronto: McClelland and Stewart, 1976.

Chambers-Schiller, Lee Virginia. *Liberty, A Better Husband: Single Women in America – The Generations of 1780-1840.* New Haven, CT: Yale University Press, 1984.

Clark, S.D. *The Developing Canadian Community.* 2nd ed. Toronto: University of Toronto Press, 1968.

Clarkson, Chris. *Domestic Reforms: Political Visions and Family Regulation in British Columbia, 1862-1940.* Vancouver: UBC Press, 2007.

Cohen, Gary. *Enterprising Canadians: The Self-Employed in Canada.* Ottawa: Statistics Canada, 1988.

Cohen, Marjorie Griffin. *Women's Work, Markets, and Economic Development in Nineteenth-Century Ontario.* Toronto: University of Toronto Press, 1988.

Converse, Cathy. *Mainstays: Women Who Shaped BC.* Victoria: Horsdal and Schubart, 1998.

Cooper, Patricia. *Once a Cigar Maker: Men, Women, and Work Culture in American Cigar Factories, 1900-1919.* Urbana: University of Illinois Press, 1987.

Cott, Nancy F. *The Bonds of Womanhood: Women's Sphere in New England, 1780-1835.* New Haven, CT: Yale University Press, 1977.

Courchane, Marsha, and Angela Redish. "Women in the Labour Force, 1911-1986: A Historical Perspective." In *False Promises: The Failure of Conservative Economics,* ed. Robert C. Allen and Gideon Rosenbluth, 146-62. Vancouver: New Star Books, 1992.

Creese, Gillian, and Veronica Strong-Boag, eds. *British Columbia Reconsidered: Essays on Women.* Vancouver: Press Gang, 1992.

–. "Taking Gender into Account in British Columbia: More Than Just Women's Studies." *BC Studies,* nos. 105-6 (Spring/Summer 1995): 9-27.

Dagg, Anne Innis. *The Feminine Gaze.* Waterloo, ON: Wilfrid Laurier University Press, 2001.

Davis, Chuck, ed. *The Greater Vancouver Book: An Urban Encyclopaedia.* Surrey, BC: Linkman Press, 1997.

Dawson, Michael. *Selling British Columbia: Tourism and Consumer Culture, 1890-1970.* Vancouver: UBC Press, 2004.

Faderman, Lillian. *Surpassing the Love of Men: Romantic Friendships and Love between Women from the Renaissance to the Present.* New York: William Morrow, 1981.

Farmer, Diane. "Widowhood in the Parish of Notre Dame: An Examination of Death and Remarriage in Mid-Nineteenth-Century Lower Town." Master's research essay, Carleton University, 1981.

Ferris, Lesley. *Acting Women: Images of Women in Theatre.* New York: New York University Press, 1989.

–, ed. *Crossing the Stage: Controversies on Cross-Dressing.* London: Routledge, 1993.

Fine, Lisa M. "Between Two Worlds: Business Women in a Chicago Boarding House, 1900-1930." *Journal of Social History* 19 (Spring 1986): 511-19.

–. *The Souls of the Skyscraper: Female Clerical Workers in Chicago, 1870-1930.* Philadelphia: Temple University Press, 1990.

Fisher, Robin. *Contact and Conflict: Indian-European Relations in British Columbia, 1774-1890.* 2nd ed. Vancouver: UBC Press, 1992.

–. "Matters for Reflection: *BC Studies* and British Columbia History." *BC Studies,* no. 100 (Winter 1993-94): 59-77.

Freund, Alexander, and Laura Quilici. "Exploring Myths in Women's Narratives: Italian and German Immigrant Women in Vancouver, 1947-1961." *BC Studies,* nos. 105-6 (Spring/Summer 1995): 159-82.

Friesen, J., and H.K. Ralston, eds. *Historical Essays on British Columbia*. Toronto: Mc-
Clelland and Stewart, 1976.

Gaffield, Chad. "Historical Thinking, C.P. Snow's Two Cultures, and a Hope for the
Twenty-First Century." *Journal of the Canadian Historical Association*, new series, 12
(2001): 3-25.

Gamber, Wendy. *The Female Economy: The Millinery and Dressmaking Trades, 1860-1930*.
Urbana: University of Illinois Press, 1997.

–. "Gendered Concerns: Thoughts on the History of Business and the History of Women."
Business and Economic History 23, 1 (Fall 1994): 129-40.

–. "A Gendered Enterprise: Placing Nineteenth-Century Businesswomen in History."
Business History Review 72, 2 (Summer 1998): 188-218.

–. "A Precarious Independence: Milliners and Dressmakers in Boston, 1860-1890." *Journal
of Women's History* 4, 1 (Spring 1992): 60-88.

Gay, Katherine. *In the Company of Women: Canadian Women Talk about What It Takes to
Start and Manage a Successful Business*. Toronto: HarperCollins, 1997.

Giddens, Anthony, and David Held. *Classes, Power, and Conflict: Classical and Contemporary Debates*. Berkeley: University of California Press, 1982.

Goldin, Claudia. *Understanding the Gender Gap: An Economic History of American Women*.
Oxford: Oxford University Press, 1990.

Gossage, Carolyn. *A Question of Privilege: Canada's Independent Schools*. Toronto: Peter
Martin Associates, 1977.

Gough, Barry M. "The Character of the British Columbia Frontier." *BC Studies*, no. 32
(Winter 1976-77): 28-40.

Gould, Jan. *Women of British Columbia*. Saanichton, BC: Hancock House Publishers, 1975.

Graydon, Shari, and David Mitchell, eds. *British Columbia's Business Leaders of the Century*. Vancouver: BIV Special Publications, Quebecor Printing, 1999.

Harris, Cole. *The Reluctant Land: Society, Space, and Environment in Canada before Confederation*. Vancouver: UBC Press, 2008.

–. *The Resettlement of British Columbia: Essays on Colonialism and Geographical Change*.
Vancouver: UBC Press, 1997.

Herr, Elizabeth. "Women, Marital Status, and Work Opportunities in 1880 Colorado."
The Journal of Economic History 55, 2 (June 1995): 339-66.

Herrmann, Anne. "Imitations of Marriage: Crossdressed Couples in Contemporary Lesbian
Fiction." In *Lesbian Subjects: A Feminist Studies Reader*, ed. Martha Vicinus, 102-15.
Bloomington: Indiana University Press, 1996.

Hilton, Matthew. *Smoking in British Popular Culture, 1800-2000*. Manchester, UK: Manchester University Press, 2000.

Hobbs, Margaret. "Equality and Difference: Feminism and the Defence of Women Workers during the Great Depression." In *Canadian Women: A Reader*, ed. Wendy Mitchinson, Paula Bourne, Alison Prentice, Gail Cuthbert Brandt, Beth Light, and Naomi
Black, 251-68. Toronto: Harcourt Brace, 1996.

–. "Gendering Work and Welfare: Women's Relationship to Wage-Work and Social Policy
in Canada during the Great Depression." PhD dissertation, University of Toronto, 1995.

Howard, Irene. *The Struggle for Social Justice in British Columbia: Helena Gutteridge, the
Unknown Reformer*. Vancouver: UBC Press, 1992.

Iacovetta, Franca, and Mariana Valverde, eds. *Gender Conflicts: New Essays in Women's
History*. Toronto: University of Toronto Press, 1992.

Jeffreys, Sheila. "Does It Matter If They Did It?" In *Not a Passing Phase: Reclaiming Lesbians in History, 1840-1985,* ed. Lesbian History Group, 19-28. London: Women's Press, 1989.

Johnston, Hugh J.M. "Native People, Settlers and Sojourners, 1871-1916." In *The Pacific Province: A History of British Columbia,* ed. Hugh J.M. Johnston, 165-204. Vancouver: Douglas and McIntyre, 1996.

Kanes, Candace. "American Business Women, 1890-1930: Creating an Identity." PhD dissertation, University of New Hampshire, 1997.

Kinnear, Mary. "'Do You Want Your Daughter to Marry a Farmer?' Women's Work on the Farm, 1922." In *Canadian Papers in Rural History,* vol. 6, ed. D.H. Akenson, 137-53. Gananoque, ON: Langdale, 1988.

Korinek, Valerie J. "'Mrs. Chatelaine' vs. 'Mrs. Slob': The Contestants, Correspondents and the *Chatelaine* Community in Action, 1961-1969." *Journal of the Canadian Historical Association* 7 (1996): 251-75.

–. *Roughing It in the Suburbs: Reading Chatelaine Magazine in the Fifties and Sixties.* Toronto: University of Toronto Press, 2000.

Krasnick Warsh, Cheryl. "Smoke and Mirrors: Gender Representation in North American Tobacco and Alcohol Advertisements before 1950." *Histoire sociale/Social History* 31, 62 (1998): 183-222.

Kwolek-Folland, Angel. *Engendering Business: Men and Women in the Corporate Office, 1870-1930.* Baltimore: Johns Hopkins University Press, 1994.

–. *Incorporating Women: A History of Women and Business in the United States.* New York: Twayne, 1998.

Lang, Joan. *Lost Orchards: Vanishing Fruit Farms of the West Kootenay.* Nelson, BC: Ward Creek Press, 2003.

Lang, Marjory, and Linda Hale. "Women of the *World* and Other Dailies: The Lives and Times of Vancouver Newspaperwomen in the First Quarter of the Twentieth Century." *BC Studies,* no. 85 (Spring 1990): 3-23.

Latham, Barbara, and Cathy Kess, eds. *In Her Own Right: Selected Essays on Women's History in BC.* Victoria: Camosun College, 1980.

Latham, Barbara, and Roberta Pazdro, eds. *Not Just Pin Money: Selected Essays on the History of Women's Work in British Columbia.* Victoria: Camosun College, 1984.

Lay, Jackie. "To Columbia on the Tynemouth: The Emigration of Single Women and Girls in 1862." In *In Her Own Right: Selected Essays on Women's History in BC,* ed. Barbara Latham and Cathy Kess, 19-41. Victoria: Camosun College, 1980.

Leffler, Marjorie. "The Island Hall Hotel History." *British Columbia Historical News* 27, 2 (Spring 1994): 21-22.

Lewis, Susan Ingalls. "Beyond Horatia Alger: Breaking through Gendered Assumptions about Business 'Success' in Mid-Nineteenth-Century America." *Business and Economic History* 24, 1 (Fall 1995): 97-105.

Lowe, Graham. *Women in the Administrative Revolution: The Feminization of Clerical Work.* Cambridge, UK: Polity Press, 1987.

Lutz, John, ed. *Myth and Memory: Stories of Indigenous-European Contact.* Vancouver: UBC Press, 2007.

MacGill, Elsie. *My Mother, the Judge: A Biography of Judge Helen Gregory MacGill.* Toronto: Ryerson Press, 1955.

Makabe, Tomoko. *Picture Brides: Japanese Women in Canada.* Translated by Kathleen Chisato Merken. Toronto: Multicultural History Society of Ontario, 1995.

Marx, Karl. *Capital.* Moscow: Foreign Languages Publishing House, 1957.

Marx, Karl, and Friedrich Engels. *The Communist Manifesto.* Translated by Samuel Moore. Chicago: Charles H. Kerr, 1945.

Matthaei, Julie A. *An Economic History of Women in America: Women's Work, the Sexual Division of Labor, and the Development of Capitalism.* New York: Schocken Books, 1982.

McCormick, Virginia E. "Butter and Egg Business: Implications from the Records of a Nineteenth-Century Farm Wife." *Ohio History* 100 (Winter/Spring 1991): 57-67.

McDonald, Robert A.J. *Making Vancouver: Class, Status, and Social Boundaries, 1863-1913.* Vancouver: UBC Press, 1996.

McLean, Lorna R. "Single Again: Widow's Work in the Urban Family Economy, Ottawa, 1871." *Ontario History* 83, 2 (June 1991): 127-50.

McMaster, Lindsey. *Working Girls in the West: Representations of Wage-Earning Women.* Vancouver: UBC Press, 2008.

Meyerowitz, Joanne. *Women Adrift: Independent Wage Earners in Chicago, 1880-1930.* Chicago: University of Chicago Press, 1988.

Michals, Debra. "Toward a New History of the Postwar Economy: Prosperity, Preparedness, and Women's Small Business Ownership." *Business and Economic History* 26, 1 (Fall 1997): 45-56.

Mitchell, David, and Shari Graydon, eds. *British Columbia's Business Leaders of the Century.* Vancouver: BIV Special Publications, Quebecor Printing, 1999.

Monod, David. *Store Wars: Shopkeepers and the Culture of Mass Marketing, 1890-1939.* Toronto: University of Toronto Press, 1996.

Muhlert, Devon L. "Armstrong Hotel Fits a Dowager's Role." *Okanagan History: The Sixty-First Report of the Okanagan Historical Society* 61 (1997): 84-89.

Murphy, Lucy Eldersveld. "Business Ladies: Midwestern Women and Enterprise, 1850-1880." *Journal of Women's History* 3, 1 (Spring 1991): 65-89.

Neering, Rosemary. *Wild West Women: Travellers, Adventurers and Rebels.* Vancouver: Whitecap Books, 2000.

Nenadic, Stana. "The Social Shaping of Business Behaviour in the Nineteenth-Century Women's Garment Trades." *Journal of Social History* 31, 3 (Spring 1998): 625-45.

Neth, Mary. *Preserving the Family Farm: Women, Community, and the Foundations of Agribusiness in the Midwest, 1900-1940.* Baltimore: Johns Hopkins University Press, 1995.

Ollman, Bertell. "Marx's Use of 'Class.'" *Dialectical Marxism: The Writings of Bertell Ollman.* http://www.nyu.edu/projects/ollman/docs/class.php.

"100 Top Women Entrepreneurs." *Chatelaine,* November 1999: 72-118.

O'Neill, Jeff. "Changing Occupational Structure." *Canadian Social Trends* 23 (Winter 1991): 9-12.

Osterud, Nancy Grey. *Bonds of Community: The Lives of Farm Women in Nineteenth-Century New York.* Ithaca, NY: Cornell University Press, 1991.

Ostry, Sylvia. *The Occupational Composition of the Canadian Labour Force.* Ottawa: Dominion Bureau of Statistics, 1967.

Parent, Rosemarie. "The Story of Estella Hartt." *British Columbia Historical News* 32, 2 (Spring 1999): 30.

Parr, Joy. *The Gender of Breadwinners: Men, Women, and Change in Two Industrial Towns, 1880-1950.* Toronto: University of Toronto Press, 1990.

–. "The Skilled Emigrant and Her Kin: Gender, Culture, and Labour Recruitment." *Canadian Historical Review* 68, 4 (December 1987): 529-51.

Pearce, Tralee. "Mompreneurs." *Globe and Mail,* 7 August 2004, L1.

Peiss, Kathy. "On Beauty ... and the History of Business." In *Beauty and Business: Commerce, Gender, and Culture in Modern America,* ed. Philip Scranton, 7-22. New York: Routledge, 2001.

–. "'Vital Industry' and Women's Ventures: Conceptualizing Gender in Twentieth-Century Business History." *Business History Review* 72, 2 (Summer 1998): 219-41.

Perry, Adele. "Oh I'm Just Sick of the Faces of Men: Gender Imbalance, Race, Sexuality, and Sociability in Nineteenth-Century British Columbia." *BC Studies,* nos. 105-6 (Spring/Summer 1995): 27-43.

–. *On the Edge of Empire: Gender, Race, and the Making of British Columbia, 1849-1871.* Toronto: University of Toronto Press, 2001.

Phillips, Paul, and Erin Phillips. *Women and Work: Inequality in the Canadian Labour Market.* Toronto: Lorimer, 1993.

Porsild, Charlene. *Gamblers and Dreamers: Women, Men, and Community in the Klondike.* Vancouver: UBC Press, 1998.

Rochlin, Harriet. "The Amazing Adventures of a Good Woman." *Journal of the West* 12 (April 1973): 281-95.

Sangster, Joan. *Earning Respect: The Lives of Working Women in Small-Town Ontario, 1920-1960.* Toronto: University of Toronto Press, 1995.

Scott, Joan Wallach. "Comment: Conceptualizing Gender in American Business History." *Business History Review* 72, 2 (Summer 1998): 242-49.

–. *Gender and the Politics of History.* New York: Columbia University Press, 1988.

Scranton, Philip, ed. *Beauty and Business: Commerce, Gender, and Culture in Modern America.* New York: Routledge, 2001.

Seager, Allen. "The Resource Economy, 1871-1921." In *The Pacific Province: A History of British Columbia,* ed. Hugh J.M. Johnston, 205-50. Vancouver: Douglas and McIntyre, 1996.

Shiffman, Kim. "Are You Entrepreneur Material?" *Today's Parent,* January 2009, 69.

Smith-Rosenberg, Carroll. "The Female World of Love and Ritual." *Signs* 1 (Autumn 1975): 1-29.

Solomon, Alisa. "It's Never Too Late to Switch." In *Crossing the Stage: Controversies on Cross-Dressing,* ed. Lesley Ferris, 144-54. London: Routledge, 1993.

Stansell, Christine. *City of Women: Sex and Class in New York, 1789-1860.* New York: Knopf, 1986.

Stelter, Gilbert A., and Alan F.J. Artibise, eds. *The Canadian City: Essays in Urban and Social History.* Ottawa: Carleton University Press, 1991.

Strange, Carolyn. *Toronto's Girl Problem: The Perils and Pleasures of the City, 1880-1930.* Toronto: University of Toronto Press, 1995.

Strong-Boag, Veronica. "Pulling in Double Harness or Hauling a Double Load: Women, Work and Feminism on the Canadian Prairie." *Journal of Canadian Studies* 21, 3 (1986): 32-52.

Strong-Boag, Veronica, and Kathryn McPherson. "The Confinement of Women: Childbirth and Hospitalization in Vancouver, 1919-1939." *BC Studies,* nos. 69-70 (Spring-Summer 1986): 142-74.

Taylor, Graham, and Peter Baskerville. *A Concise History of Business in Canada.* Toronto: Oxford University Press, 1994.

Thomson, Gerald. "'Through No Fault of Their Own': Josephine Dauphinee and the 'Subnormal' Pupils of the Vancouver School System, 1911-1941." *Historical Studies in Education* 18 (Spring 2006): 51-73.

Tillotson, Shirley. "'We May All Soon Be First-Class Men': Gender and Skill in Canada's Early Twentieth-Century Urban Telegraph Industry." *Labour/Le Travail* 27 (Spring 1991): 97-125.

Tinkler, Penny. *Smoke Signals: Women, Smoking and Visual Culture in Britain.* Oxford, UK: Berg Publishers, 2006.

Tippett, Maria. *Emily Carr: A Biography.* Toronto: Oxford University Press, 1979.

Van Den Broek, Astrid. "The Mother Corp.: Meet Five Mompreneurs." *Today's Parent,* March 2006. http://www.todaysparent.com.

Van Horn, Susan Householder. *Women, Work, and Fertility, 1900-1986.* New York: New York University Press, 1988.

Van Kirk, Sylvia. "A Vital Presence: Women in the Cariboo Gold Rush, 1862-1875." In *British Columbia Reconsidered: Essays on Women,* ed. Gillian Creese and Veronica Strong-Boag, 21-37. Vancouver: Press Gang, 1992.

Vicinus, Martha. *Independent Women: Work and Community for Single Women, 1850-1920.* Chicago: University of Chicago Press, 1985.

–, ed. *Lesbian Subjects: A Feminist Studies Reader.* Bloomington: Indiana University Press, 1996.

Wilson, J. Donald. "I Am Ready to Be of Assistance When I Can': Lottie Bowron and Rural Women Teachers in British Columbia." In *Women Who Taught: Perspectives on the History of Women and Teaching,* ed. Alison Prentice and Marjorie R. Theobald, 202-29. Toronto: University of Toronto Press, 1991.

Wilson, Lisa. *Life after Death: Widows in Pennsylvania, 1750-1850.* Philadelphia: Temple University Press, 1992.

Wilson Waciega, Lisa. "A 'Man of Business': The Widow of Means in Southeastern Pennsylvania, 1750-1850." *William and Mary Quarterly* 44 (1987): 40-64.

Wong, Tun. "Sue Lee Ping Wong." *Okanagan History: The Sixty-Third Report of the Okanagan Historical Society* 63 (1999): 156-59.

Yeager, Mary A., ed. *Women in Business.* Vol. 1. Northampton, MA: Elgar, 1999.

Index

Printed in Canada by Friesens

Set in Garamond by Artegraphica Design Co. Ltd.

Copy editor: Audrey McClellan

Proofreader: Lesley Erickson